*Community that pleases God is almost always intentional. Often it is strategic and sacrificial, yet always it is driven by the purposes of Scripture. Bruce Fong challenges us to become considerably more intentional in our Christian community. Followers of Jesus are ready for this challenge and a watching world awaits our response!*

Brian Doyle, Founder and President
Iron Sharpens Iron

*Have you ever felt that the people of God don't act like Jesus? Or that the Body of Christ better models pragmatism and civil religion that the lordship of Christ? Or that the church may be the most racially segregated organization these is on Sunday mornings? If so, Dr. Bruce Fong's book will dish up meaty grist for your mental mill and offer fresh insights on how your church can grow, in a truly biblical sense. The heart of Bruce's work begins with an insightful biblical theology centered in Ephesians 2:11-22— the breaking down of hostility between Jew and Gentile. But it goes so much farther: exploring the implications of sanctification, the headship of Christ, the Imago Dei, and the divine Trinity. He calls us, whether in an ethnic, multicultural, or majority church, to put display the full richness of the Church as Christ intended it to be.*

Dr. Daniel R. Lockwood, President
Multnomah University, Portland, Oregon

*Mutual Acceptance in the Church? This past year, 540 churches became 1 Church in metro-Detroit in a historic campaign to give Everyone A Chance to Hear (E.A.C.H.). We crossed racial, geographical, denominational and economic lines to work as 1 body to bring good news and good deeds to our region. The impact on our individual churches was monumental. Never before had we experienced such unity, such mutual acceptance, such cross-pollination in the body of Christ in this region. Having tasted such sweet unity, we don't want to go back! What Bruce Fong is writing about in this book – the unity of the body of Christ across all lines – is, in fact, the most potent evangelistic tool the church has. The more integrated the church is, locally and regionally . . . the more powerful and persuasive she becomes. Isn't that what Jesus said (Jn.17:23)?*

Dr. Robert Shirock
Senior Pastor – Oak Pointe Church, Michigan
Lead Pastor – E.A.C.H. (Everyone A Chance to Hear)

*"Thank you, Bruce for such a timely, prophetic resource. It is God's heart that His Church be the visible representation of the supernatural work of God in abolishing what divides us and reflecting authentic unity. Too often, the Church has accepted a pragmatism that may produce numerical growth but also may be a veiled justification for racism and exclusion. I am so grateful to God, Bruce, for this compelling call "to biblical unity."*

Dr. Crawford W. Loritts, Jr.
Author, Speaker, Radio Host
Senior Pastor, Fellowship Bible Church, Roswell GA

The church should be one... no more
cultural or ethnic separation.

# The
# WALL

Jesus destroyed the wall of
hostility; His church must never
rebuild it.  Ephesians 2:14

# Bruce W. Fong, Ph.D.

Copyright © 2011 by

Bruce W. Fong

Fong, Bruce W.
The Wall : The church should be one…
no more cultural or ethnic separation.

## Dedication

I dedicate this book in honor of my family:

Yvonne is my fabulous wife and amazing friend, who
believed in me and trusted in me enough to leave the security of
home, friends, and country to encourage me through the
arduous task of research, thinking and writing.
I am blessed to have her by my side.

Kristin, our super one-and-only special daughter is
the apple of her father's eye.
Dustin, our son-in-law set the standard for all
outstanding family additions.
Justin, our remarkably talented and bright son,
is a man of integrity and honor.
Breanna, our special daughter-in-law defines
sweetness and loyalty.
Jeremy, is our action-packed son and the one who
brings so much energy into life.

*It's always about family…always.*

# CONTENTS

## CHAPTER II –

## THE HISTORICAL DEBATE SURROUNDING

### THE HUP THEORY

**Part 2**

**FORMULATING A GROWTH PHILOSOPHY FOR THE
CHURCH ACCORDING TO THE CHRISTOCENTRIC
BIBLICAL THEOLOGY**

# CHAPTER IV – THE APPLICATION OF MUTUAL ACCEPTANCE TO THE CHURCH AND ITS MISSION

**CONCLUSION**

## PREFACE

I grew up in a church that was comprised predominantly of people who were of Chinese descent. In my youthful thinking I assumed that all Christians were like the ones at the church that I attended, namely, Chinese. I remember my surprise when our youth group went to a youth rally and the majority of Christians who attended the rally were not Chinese. It was an awakening that has never cease to spur my thinking. From the earliest days of Christian experience, I have had a curiosity to explore the phenomenon of racially segregated churches.

Over the years I have been involved in churches of different ethnic flavors. Yet, while they were ethnically segregated, they sang the same songs, participated in the same kind of activities, observe the ordinances of the church in roughly the same manner, they read the same books written by the same authors, and they gave high regard to the same nationally known Bible teachers and speakers. These are some minor difference like the kind of food served at a church meal or an occasional phrase distinction to ethnic origins or the traditions at festive occasions as a wedding. However, by in large those difference weigh lightly against what the church would describe as its essential commitment, namely its theological heritage. This contrast is intriguing.

On the one hand, there has been no church with which I have been associated that has ever been willing to "die on the hill" of keeping itself racially homogeneous. On the other hand, most of these Evangelical churches eagerly raise the banner of the Bible being the Word of God. They have proclaimed the Trinity as a vital doctrine. Furthermore, the deity of Christ and His Resurrection are uncompromising doctrines of their heritage. Nevertheless, while the essential topics of the Evangelical faith continue beyond these, none of these churches has ever written that racial homogeneity is on an equal level of importance as any of these doctrinal issues. Yet, the result of who comes to church and how they have come is self-evident. This gap between what a church believes that it must believe and what a church actually does in practice with regard to racial issues is both my curiosity and concern. While churches practice racial homogeneity, their doctrinal belief actually teaches –a different model. This model is what I hope to describe in this volume.

Having served in pastoral positions in both ethnic and non-ethnic churches has reinforced my resolve to emphasize the common ground that Christianity has put forward as one of its most important tenants, namely, all Christians are members together in the family of God. We are sisters and brothers together in Jesus Christ. Unfortunately, while this is true, racism has been present throughout the church's history. However, the presence of this problem does not need to continue. Ironically, the solution to the problem has always been a part of the Church's theology. When Jesus Christ reconciled the world to Himself it was not to a different lord for each ethnic group. But,

He reconciled each individual regardless of racial background to Himself as the one Lord of all.

The church, formed out of this reconciliation to Christ should practice the same acceptance of whoever has been reconciled. God does the inviting. The guests simply enjoy not only having been invited but also the thrill of enjoying others who are invited guests as well. When there is personal selectivity that marks the make-up of a church along racial lines, then, there is an appearance that the guests have taken over the prerogative that exclusively belongs the host. Since every Christian enjoys a new relationship that has been established with Jesus Christ; then, every Christian can also enjoy a new relations with one another regardless of race. That is the message of the Gospel. This should also be the testimony of the church and all of its members.

## ACKNOWLEDGEMENTS

I thank God for the vision and the provision to assume the enormous task involved in this writing project. It is my prayer that He will be pleased and honored with all that this document represents.

I am indebted to Ainslie Walton, my dissertation supervisor, for his guidance. Tim Dearborn taught me how to argue more precisely and write more clearly. During this project, I was reminded of how valuable gifts of encouragement, support and love can be when given by special friends like Bob and Marj, Art and Karen, Lindy, Harold and Jolene. They are my personal cheerleaders. Also, my brothers Craig and Vernon were like what all great brothers ought to be. Bell is my one and only sister, taking good care of her little brother.

The production of this volume required extensive travel, specialized skills, large doses of encouragement and attention to many mundane tasks. For their invaluable assistance in these areas I am grateful to Colin and Moira, Anne, Greg and Ronna, Derek, Ken and Moira, Ben and Patty, Num Kock and Kim, Douglas and Helen, Brian, Al and Ev, Andrew and Libby, Keith and Lily, Don and Linda, Mark and Roxanne, Harry, Dennis and Kathy, Richard, Cedric, Gil, Paul and Meg, Stephen and Cynthia.

Also I am grateful for my students at Multnomah Seminary and the former Michigan Theological Seminary for the hours of discussion and trimming of many of the ideas represented in this volume. Several church leaders and colleagues gave me their time to discuss vital issues on this topic. Their contributions were formative and defining in my thinking. For that I am grateful to: Leslie Newbigin, John Stott, James Torrance and Roland Walls. Dan Lockwood generously created the time, effort and resources to pursue this project in the middle of a busy seminary teaching duties.

The reintroduction to this once "out of print" piece has the encouragement thumbprint of some very special people. Dave is my literary agent. Sandy is a great friend and gifted writer who gave me invaluable advice in this endeavor. Mike Fezzey, Jay Hull, Rick Spurlock, Gary Tribbett, Drew Wolford and Bob Wong are like brothers to me. Their friendship and encouragement make my life rich.

Throughout the years many believers from various local churches have helped me shape my values and test the theology that is at the heart of this research: Sunset Church of San Francisco, Grace Bible Church of Ann Arbor, Highland Park Baptist Church of Southfield, Clear Creek Community Church of Gresham, Good Shepherd Community Church of Boring, Bridge of Don Baptist Church of Aberdeen, Chinese Baptist Church of Portland, Grace Bible Church of Dallas, Nooksack Valley Baptist

Church of Everson, Faith Baptist Church of Salem and Chinese Grace Bible Church of Sacramento.

My gratitude to each is unending. I am blessed with amazing people that God has placed in my life. It is my great hope is that this arduous research project will result in praise to the Lord's name in which all of these will rightfully share.

*This book was originally released under the title* <u>*Racial Equality in the Church*</u> *with the University Press of America.*

# INTRODUCTION

"Bigotry's ugliness, whether it's expressed in subtle code words of a verbal affront or in the violence of a street attack, continues to pervade society."[1] In the United States during the early 1930's white groups expressed their racial animosity against blacks through lynchings and terrorist activities. Then, in the next decade racial tensions were also expressed through the "legalized" internment of many Japanese American citizens during the initial stages of World War II. Racial tensions continued to persist with fears over the "Browning" of America, the tensions associated with the growing Hispanic population. "Yellow fear" surfaced again as a result of economic competition with Japan and the surge of refugees relocating to America from Southeast Asia. Racial tension continues to appear on the world scene, but any means to address the problem more successfully have eluded society. Communities have not learned preventative solutions from past struggles nor have they discovered how to successfully guide themselves through inevitable racial mixing.

Decades ago the Kerner Commission reported that the United States was becoming two nations, one white and one black, separate but unequal. The study served as a warning. Has America taken heed to this internally divisive dynamic? The recent measure of people's attitudes is not encouraging. In a

---

[1] William Hilliard, "Two Views in Black and White," *The Sunday Oregonian, Forum*, section B1, July 7, 1991.

poll sponsored by *Life* magazine it was discovered that racism persists largely as an unresolved issue and it is characterized by continuing mistrust and suspicion.[2] Some believe that integration has definite limits and cannot be totally achieved.[3] Yet others suggest only a short-term solution designed to cope with the racist indignities of daily life. Their reasoning suggests that such social pressures are inevitable, an unalterable feature of real life and at least for the time being are too big to be overcome.[4] The consensus is that racism has not dissipated in society. On the contrary, it has increased.[5] Also, there is evidence that it has become more complex.[6]

Now, if society cannot find a solution to the issue of racial tension, can the church help? Unfortunately, the general population places little confidence in the church as a leader in social issues, including providing some resolution to the problems of racism. This may be due to the loss of distinctiveness by the church. The church has become

---

[2] "What We Believe," Editors, *Life* (Special Issue, Spring 1988), 69-70.

[3] See further Isabel Wilkerson, "Separate Proms Divide Seniors, Point out Limits of Integration," *The Sunday Oregonian, National,* (May 5, 1991, section E2).

[4] For a further discussion see Janet Filips, "I Was Embarrassed for My Race," in *The Sunday Oregonian, Forum,* (July 7, 1991, section B1, B4).

[5] George Barna, The Frog in the Kettle (Ventura, California Regal Books, 1990), 160.

[6] *Time* magazine reports the increase of racial tension between ethnic minority groups. Black oppression has been the largest as well as "...the longest and most bitter tasting..." (Editors, "Putting Past and Present in Perspective." *Life*, Special Edition, Spring 1988, 3.) but now the Hispanic (Brown) population is growing and statistically will overtake blacks as American's largest ethnic minority. There is growing tension between these two groups for controlling power in pressing for ethnic considerations. For a further discussion see Ricardo Chavira, Sylvester Monroe and Richard Woodbury, "Browns vs. Blacks, "" Time J (July 28, 1991,) 14-16

secularized. It possesses a created illusion of separateness but has in fact ". . . become a moral mirror image of the larger culture."[7] The church in the eyes of some is no different than its surrounding society. "The life of North American churches has become utterly predictable on sociological grounds. Factors of race, class, sex and national identity shape and define the lives of Christians just like everybody else. No one expects anything different of Christians."[8] Not only do people not expect anything different from Christians, Christians do not expect themselves to be different from the world around them. The community realizes its problems with racism but does see the church as a source for a solution. On the one hand, the church preaches love. But, on the other hand, it exhibits ". . . rancor and division regarding denominational lines, theological distinctives or ethnic distinctives."[9] Such a perception produces skepticism over the church's claims. Few will patronize an institution that is apparently openly hypocritical over its essential message.

When the church steps back from its community involvement and evaluates its mission of influence, what is it to conclude? Is the church able to address the human problem of racism and discrimination? If it is able to do so, then how can it effectively do so? Is it to model something different in its churches and then to display it to the world? Or is it to avoid

---

[7] Fran Sciacca, Generation at Risk (Minneapolis: World Wide Publications, 1990), 141.
[8] Jim Wallis, The Call to Conversion (Herts, England: Lion Pub., 1981), 19.
[9] Barna, Frog, 137

social issues that distract from its evangelistic pursuits and leave those to the hereafter?  The particular issue of relating these matters to ethnic churches is a particular concern to this author.

Regarding ethnic churches some perceive sociological trends as a basis for structuring church strategy.  To them a pluralistic society is a reality.  Managing a harmonious community that is comprised of different kinds of people in separate churches is tantamount to "getting the job done."[10] This attitude in church circles is advanced by the school of Church Growth through one of Otis primary teaching tenets known as the Homogeneous Unit Principle ((hereafter HUP theory).

The HUP theory describes the world as a "vast mosaic" with each piece a homogeneous unit defined by its linguistic, ethnic, economic or other unique characteristic.  It states that, "People like to become Christians without crossing racial, linguistic, or class barriers."[11] Such a statement affirms that far from being contrary to Christian habit, this strategy is proper, Biblical and should be allowed and encouraged.[12] Advocates insist that any view to the contrary ignores the indigeneity of a

---

[10] A major American corporation operates its management principles based upon this scheme.  Pluralism is basic to its hiring and advancement procedures.  For a further discussion see Lynne Duke, "Road to Pluralism Requires a Complex Map," in *The Sunday Oregonian, National* (August 4,1991).

[11] Donald McGavran, Understanding Church Growth, 3rd ed., ed. C. Peter Wagner (Grand Rapids: Wm. B. Eerdmans Pub Co., 1990), 163.

[12] Lausanne Education and Theology Group, "The Homogeneous, Unit Principle: Definition and Clarification," preliminary explanation sheet in preparation for the Pasadena Consultation (Lausanne Archives, London), 1977.

homogeneous unit.[13] They argue that to perpetuate the traditional idea of a non-cultural church is to stifle evangelism. Donald McGavran[14], originator of the HUP theory, reasons, "The principle here is that when 'becoming Christian' means joining another culture, kindred, and marriage market, the Church grows slowly, it at all."[15] Accordingly, they suggest that the church which receives new converts ought to identify with each homogeneous unit sufficiently for them to feel at home in it.[16] This explanation of the HUP theory will be detailed in Chapter 1 of this writing.

Responses to the HUP theory have come from a variety of backgrounds and have challenged this new[17] idea on several different grounds. Some of the criticisms have been uninformed and unfair.[18] But, certain arguments are worthy of careful scrutiny and wise attention. In particular, brotherhood and unity are essential to the church; but, they would be damaged by the application of the HUP theory. The application of the HUP

---

[13] Donald McGavran, "The Genesis and Strategy of the Homogeneous Unit Principle" (Lausanne Theology and Education Group, consultation on the Homogeneous Unit Principle, May 31 to June 2, 1977), 6.

[14] Late Dean Emeritus and Senior Professor of Mission, Church Growth and South Asian Studies at the School of World Mission, Fuller Theological Seminary, Pasadena, California.

[15] McGavran, "Genesis", 7.

[16] The Pasadena Consultation _ Homogeneous Unit, Lausanne Occasional Paper No. 1, Lausanne Education and Theology Group (London: Lausanne Committee for World Evangelization Archives, 1978), 3.

[17] Donald McGavran called the HUP theory "one of the new ideas in Church and Mission." ("Genesis and Strategy", 1.)

[18] It is clear that neither McGavran or Wagner are perpetuating a racist ideal. Neither is a racist. Also, their concern is not "numbers" for numbers sake. Neither of these criticisms are legitimate.

theory would excuse the church from standing apart from the world on the matter of racial unity. In response, proponents admit to the potential misuses of the theory but also clarify that their intent is theologically, Biblically, and practically defensible.[19]

Through the early 1970's a number of publications either advocating or criticizing the HUP theory appeared. The escalation of the exchange precipitated a consultation sponsored by the Lausanne Theology and Education Group in 11977 in Pasadena, home of Fuller Seminary and the School of World Missions, principle center for the promoting the HUP theory. John Stott moderated the consultation. Five participants, representing the Fuller position,[20] met with five respondents, representing those who opposed the HUP theory.[21] The results from the consultation indicate that neither side adjusted their position to any measurable degree as a result of the interaction. The Lausanne Theology and Education Group published an enlightening paper on the results of the consultation. In a carefully worded document the areas of agreement and disagreement are outlined. Chapter II of this

---

[19] Pasadena, 1.
[20] The five participants who argued in favor of the HUP theory were: Charles H. Kraft, Arthur F. Glasser, Donald A. McGavran, Ralph D. Winter and C. Peter Wagner.
[21] Respondents who represented the position opposed to the HUP theory were: Harvie M. Conn, Victor E. W. Hayward, C. Rene Padilla, Robert L. Ramseyer and John H. Yoder.

writing will detail the history of this debate surround the HUP theory.[22]

Subsequent to the Pasadena Consultation both McGavran and Wagner[23] published independent volumes[24] promoting the HUP theory for church use. Separation is celebrated under the banner of individuality and cultural preservation. Their position is that cultural abandonment should never be made a prerequisite for conversion. Furthermore, it is believed that to guard against this misunderstanding will result in a more attractive church and hence greater church growth.

Throughout the 1980's the HUP theory was actively promoted as a legitimate strategy for the church. Possibly through the debate, the HUP theory places a greater emphasis on the evangelistic mandate, the temporary nature of the principle, and the allowance for other options. However, the essential idea continues to be concerned with not adding culturally offensive prerequisites to conversion. This is translated into matters of joining a church comprised of people that one's culture despises. Allowing a person to accept Christ among people at his "own level of society"[25] is presented a s more likely context for conversion. Illustrating from the caste system of India Glasser writes, "Let him join a group of believers

---

[22] Pasadena, 7.

[23] Associate Professor Church Growth and Latin American Affairs, School of World Mission, Fuller Theological Seminary, Pasadena, California.

[24] Ethnic Realities and Our Kind of People respectively.

[25] Arthur F. Glasser, "Church Growth at Fuller, "Missiology: An International Review (14, no. 4, October 1985), 416-417.

of his own caste, and as he grows in his understanding he will learn that in Christ there is neither Jew nor Greek, and that all believers are members of the family of God. But should we require him to accept this understanding before he is baptized?"[26] Captured in Glasser's probing is an essential line of reasoning used by the HUP theory advocates: be deliberate in the baptizing of people but do so in their ethnically distinct groups. Great care is given to be as non-disruptive as possible to group identity with spiritual conversion. An understanding of essential Christian unity is separated from and kept distinct from the initial decisions of coming to Christ.

While the HUP theory deals with the three general areas of race, language and class differences, it is the issue of race or ethnicity that will dominate this discussion. There is no lack of illustrations used in connection with the defense of separating congregations based upon their ethnic differences. Glasser makes the following statement in this regard: "In America no one says that the Chinese in our midst should not have their own churches. Why can't we allow various types of churches to emerge and function within separate language and cultural groups? People prefer to come to Christ with their own kind of people, their own piece of the mosaic."[27] Several questions come to mind in light of this HUP theory reasoning. First, what

---

[26] Ibid.
[27] Glasser, "Church Growth," 417.

does Glasser mean by "Chinese"? Is he referring to newly

arrived immigrants? Could he be thinking of those who have a Chinese ancestry but are second or third generation in this country? If the latter, then, why does he not refer to them as Americans? One wonders if his reference to second or third generation Europeans in America would be consider by their ethnic roots. Categorizing all Christian from a common ethnic heritage as "Chinese" and failing to observe the generational tensions that exist is not a helpful generalization. This is a common danger of stereotyping that frustrates solutions to racial problems.[28] Second, it is not certain that "no one" is challenging the strategy of segregated churches that gather Christians into a congregation based upon their ethnic heritage. This author's personal experience is that subsequent generations of ethnic-Americans regularly question and challenge the existence of ethnic churches based upon new Testament grounds. Third, even though it is clear that many ethnic congregations do exist in America, do proponents of the HUP theory advocate that such a phenomenon actually proves theological truth? Could it not also be possible that while congregations and ethnic congregations in America may be conveniently ignoring the negative issue, namely, that although they are one in Christ, they choose not to fellowship with each other solely on the basis

---

[28] Editors, *Life*, 3.

of ethnic difference?  Also, is this not a subtle form of racism in itself?  If this problem exists, then is it possible that both kinds of congregations have a maladjusted attitude about their basis for fellowship?

It is possible to re-position the starting point of this discussion.  That is, racial tension in the church must be firmly resisted.  This stand is not to be a passive one but a deliberate and open one.  Some may choose a radical approach of civil disobedience but that is not the emphasis of this thesis.  Rather, the key is contrast.  Well aware of the sensitivity ingrained in ethnic minorities who are converted out of a racially distinctive and oppressive world, the church offers a visible difference directly affecting this issue of equality.  Every church, realizing the inhumanity and inherent wickedness of racism, must take every opportunity to demonstrate that once "in Christ" all are brothers and mutually accepted into any Christian fellowship.

When two Christians of different ethnic heritages meet they share more in common than in differences.  They are both recipients of the grace of God, they are both sons of God, they are both recipients of eternal redemption and the forgiveness of their sins, they are both sharers of a common eternal hope, they are both sharers of the seal of the Spirit, and they are both sharers in the inheritance of God's possession. [29]  Their

---

[29] The Apostle Paul identifies specific spiritual benefits common among all Christians with no differentiation due to ethnic heritage. He discusses the divine prerogative of being chosen resulting in being made "holy and blameless" (for a discussion see T. K. Abbott, A Critical and Exegetical Commentary on the Epistles

"newness" in Christ and their new "commonness" in Christ seem to give them a basis for coming together. Yet, their ethnic differences remain and are deeply ingrained in their minds and the racial dangers of the world are memories that are still fresh. Chapter III of this thesis addresses these factors, developing the philosophical ministry perspective of "Mutual Acceptance". It will exegete a key New Testament passage outlining the basis of Christian unity, discuss the need of an adequate inclusion of sanctification in a strategy for church development, and describe an alternative philosophy for church development regarding ethnic churches.

Chapter IV will make a practical application of Mutual Acceptance. Practical suggestions for the ministry, lay leaders, church associations, mission agencies and theological training centers will be made. With true conversion comes a radical new way of thinking. Conforming to the world is not the way of Christ but transformed thinking is. Those who pick up their cross and follow Jesus no longer reason as those who are of the world. To the world the "Good Samaritan" is a shocking story that conflicts with all of their values of class and race. To the disciple of Christ it is the proclamation of the grace of God. Those who

---

to the Ephesians and to the Colossians, The International Critical Commentary, reprint [Edinburgh: T. & T. Clark, 1977], 6-8 and E. K. Simpson and F. F. Bruce, Commentary on the Epistles to the Ephesians and the Colossians [Grand Rapids: Wm. B. Eerdmans Pub. Col, 1957], 25,26.) Also, the Apostle expands the description of every Christian's common spiritual heritage speaking of "adoption," "redemption," "forgiveness," "the seal," and the "promised Spirit." (For a discussion see Abbott, Ephesians, 8-23 and Simpson and Bruce, Ephesians, 25-35.)

have been unconditionally accepted by the Father are called upon to unconditionally accept one another.

The infrastructure to this critique is the priority of developing a philosophy of ministry first, then, creating methods based upon that philosophy. To reverse that order leads to potential violation of New Testament principles. This approach can best be tested by asking what is the beginning point of developing a ministry approach? There is one of at least two choices. One could begin with an analysis of people and their problems,. As a result, solutions to resolve those problems are constructed. Here "method" assumes the first position of a ministry approach. However, the other choice, the opposite of the first, is the preference of this discussion, namely, "methods grow out of philosophical objective."[30] A philosophy based upon New Testament principles must be established, then, the needs of people and the church must be addressed from the base with effective methods to achieve proper church development.

---

[30] Hull describes this as "philosophical purity." For a further discussion see Bill Hull, The Disciple Making Pastor (Old Tappan, New Jersey: Fleming H. Revell, 1988.), 146-189.

"newness" in Christ and their new "commonness" in Christ seem to give them a basis for coming together. Yet, their ethnic differences remain and are deeply ingrained in their minds and the racial dangers of the world are memories that are still fresh. Chapter III of this thesis addresses these factors, developing the philosophical ministry perspective of "Mutual Acceptance". It will exegete a key New Testament passage outlining the basis of Christian unity, discuss the need of an adequate inclusion of sanctification in a strategy for church development, and describe an alternative philosophy for church development regarding ethnic churches.

Chapter IV will make a practical application of Mutual Acceptance. Practical suggestions for the ministry, lay leaders, church associations, mission agencies and theological training centers will be made. With true conversion comes a radical new way of thinking. Conforming to the world is not the way of Christ but transformed thinking is. Those who pick up their cross and follow Jesus no longer reason as those who are of the world. To the world the "Good Samaritan" is a shocking story that conflicts with all of their values of class and race. To the disciple of Christ it is the proclamation of the grace of God. Those who have been unconditionally accepted by the Father are called upon to unconditionally accept one another.

---

description of every Christian's common spiritual heritage speaking of "adoption," "redemption," "forgiveness," "the seal," and the "promised Spirit." (For a discussion see Abbott, Ephesians, 8-23 and Simpson and Bruce, Ephesians, 25-35.)

The infrastructure to this critique is the priority of developing a philosophy of ministry first, then, creating methods based upon that philosophy. To reverse that order leads to potential violation of New Testament principles. This approach can best be tested by asking what is the beginning point of developing a ministry approach? There is one of at least two choices. One could begin with an analysis of people and their problems,. As a result, solutions to resolve those problems are constructed. Here "method" assumes the first position of a ministry approach. However, the other choice, the opposite of the first, is the preference of this discussion, namely, "methods grow out of philosophical objective."[30] A philosophy based upon New Testament principles must be established, then, the needs of people and the church must be addressed from the base with effective methods to achieve proper church development.

---

[30] Hull describes this as "philosophical purity." For a further discussion see Bill Hull, The Disciple Making Pastor (Old Tappan, New Jersey: Fleming H. Revell, 1988.), 146-189.

CHAPTER I    Hidden Tension in the Church

# AN EXPLANATION OF THE HOMOGENEOUS UNIT PRINCIPLE

## *Introduction*

Only a very few believers initiate the discussion of racial or ethnic tension in the church.[1] When the church downtown is filling the air with high energy worship, pumping out rhythmic preaching that stirs the congregation to verbally physically engage, we feel comfortable. The church down the street is singing familiar music, organizing their service much like ours but the language is foreign to us, we are pleased that the church is so diverse and that they can meet with people like themselves in a language that they understand. Then, we wonder why those few in our church don't go to one of those churches where surely they would feel more comfortable.

---

[1] Paul Metzger writes, "Many Americans, including evangelicals, believe that race barriers and their impact on class are in the past … I would counter that segregation is still a fact of life: though it is perhaps no longer based on enforced legal structures, it is based on the norms of consumer preference." Metzger, Consuming Jesus: Beyond Race and Class Divisions in a Consumer Church, 2007.

Some believe that churches that are organized according to ethnicity, unique language specific or even cultural leanings is not only an acceptable strategy but preferred. One popular perspective is called the Homogeneous Unit Principle. The proponents of this view address one of the hidden tensions of the church, especially in the USA.

The material in this chapter will present the argument in favor of the Homogeneous Unit Principle (hereafter the HUP theory) as developed by the School of Church Growth. First, the historical context of the philosophy of Church Growth (from which the HUP theory emerges) will be outlined. Second, the unique features of Church Growth as they pertain to the HUP theory will be identified. Third, the HUP theory itself will be defined and explained. And finally, the Biblical, practical and Theological arguments in favor of the HUP theory will be traced.

**The Historical Context of the Theory[2]**

The phenomenon known as Church Growth had its beginnings in the mid-1950's. It was a new approach to missions

---

[2] What follows is a brief overview from a third party perspective of the historical context from which Church Growth and ultimately the Homogeneous Unit Principle developed. Similarly, McGavran traces the HUP history himself by identifying three major stages in the history of Church Growth: 1933-65 tracing McGavran's early missionary service up to the fledgling school of Church Growth in Oregon; 1965-71 incorporating the new relationship with Charles Fuller and Fuller Seminary up through the formative years of organizing the School of Church Growth; and 1971-85 accounting the impact of Church Growth concepts on the U.S.A. For a more detailed discussion of these eras see chapters 7-9, 64-101, in McGavran, Effective Evangelism: A Theological Mandate,

developed by Donald McGavran, as an outgrowth of his missionary endeavors in the third world.[3] "Church Growth" began as a missions movement with a desire to re-ignite an evangelistic fervor that would rival the exploding population of the earth.

An enormous task, such as this, which attempts to convert the world's unconverted billions reflects the degree of enthusiasm with which McGavran has lived his life. One writer describes McGavran's life: "At the age of 88, a small, bespectacled man with a barren scalp and impish eyes that no longer see to read, Donald McGavran still seems - there is no other word for it - young. He has a young man's barely restrained impatience to get on with it – 'it' being, always, the task of drawing every people group on earth to Jesus Christ."[4] His life and philosophy of ministry has been to find a strategy to make evangelism happen more efficiently and more quickly.

---

1988.

[3]  This point is helpful for it lends itself to the notion that "Church Growth" may have an other-than-American origin. For a further discussion see C. Peter Wagner, Leading Your Church to Growth, (Ventura, California: Regal Books, 1984) 13, 14.   Also, Wagner notes that in its early stages the Institute of Church Growth attracted students who were interested in applying growth principles to the overseas populations and "did not think of church growth as applying to America." (C. Peter Wagner, Your Church Can Grow [Glendale: Regal Books, 1976], 13.)   For further evidence of this see McGavran's two chapters "The God-given People Movements" (chapter VI, 69-99) and "Gathered Colony Strategy in the Light of People Movements", chapter VII, 100-108, in The Bridges of God (New York: Friendship Press, 1955).

[4]  Tim Stafford, "The Father of Church Growth", Christianity Today [February 21, 1986], 19.  For a further biographical discussion of McGavran see "Part 1: Donald Anderson McGavran: Three Portraits", 5-43 in A. R. Tippett, ed., God, Man and Church Growth (Grand Rapids: Wm. B. Eerdmans Pub. Co.), 1973.

McGavran's particular emphasis that is of interest to this study is that churches usually grow along ethnic or family lines.

Twenty years after its inception in India, the principles of Church Growth were introduced into the United States in the early 1970's.[5] And, as a result, Donald McGavran was been dubbed the "Father of Church Growth."[6] Both he and his passion for evangelism stimulated discussion among church leaders who were asking for specific data that could analyze why certain churches grew and why others did not.[7]

**The Historical Beginnings of Church Growth and McGavran**

The principles of Church Growth formed in the mind of Donald McGavran during his life as a third-generation missionary to India over a 30 year span of time. These ideas were published in two subsequent volumes: The Bridges of God[8] and How Churches Grow[9]. Both works developed thoughts of

---

[5] Wagner notes that through the mid-1970's reception of Church Growth by mainline denominations was not enthusiastic. Criticism of the principles was largely the effort of Christian social activists. But, this reticence dissipated after these same denominations began to experience serious decline in their memberships. To see Wagner's response to these criticisms see further Church Growth and the Whole Gospel (San Francisco: Harper & Row, 1981).

[6] Stafford, "Father," 19,20.

[7] Wagner, Your Church, 10.

[8] In this volume McGavran traces the evidence, which substantiates the phenomenon of "people movements". He presents evidence of group salvation experiences that are found in both ancient and current settings, namely, the third world. These illustrative observations lead McGavran to postulate several ideas that form the core of the Church Growth Movement philosophy. See further: McGavran, Bridges.

[9] Donald McGavran, How Churches Grow (New York: Friendship Press, 1959).

4

Church Growth within the context of world evangelism.[10] The latter work had application to the United States.[11]

## A Definition of Church Growth

McGavran's thoughts on world missions and the church needed a term to communicate his deepest concern. His choices of the traditional ideas of "evangelism" or "missions" were unsatisfactory because they had been over-used, over-defined and over-generalized. To McGavran these terms had come to mean all that Christians do and therefore were not specific enough for him.[12]

Precision and articulation were his goal. To achieve this he combined the two terms "Church" and "Growth". Together, they formed a technical phrase that makes it independent from what either term means alone.[13] The meaning of "Church Growth" is "all that is involved in bringing men and women who do not have

---

[10] For a further development of McGavran's personal recounting of the formulation of Church Growth and his part in it see chapter 1, "The Discovery of Church Growth," 13-27 in McGavran and Hunter, Church Growth: Strategies that Work (Nashville: Abingdon, 1980).

[11] Wagner, Your Church, 11.

[12] Ibid. 12.

[13] Wagner describes this technical term with an illustration of a common American breakfast cereal called "Grape Nuts". It is a grain cereal that neither has grapes in it nor nuts. But, the name refers to that brand name cereal. In the same way, he describes "Church Growth" as a technical name for McGavran's philosophy (Wagner, Your Church, 12).

a personal relationship to Jesus Christ into fellowship with Him and into responsible church membership."[14]

At the center of the Church Growth philosophy are four principles. These four principles are: (1) God wants His lost sheep found.[15] While effort is admirable, more must be expected. Namely, results determine success not attempts. If people do not become countable responsible members of the church then Christians have failed.[16] (2) Our choice of method must be based on fact.[17] Technique is accepted or rejected based upon the growth it produced. Hard evidence, however, is demanded to prove results. (3) Pour your resources into winning channels.[18] Mobility of resources and administrative awareness must quickly respond to wherever the spiritual opportunities are. (4) People like to stay with their own people.

---

[14] Wagner, Your Church, 12.

[15] McGavran argued that the traditional "Mission Station" approach to evangelism produced few results in comparison to the "People Movement" approach. He further notes that "more" is not depersonalizing but that each convert is a beloved person of God. Simply, " . . . the more who come to Christian faith the better." (McGavran, Bridges, 97. See further chapter 6, 68-99)

[16] Essential to Church Growth principles is the postulate that it is God's will for churches to grow. Both Biblically and Theologically, it is attested that evangelism is intended to successfully produce converts and hence, Church Growth. (Wagner, Leading, 13.) See further chapter 1, 13-40.

[17] Church Growth puts an emphasis on what "works". Pragmatism, a consecrated pragmatism is central. Results are a constant demand. (Wagner, Your Church, 135.) See further chapter 10, "Decisions or Disciples" - the sixth vital sign of a healthy church, 135-146.

[18] McGavran poses the following question to aid in determining where mission resources should be channeled: "From the point of view of the greatest possible extension of Christianity during the foreseeable future, which growing churches should receive priority." (McGavran, Bridges, 115. See further chapter 8, 109-125.)

Let them do so.[19]  McGavran views a multiethnic church as counterproductive to evangelism.[20]  This perspective is based again upon the emphasis of measurable evangelistic results, not attitudes toward different cultural or ethnic groups.

## Moving to Influence Missions through Education

As a direct result of McGavran's first two publications, he became in high demand as a speaker on his ideas.  However, he soon concluded that the overall impact on missions thinking via the speaking circuit was minimal.  Therefore, the Institute of Church Growth was formed to generate a lasting influence on world missions. The strategy for the Institute was simple: gather career missionaries on furlough, introduce them to the principles of Church Growth on a graduate level, demonstrate them in real church situations and finally, pass these concepts on to others.[21]  Classes began in 1961 within the hospitality of Northwest Christian College in Eugene, Oregon.  By 1965 the Institute outgrew its beginnings and moved to Fuller Theological Seminary in Pasadena, California.  There, it became the School of World Missions and Institute of Church Growth.[22]

---

[19] This is the principle under critique in this dissertation.  Wagner identifies it as the fifth of seven vital signs of a growing church. (Wagner, Your Church, 110.)

[20]  Stafford, "Father," 21.

[21]  Wagner, Your Church, 12.

[22]  Ibid. 12-13.

McGavran began to build the teaching staff of the Institute with men of missionary experience and like-minded perspective. Alan Tippett, who was already a colleague of McGavran's in Eugene, was the first faculty addition at Fuller. He came with 20 years of missionary experience in the Fiji Islands and with similar but independently derived growth principles as McGavran. Subsequent additions to the Institute expanded the trans-cultural, missionary and anthropological experience of its staff. Additions included Ralph Winter, who served as a missionary in Guatemala, Arthur Glasser, a former missionary in China, Charles Kraft, whose missionary field was Nigeria, C. Peter Wagner, whose missionary experience was Bolivia, and finally J. Edwin Orr.[23]

## The Essential Objective of Church Growth

Central to McGavran's development of his theories and institute was a single objective: ". . . to make more effective the propagation of the gospel and the multiplication of churches on new ground."[24] At the time of its inception, McGavran estimated that $300 million a year were spent by North America for missions overseas and he believed that the yield of Christian growth could be raised significantly if his theories were adopted into missionary thought. Therefore, he desired to influence

---

[23] Ibid. 13.
[24] Ibid.

8

mission executives, career missionaries, and national church leaders who were the key mission thinkers working in Asia, Africa, and Latin America.[25]

## The Wagner-McGavran Connection

If Donald McGavran is considered the father of "Church Growth", then C. Peter Wagner would certainly be the first disciple. Now an ardent follower of Church Growth principles, Wagner reflects on his originally negative attitude toward McGavran's ideas. As a missionary in Bolivia, he was <u>not</u> an admirer of McGavran's concepts. Instead, Wagner completely dismissed much of McGavran's thinking, largely because they were in conflict with his own training.[26]

The change for Wagner came when he studied with McGavran at Fuller Seminary during a furlough from Bolivia. Reflecting over that change, Wagner describes the shift, " . . . I entered his program in 1967 as a skeptic. But I emerged an enlightened person."[27] Wagner became convinced that the Church Growth approach is both Biblical and pleasing to God

---

[25] Ibid.

[26] Wagner recalls his original opinion of McGavran referring to him as an "outright quack". As a graduate of Fuller Seminary, Wagner was the opinion that McGavran's ideas were in conflict with his own training at the very same institution. To review more of Wagner's reflections on his original reaction to McGavran and his ideas see the introduction to chapter 2 "What is Church Growth All About?" in Wagner, <u>Your Church</u>, 34-35.

[27] Wagner, <u>Your Church</u>, 33.

and has emerged as a leader in persuading others to adopt this position as well.[28]

## *Unique Features of Church Growth*

The philosophy of Church Growth finds its meaning best expressed in three important areas. There is a Biblical foundation that is at the root of its thinking. Then, there is the matter of Science, which is integral to this perspective. And finally, there is the need in Christianity to stimulate churches that are stagnated in their development.

## The Biblical Argument Used by Church Growth

Essential to the development of the Church Growth philosophy is an understanding of God's purpose for the unsaved people of the world. The God of the Bible is both a God who seeks after those who are lost and also finds those whom He seeks.[29] To accomplish this, God has provided the Gospel, the provision to bring lost people to Himself.

---

[28] It is important to note that while Wagner strongly supports the precepts of Church Growth, he is also gracious toward those who do not accept this position. He further acknowledges that their use by God may be better achieved outside the framework of the church growth philosophy. To view this generous testimony in greater detail please see the introduction to chapter 2 "What is Church Growth All About?" 34,35 in Wagner, Your Church.

[29] The two verses cited to substantiate this perspective of God's pursuit of the unsaved are Luke 19:10 and 2 Peter 3:9. These texts represent the intent of God to bring all men to conversion, a disposition of God's ever since seeking Adam in the garden. (Wagner, Your Church, 35,36.)

10

However, God has also designed a mechanism to make this provision of the Gospel functional. That is, God could have communicated the Gospel message to the world Himself; but, instead chose to use Christians to be His witnesses. As a steward carries out his duties when ordered by his master, so Christians are given the duty of spreading the news of the Gospel to the world. Facilitating this important task is the desire of Church Growth.[30]

## Pragmatism

Since the Church Growth philosophy believes that it is vital to carry out the task of evangelism, it also expects evangelistic results. That is, it believes that the church must grow and that growth is not just a good idea but it is the will of God.[31] This to them requires a pragmatic strategy.[32] Church Growth describes its position as consecrated pragmatism.[33] McGavran's spirit illustrates this perspective of getting the job

---

[30] Wagner, Your Church, 36-38.

[31] Wagner, Leading, 13.

[32] For a further discussion of the Church Growth's concepts on "consecrated pragmatism" please see Wagner, Whole Gospel, chapter 4, "Consecrated Pragmatism," 69-86.

[33] Wagner stresses the commitment of the Church Growth School to pragmatism but to a "consecrated pragmatism". He shuns any functional choices that lead to doctrinal or unethical compromise. He opposes a pragmatism that dehumanizes people by emphasizing the importance of an end over a priority on those people. However, he advocates the rigorous testing of "traditional" methodologies and programs with hard questions. When any method fails to achieve their designed purpose or reach their stipulated goal, then, the School of Church Growth calls for correction. (Wagner, Leading, 201.)

done: The fundamental presupposition of [McGavran's] entire thought is that the growth of the church is always and everywhere God's purpose. God desires a harvest. Thus, a stagnant or declining church is never the will of God.[34] Thus, an interest in numerical church growth is viewed as a natural part of church life. The shepherding minister knows that counting his sheep is of vital importance. He not only accounts for a current total but he also finds an even greater delight in an ewe having twins over a single lamb.[35]

## Accounting the Data

It is no mistake to observe that Church Growth places an emphasis on numerical growth as a priority. McGavran writes, "Numbers of the redeemed are important. When good shepherding is provided, growth improves quality.[36] He reasons that the normal course of a routine life illustrates that two can accomplish more than one. Also, he sees a direct proportion between the size of a group and its affect when involved in worship and ministry. Bigger churches sing better, do more

---

[34] David Smith, "The Church Growth Principles of Donald McGavran," in Transformation, 2 (1985), 25.

[35] Wagner, Leading, 22.

[36] Donald McGavran, Ethnic Realities and the Church, "Lessons from India" (South Pasadena: William Carey Library, 1979), 149. For a further discussion of the philosophy and attitude of Church Growth on numerical analysis see chapter 4 "Measurement and Meaning", 104-133 in Eddie Gibbs, I Believe in Church Growth (London: Houghton and Stoughton, 1981).

12

ministry, send out more missionaries, and begin more churches.[37]

Numerical results are described as the consequence of effective evangelism.[38] Large numbers of converts are not only the goal of Church Growth but they also become an asset in continuing the success of more evangelism. It is part of the dynamic of people with other people. Gibbs emphasizes that numerical increase is not an end itself but part of the whole planning process of Church Growth. He firmly states that he is as . . . concerned with quality control as much as quantity performance.[39]

## The Use of Science in Church Growth

Church Growth introduces the use of science[40] by noting that the difference between humans and animals is that God

---

[37] McGavran, Ethnic Realities, 149.

[38] McGavran explains that an interest in quantitative results does not diminish Church Growth in the individual. On the contrary, the more that are converted simply gives more reason for delight with more Christians. See further "Should We Be So Concerned with Mere Numbers?" in McGavran, Bridges, and 97,98.

[39] Gibbs, I Believe, 128.

[40] "Science" is the term that McGavran uses to describe the practical purpose of the church, nearly a synonym for "mission". And he understands that the purpose of the church is evangelism, propagating the gospel. The carrying out of evangelism (which is the mission of the church) is the science of the mission (which is his definition of what Missiology is). For a further development of this see McGavran, "Missiology Faces the Lion," Missiology 17(July 1989): 335-341. In particular, note pages 335, 338, and 340. McGavran begins this article describing his understanding of science, which serves as a backdrop for a Missiological statement to preserve the church's mission - hence, science is in action. The main point of the article is to alert the church

made man in His image. Man has a mind with which he can be rational. Hence, God calls for His followers to love Him with all their minds. Then a transition is made: Using the mind well to understand, plan, and implement a specific task brings science into the picture.[41] Doing the task of stewardship, spreading the Gospel, can be done well or not well.

According to Church Growth the spiritual dimension of making missions work is granted; but, much more is involved. Historically, missionaries were burdened with more guilt when their efforts saw little fruit in spite of following the admonition of others to pray more or study more. Too often the spiritual problem approach was in fact simplistic and resulted in more harm than good. Some of the changes that are sought by missions require more complex thinking. This is where Church Growth sees the value of adding science to missions: The scientific aspect of church growth is vitally interested in understanding and describing all the factors which enter into cases of failure and success in evangelistic efforts.[42]

McGavran incorporates in his analyses the tools of statistics, careful documentation, and sociological theorizing. According to Donald McGavran, these tools are essential in

---

to the danger of substituting efforts that improve human living in place of direct evangelism. For a further discussion see "Church Growth as a Science" 75-77 in Wagner, Whole Gospel, 1981.

[41] Wagner, Your Church, 38.

[42] Ibid. 39.

14

helping the church to grow. This perspective of the church-growth movement perceives evangelism techniques from a functional angle. It is interested in the production of results. If the method works then it has merit. If it does not produce, then, the technique must be altered or replaced. For fundamental to the School of Church Growth is that God wants people to be converted. Evangelism is God's method of accomplishing this. Therefore, whatever techniques are used to carry out the mission of the church must produce results.[43] This is the essential test to the church's strategy: does it work? In the area of reaching people who are from different ethnic groups within a culturally mixed environment like the USA, what strategy will work the best in converting different ethnic groups to Christianity?

## Sociology and Evangelism Strategy

The zeal behind the Church Growth and HUP theory is the urgency to make evangelism[44] the first priority of the church. One way in which McGavran has developed his emphasis for

---

[43] Stafford, "Father," 19,20.

[44] Evangelism strategy is an important detail in Church Growth. Gibbs elaborates on Wagner's three-pronged system of celebration, congregation, and call. He notes that evangelism can happen successfully in any of these layers but the closer and more intimate the group, the more homogeneous the group should be to make evangelism successful. For a further discussion of this see "Structures and Strategies", chapter 7, 192-220 in Gibbs, I Believe, 1981.

results is by utilizing sociology as an important tool in reckoning the course of the Church. McGavran believes that sociology contributes to an understanding of how churches flourish in new areas, how churches reproduce, how the Christian faith is communicated and how the church influences its nation. Since the developing church follows sociological and anthropological characteristics, then, an understanding of these sciences can only lead to a greater understanding of the church. They add a depth of comprehension that remains hidden if we employ only ecclesiastical or theological frames of reference.[45] Wagner reveals that he concurs with this view when he states that: . . . God's will must always be socially interpreted.[46] According to the constitution of the Church Growth school, their philosophy rests upon principles derived from the Bible and developed through a theological matrix. But, in the application of its goals, namely, the task of world evangelism, it also utilizes both data and methods from the social sciences as helpful insights in the accomplishment of its mission.[47] In particular cultural anthropology[48] is noted as the "key social science in the church growth paradigm."[49]

---

[45] McGavran, Ethnic Realities, 2.

[46] Ibid. 5.

[47] Wagner, Whole Gospel, 149.

[48] For a further discussion of the balanced use of cultural anthropology in missions see Orlando E. Costas, The Church and Its Mission: A Shattering Critique from the Third World (Wheaton: Tyndale, 1974.)

[49] Wagner, Whole Gospel, 150.

16

Much of the HUP theory derives its supportive data from observing the human preference to associate with familiar or like features in other human groupings.[50] This is an undeniable observable phenomenon of human behavior. The HUP theory is an acknowledgment of this preference along with a strategy to utilize the dynamic in accomplishing evangelistic results; namely, starting churches along the lines of these preferences where feasible.

Furthermore, this phenomenon not only is observable on the level of preferred association but also in the area of desired ecclesiastical leadership. The reasoning behind the implementation of the HUP theory is a pragmatic one. Ideally it is acknowledged that a pastor ought to be accepted to care for the people regardless of his ethnic background. Nevertheless, the HUP theory maintains a contrary philosophy and strategy. It is their conclusion that a congregation is best lead by "one of its own sons." Calling a pastor is admittedly easier when racial or ethnic background is totally disregarded, nevertheless, " . . . one continually sees pastors who do not fit their congregations simply because they are not of the homogeneous unit

---

[50]   The HUP theory is in agreement to Niebuhr's sociological comments on denominationalism.   Niebuhr argues that the origins of U.S. denominations parallel cultural rather than distinctly religious causes.  Furthermore, it is observed that Niebuhr shows that though denominations are religious they have developed or conformed to the social order of classes or castes.  For a further discussion of this see Richard Niebuhr, The Social Sources of Denominationalism (Cleveland and New York: The World Pub. Co., 1929).

concerned."[51] This philosophy of church development, then, assumes an unmistakable distinction between theology in the classroom and theology that actually operates in the church. The former can be understood and acknowledged but the latter is the adjustment necessary to the actual working environment of everyday parish and church life.

## An Explanation of the Homogeneous Unit Principle

The HUP theory of church growth can best be linked to the following statement: "Men like to become Christians without crossing racial, linguistic, or class barriers."[52] And just as well it could be identified with Wagner's statement: "Disciples are more readily made by people within their own homogeneous unit, and congregations develop into healthy communities when they concentrate on only one kind of people."[53] According to Wagner the general consensus acknowledges that it is _easier_ for churches to develop around just one kind of people. His conclusion is based upon a biblical, theological and sociological search that leads him to adhere to the HUP theory. He also believes " . . . that the weight of the cumulative data supports the

---

[51] McGavran, Ethnic Realities, 147.
[52] McGavran, Understanding (revised 1980), 223. This observation was first published by McGavran, Bridges, 1955.
[53] Ibid. 4.

18

homogeneous unit approach to the development of Christian churches."[54]

This concept was introduced[55] into the United States in the 1972. Then, in 1979 two volumes were published to discuss the HUP theory. Ethnic Realities by Donald McGavran illustrated the HUP theory with India as a case study. Our Kind of People by C. Peter Wagner illustrated the HUP theory with the United States of America as a case study.[56] Subsequent to these two major works that argue in favor of the HUP theory, several articles and chapters in later volumes continue the discussion over this perspective of Church Growth. The following is a summary of this strategy for evangelism and Church Growth.

**The Definition of a Homogeneous Unit**

A major consideration in the development of the HUP theory is the definition of a Homogeneous Unit. In the second chapter of Our Kind of People the view that an ethnic group and a homogeneous unit are not necessarily the same thing is made clear. To clarify a definition of ethnicity an elimination process is

---

[54] Ibid.
[55] By "introduce" I mean that this practice was described in detail from an ecclesiastical perspective. The practice of human bias and prejudice is an old one. I am grateful to Ainslie Walton for this clarification.
[56] Wagner, Whole Gospel, 166.

19

used. First, it is stated that ethnicity is not national. A nation has a common government at a particular time and place with the qualifications to membership in the United Nations. It is further noted that a nation can be comprised of several ethnic groups. Second, an ethnic group is not a race. A race is related to genetics. Each member of a race shares prominent physical characteristics. Third, an ethnic group is not a tribe. Fourth, it is not a social class. Fifth, it is not a minority group. A minority group experiences a common feeling of discrimination. Sixth, it is not a homogeneous unit. To positively define an ethnic group this work quotes Shibutani and Kwan: "An ethnic group consists of those who conceive of themselves as being alike by virtue of their common ancestry, real or fictitious, and who are so regarded by others."[57]

Sociologist, Alfred Schultz, helps to explain the idea of a Homogeneous Unit. Individual members of a given group are "at home" with each other and in their community setting. That is, they are comfortable in the common surroundings, where institutionalized habits, mores, and folkways provide a sense of direction that provide the necessary adjustments to fit in with other people belonging to the same situation. Thus, similar symbols, customs, and habits shared with other members of the

---

[57] Tamotsu Shibutani and Kian M. Kwan, Ethnic Stratification: A Comparative Approach (New York: MacMillan, 1965), 47; quoted in C. Peter Wagner, Our Kind of People, "The Ethical Dimensions of Church Growth in America," (Atlanta: John Knox Press, 1979), 39.

20

group define the social roles, positions, and statutes of each. This acceptance of a common system of lifestyle and custom leads the members of the group to identify with a homogeneous self-typification.[58] A view of this nature acknowledges that some group association is essential on a daily basis for each individual. The most fluent and meaningful communication takes place within the group. Mutual signs for communication are clear and easily understood. People naturally gravitate to what is comfortable. They find security and meaning where they can communicate. Hence, interaction across mixed lines is very difficult. Usually such occurrences result when a minority group adopts the communication features and signs of the dominant group.[59]

It is from this sociological analysis that the HUP theory argues sympathetically against mixing Homogeneous Units. Illustrating the difficulty of mixing groups, the following is noted: " . . . American whites, accustomed to their dominant position in society as a whole, are less willing than blacks to go through the difficult and uncomfortable process of altering their system of relevances."[60] According to this position, the expectation of Homogeneous Units to both mix and maintain original group

---

[58] For a further discussion see the Collected Papers, Vol. II: Studies in Social Theory, ed. by Arvid Brodersen (The Hague: Nijhoff, 1964), 251-52 quoted in Wagner, Our Kind, 59.

[59] Wagner, Our Kind, 59.

[60] Ibid., 60.

communication is elevated to a level of difficulty too great for common application.[61]

Then, to further identify a Homogeneous Unit, the HUP theory adopts Milton Gordon's "ethclass" model, a combination of vertical ethnic stratification and horizontal social class stratifications.[62] To this model Wagner adds his "A-factor" (rate of assimilation) and "C-factor" (degree of acculturation). In detail Wagner outlines his selection of factors that must be considered for Homogeneous Unit identity. Yet, he cautions at the end that "Every human group is not automatically a homogeneous unit."[63] Rather, it is where distinctions as "ours" and "theirs" are apparent.[64]

Several precautions are raised at this point. First, groups with an intrinsically sinful common habit (crime or perversion for example) cannot be celebrated by Christians and therefore must be avoided in strategic planning. Second, Wagner states, "The

---

[61] Ibid., 61.

[62] Ibid., 61.

[63] Ibid., 75.

[64] A common approach in applying the HUP theory to a church situation is to consider the three factors of socio-economic status, age, and education. In considering the five traditional socio-economic levels (upper, upper-middle, middle, lower-middle and lower) it is observed that the socio-economic level of the church had no bearing on a church's growth but what relationship the church had to the surrounding community did affect its growth. Similarly, in both the categories of age and education, the closer in proximity that these features were to their community the more apparent the church's growth. For a further discussion of this see chapter 6, "Growth through Assimilation", 93-116 in Charles Arn, Donald McGavran, and Win Arn, Growth: A New Vision for the Sunday School (Pasadena, Calif.: Church Growth Press, 1980).

22

homogeneous unit principle need not and should not be pushed to ridiculous extremes in any direction."[65]

At the same time, however, both the population in the church and out of the church indicate that any non-racist "ideal" is currently absent and may be unreachable. Therefore, the need to accelerate the evangelistic result in such a situation is self-evident: "The new climate for accepting a diversity of peoples as proper in American society favors the development of Christian churches along homogeneous lines. The great majority of America's 330,000 churches are, of course, already homogeneous." What Church Growth people object to is the unfounded guilt generated by pressures to become heterogeneous.[66]

**The Church and Cultural Heritage**

One of the fundamental concerns of the HUP theory is that when a person converts to Christianity, his or her decision does not alienate others within their same homogenous unit. The HUP theory observes that Christianity is sometimes perceived as a threat to homogeneous unit identity and

---

[65] Ibid., 77. Wagner elaborates on the importance of balancing the application of the HUP theory in light of what he describes as a "*penultimate dynamic*" in contrast to an "*ultimate ideal*". This translates into a willingness to begin churches that are homogeneous in nature if by doing so evangelism results can be better achieved. However, this should be seen only as a beginning to move a group of people toward a Biblical heterogenous ideal. For a further discussion see "What a Homogenous Unit Really Is" 167-168 in Wagner, Whole Gospel.

discourages continued evangelistic potential if converts abandon their cultural roots. The rationale is as follows: " . . . in regard to certain matters, the Christian and the congregation must think of itself as a new creation, which has repented of its sins and walks in the light. It must do this while speaking the old language, living in ancestral houses, earning its living in accustomed ways, and being thoroughly a part of its culture and its ethnic linkage. Christians must not betray and abandon their ethnic units in becoming Christian. They must not think of themselves as doing this, and they must not seem to others to have done this."[67]

The topic of group identity is surfaced to explain the HUP theory. It gives ethnicity a high place in determining the morality of people-group interaction: "Ethnicity becomes a moral issue because though it unites people, it also divides them."[68] This topic of ethnic dynamic is explored by addressing a classic race travesty. The reasoning grants for the moment that the church and its 11 o'clock Sunday service is the "most segregated hour" in America. But, having granted that it asks whether that is necessarily bad. Furthermore, it inquires, "Does the Christian ethic demand that congregations be characterized by a mixture of the ethnic groups present?"[69]

---

[66] Ibid., 79.
[67] McGavran, Ethnic Realities, 14.
[68] Ibid., 9.
[69] Ibid.

24

Gerald Palmer, director of the Missions Section of the Home Mission Board of the Southern Baptist Convention, wins the HUP theory's approval in his strategy to apply the HUP theory to church growth. Palmer suggests that the alternative to this HUP theory is ineffectiveness: "We cannot afford to address our mission work to the median-range Anglo-Saxon culture and wait for the ones outside this range to become like us . . . "[70]

Another precaution is raised at this point. The HUP theory disavows total separation. Unity among Christians is a priority that must be maintained. But, this unity can be expressed on different levels of Christian interaction. The HUP theory " . . . applies chiefly not on the denominational level, but on the congregational level where the fellowship of church life becomes prominent."[71] Therefore, integration can and should be visibly demonstrated by the leaders of each denomination as a mature example to the members of the many churches that they represent of the ideal toward which all the churches are striving.

**Indian Culture Problems and the HUP Theory Philosophy**

The philosophy behind the HUP theory is illustrated in the complexities of Indian society and its caste structure. It is explained that the churches of India do not <u>promote</u> either the

---

[70] Wagner, <u>Our Kind</u>, 12.
[71] Ibid., 14.

25

caste system or segregation. Their Christian faith will not permit this methodology. However, the church does promote an essential of Indian culture: " . . . namely, that it highly values the ethnic composition of all its peoples."[72] The variety of Indian subcultures is listed in the thousands and it is supposed as natural for each separate group to convert to Christianity " . . . while yet in the stage of maintaining its high sense of peoplehood."[73] Caste itself is not a structure that Christians can morally espouse, but, they can and should recognize it as part of the fabric of the culture of India. Hence, they act properly by advancing the Gospel in that context without attempting to disrupt the society in which the church exists.

Thus, in this context, it seems reasonable to allow new converts to have time to grow into their new found Christian faith. And if homogeneous churches allow for spiritual growth and at the same time encourage others of the same homogeneous group to be attracted to convert to Christianity, then, homogeneous churches should be commended and duplicated.[74]

---

[72] McGavran, Ethnic Realities, 125.

[73] Ibid.

[74] In a society where there are several homogeneous groups responding to the Gospel at the same time, McGavran and Wagner suggest that each group must be separately "discipled" to the furthest possible extent. They suggest that group loyalty is a high priority and must become the avenue by which Christ is introduced to the others. Building a single brotherhood of believers before 2% of a particular group is converted will have a negative affect on the 98% of any unconverted homogeneous group. (McGavran, Understanding, third ed., 177.)

26

## Mission Lessons from India

The Indian society is permeated with the problem of racial bias. As such, Church Growth is not denying that reality; instead, it attempts to develop a strategy that works in spite of it. Dealing with the racial bias of a massive population such as India, leads McGavran to conclude the following: " . . . caste feeling, caste prejudice, the awareness of profound difference, and strong ethnic pride are quite common. It is of no use, I believe, simply to ignore these things. They will not go away through mere denial that they exist."[75] Thus, the HUP theory is an attempt to fulfill the church's mission in the context of a world that is severely handicapped with racial bigotry.

Consequently, McGavran reasons as follows: "I believe the solution is to permit, and indeed in suitable circumstances to encourage, each homogeneous unit . . . to form a cluster of congregations within itself."[76] An obvious predicament arises; namely, the Hindu-thinking Indian will not accept Christianity for fear of violating his social order. This is a major concern expressed and addressed by the HUP theory. While Christian brotherhood is acknowledged as a feature of true Christianity, it is emphasized that such unity is " . . . a result of the operation of

---

[75] McGavran, <u>Ethnic Realities</u>, 252.
[76] Ibid., 252.

27

the Holy Spirit in the lives of Christians - not a prerequisite for baptism."[77]

## Mission Strategy and a Soteriological Foundation

The thinking behind the HUP theory concerns itself primarily with the conversion of the non-Christian. Its primary focus is on tailoring the Gospel presentation to appeal to the non-Christian. These people are not yet a part of the kingdom of God and Jesus is not the Lord of their lives. Wagner describes the thrust: "It is a principle of evangelism, not Christian nurture."[78]

In another statement the HUP theory reveals a preference in seeing the Church adapt to different cultures: "The principle is that as the Church spreads into caste after caste, it is desirable that it take on the color of each."[79] With successful evangelism taking place and thus an accurate soteriological emphasis, the resulting ecclesiastical variations are accepted as legitimate. The ideal of a single unified Christian brotherhood is

---

[77] McGavran, Understanding, 3rd ed., 177.
[78] Wagner, Whole Gospel, 167. Wagner elaborates: "If the gospel is presented in such a way that it carries racial overtones, and if becoming a Christian involves a social rather than a religious or spiritual decision, most of them will not even hear it. They will choose to remain with their people, in their sins and outside the kingdom of God." (Ibid., 167-168.)
[79] McGavran, Ethnic Realities, 201.

the desired goal but may have to be realistically preceded by a Christianity that initially identifies with a particular group.[80]

## Endogamy and the Church

The practical results of the HUP theory are further strengthened when the subject of marriage and culture is explored. Marriage mores are tightly woven into the fabric of every social group.[81] They determine values and dictate social behavior to a greater degree than most other community beliefs. Consequently, if the church aims at effectively communicating to the surrounding community without offending it, she must respect the marriage characteristics of that same community.

For example, McGavran illustrates from Indian culture what he perceives as a necessary flexibility regarding marriage between a believer and a non-believer. He argues that if the marriage of one's daughter to a non-Christian "always results" in losing that girl to the Christian faith then such arrangements should be "discouraged" on the basis of the biblical injunction forbidding Christians to be unequally yoked. If however, such marriages produce regular converts, then, such arrangements

---

[80] Wagner describes this balance as a "penultimate spiritual dynamic". See note 64.

[81] Intergroup relationships that reflect a tightly knit society also reveal restricted marriage possibilities, according to McGavran. Along with a high level of "people consciousness" he observes that " . . . all marriages take place within the segment of society concerned . . . " (McGavran, Understanding, 3rd ed., 258.)

should be viewed as acceptable. The non-Christian partners in such situations should be considered inquirers rather than an unequal partner. McGavran suggests that no biblical injunctions have been violated in such circumstances.[82] Such reasoning is defended as a perspective which gives regard to the homogeneous unit cultural value of marriage and preserves the integrity of the new Christian perspective as well.

## Exogamy and the Church

It is also noted that there is a pattern among church leaders that indicates that Homogeneous Unit lines are preferred in marriage relationships. On the one hand, leaders affirm a unified peoplehood among all Christians, denounce racism and classism, read widely including materials from all backgrounds. On the other hand, ". . . when he chooses a daughter-in-law he will get one from the right segment of the Church . . ."[83] McGavran cites church history in support of this observation. Almost in spite of the church's traditional stance in favor of a heterogeneous philosophy, its members have largely followed

---

[82] McGavran, Ethnic Realities, 131. McGavran also notes the following: "There are over three thousand ethnic units of various kinds. Each is very largely endogamous: that is, marries within itself and thus holds itself separate from all the others, or tries to. Each has a high consciousness of being itself." (McGavran, Ethnic Realities, 7)

[83] Ibid., 32.

an endogamous pattern.[84]  Wagner makes a distinction here between primary and secondary group relationships.  On levels of the latter, heterogeneous relationships are necessary, even obligatory.  However, on levels of the former, homogeneous relationships are not only acceptable but should never be hindered.[85]

In analyzing the Indian[86] culture with respect to the observance of endogamy, McGavran makes the following observation from the perspective of Indian caste observers: "If our members refuse to give husbands and wives to children of such unions, that is not a church decision but a personal one."[87]  An emphasis on freedom is made along with this reasoning.  It is stated that individuals must be allowed to make choices that allow their ethnic heritage and Christianity to exist together.  The cultural ties to established marriage mores are some of the

---

[84] McGavran traces the HUP theory through the spread of Christianity in Europe.  The Gospel moved from one people group to the next.  "In each case a one-people (monoethnic) denomination arose.  Every member of that cluster of congregations belonged to the one tribe.  Most of them practiced endogamy.  Christian men of the tribe married women of the same tribe." (McGavran, Ethnic Realities, 121.)

[85] Wagner suggests that ecclesiastical or political powers should be utilized to insure heterogeneous relationships in social institutions as employment, entertainment, schooling, recreation, et cetera but not with regard to marriage, church, medical care, or other choices related to "intimate access to the person."  For a further discussion see Wagner, Whole Gospel, 170-173 and chapter 5.

[86] McGavran also illustrates this with the Bataks of Indonesia.  "In becoming Christian the tribe maintained its ethnic purity.  With a few exceptions where Western-educated Bataks have occasionally married non-Bataks, Christian Bataks marry within the tribe.  All the Christians in this branch of the Church Universal are Bataks . . . tribal culture is enhanced, not destroyed." (McGavran, Ethnic Realities, 122.)

[87] McGavran, Ethnic Realities, 181.

strongest in any cultural group.  Bearing this in mind, the HUP theory is seeking a solution that properly observes them while continuing the mission of evangelism.

**Nationalism and the HUP Theory**

Besides the cultural factor of marriage to support the HUP theory, nationalism is also used to illustrate the strong influence of homogeneity as a factor in church history.  A historical pattern of nationalism that served in the development of the church is pointed out by McGavran.  He illustrates this from Scottish church history.  John Knox and his famous declaration "Lord, give me Scotland or I die!" are presented. Expanding on this illustration, McGavran describes Knox as both a great Christian and also a great Scot.  "In any controversy about the rights of the English and the Scots, he was solidly on the side of the Scots. No leader of the Scottish Church who maintained a strict impartiality . . . could possibly have won Scotland to the reformed faith."[88]  The homogeneous unit of John Knox was Scottish.  McGavran suggests that the Scottish spiritual response was aided because one of their own kith and kin led the way.  McGavran illustrates this point further by suggesting that the growth of the church in Korea is a direct result of nationalistic influences.  Conversely, he also suggests that the nationalistic spirit of Mexico in mid 19th century was ripe for an evangelistic effort but the church in North America failed to capture that opportunity.[89]

## The HUP's Discussion of Unity

Next, how the HUP theory handles the Biblical issue of unity is worth examining. The HUP theory does not neglect the priority of unity in the church. In fact it supports the idea vigorously. Its proponents see that the HUP theory is compatible with unity in the church. McGavran's concern is that the church not sacrifice its evangelistic effort with an over-concern to integrate converts. The matter of brotherhood is essential to Christianity but is a matter to address after conversion.[90] Wagner describes this tension in terms of prioritizing the "evangelistic mandate" over the "cultural mandate." He maintains that the HUP theory places its emphasis on accomplishing the former, while a heterogeneous emphasis emphasizes the latter.[91] Thus, the HUP theory advocates unity. Its concern is how to effectively address the matter of church diversity. As it does, it sees itself as being consistent with Biblical mandates not opposed to them.

---

[88]. Ibid., 195.

[89] McGavran, Understanding, 3rd ed., 184–185.

[90] For a further discussion of this perspective see Donald McGavran, Understanding Church Growth, revised (Grand Rapids: Wm. B. Eerdmans Pub. Co., 1980), 173-175.

[91] For a further discussion see Wagner, Whole Gospel, 169-173.

The HUP theory includes a standard for the determination of diversity. It includes "local conditions" and "historical background." These two features are inclusive of matters as language, cultural distinctives and economic environment. "The diversity must always be strictly within biblical limits; but these must neither be defined by the Church of any one nation . . . The unity of the Church is unity <u>in Christ</u>."[92] Thus, diversity[93] must be defined within the parameters of the Scriptures in order for the church to operate legitimately. These limits are in fact established by placing a priority on preserving the unity in Christ within the context of a specific culture[94].

In a further explanation of the compatibility between the HUP theory and unity the trend of declining denominational antagonism is noted. This atmosphere of growing acceptance on this broad base will enhance church growth, allowing unity to be expressed on this higher level while the HUP theory is applied to individual churches[95]. A visible unity in the church is a preference and according to Church Growth analysis is being

---

[92] McGavran, <u>Ethnic Realities</u>, 247.

[93] Gibbs argues for an ecclesiastical promotion of cultural diversity that is reflected in "the structures and institutional life of the churches." (Gibbs, <u>I Believe</u>, 99.)

[94] For an explanation of the situation in India McGavran writes, " . . . the things that really matter - intermarriage, and common sorrow at the time of death - Christians in India of most denominations act like <u>one</u> community . . . the differences of ritual, polity, and creed can easily be exaggerated." (McGavran, <u>Ethnic Realities</u>, 23.)

[95] In explaining the phenomenon of Christians forming churches with people who are like themselves, McGavran states that they " . . . they prefer to join churches whose members look, talk, and act like themselves." (McGavran, <u>Understanding</u>, 3rd ed., 167.)

34

enhanced by two movements: ". . . a spirit of mutual respect and cooperation between the various denominations marks the current scene . . ."[96] and ". . . denominations are regrouping themselves into Federations and United Churches."[97] This improving environment is a helpful climate for church growth to take place. And the HUP theory, applied with these priorities of Biblical unity and diversity in mind, will be strategic in the church's fulfillment of its mission.

An emphasis must be placed on this perspective of keeping unity at the forefront of the HUP theory. The larger churches must set the example. They must model and teach the unity of man as well as the unity of the church. They ". . . should encourage many forms of action above and beyond all ethnic differences.'[98] Practically, the use of united conventions and conferences are suggested as helpful in bringing together Christians of all parts of the Church, across all denominations. It is suggested that the training of all candidates be done without regard to ethnic differences. Literature will also be universal and non-ethnic. None will be considered nor treated as superior or inferior to another. But, there are exceptions to the HUP theory as applied in local church situations.

---

[96] McGavran, Ethnic Realities, 23,24.
[97] Ibid.
[98] Ibid., 208.

## The Test for the Heterogeneous Exception

It is cited that before any church can claim to be a heterogeneous exception it must pass three tests. Only then would it be accepted as a true exception to the HUP theory. The three tests are as follows: First, is the heterogeneity illusory? That is, if a church has an apparent visible mix, such as diverse racial backgrounds, could there be a less visible homogeneous feature that has attracted them together? For example, could their group identity actually be an intellectual or educational grouping which is a homogeneous group of its own? Or perhaps a small percentage of a contrasting homogeneous group may be present within a larger group but in no way influences the church's basic philosophy of ministry.[99] Second, is the heterogeneity transitory? For example is high and frequent social mobility present? In such cases one homogeneous unit is replacing another. Third, is the heterogeneous church growing? Essential to the HUP theory is growth. Growth is the goal and therefore significant in determining an evangelistic strategy. Wagner explains: "Although I do not have empirical evidence to confirm it, my impression is that if any truly heterogeneous

---

[99] The HUP theory assumes significant individual participation in a church situation. Thus, in large church situations, when an appearance of heterogeneity is noted the question is raised as to the actual extent of mixing. Wagner states, " . . . no more problems arise in mixing homogeneous units in that style of worship than mixing them in a baseball stadium." (Wagner, Our Kind, 16)

36

churches in America are growing, they are exceptions to the general rule."[100]

## *A Biblical Explanation by the HUP Theory*

Now, a review of the HUP theory and its Biblical explanation is in order. Beyond developing a technique or strategy for fulfilling the evangelistic mandate of the church, the HUP theory suggests that its essential premise was the pattern of growth in the early church and the philosophy of Jesus in carrying out His ministry on earth: "What were the precise sociological lines along which church growth actually took place under Jesus and the apostles? The validity of the homogeneous unit principle may stand or fall on the answer to that question."[101]

Beginning the treatment of this topic, three general observations from the Old Testament that pertain to God's relationship to the origin and development of man are made. First, the human race is one. It is explained that the ". . . biblical assertion of the creational unity of the human race is basic to the theological understanding of pluralism."[102] Second, God desired and planned for a diversity of people to develop. God's

---

[100] Wagner, Our Kind, 16.
[101] Ibid., 109.
[102] Ibid., 110.

37

scattering of people at Babel ". . . was designed to prove to men and women that they could not frustrate God's plan for human pluralism."[103]   Third, God is concerned for all people.   Even though God elected Israel to be His covenant people, this was not an act that demonstrated superiority.   Rather, all nations would enjoy the blessings of God through Israel.[104]

**The View of *ta ethne* in the HUP Theory**

The central text that is used to support the HUP is the "Great Commission" passage recorded in Matthew 28:18-20.  In particular McGavran makes the interpretive choice that *ta ethne*, which is the target of the church's evangelistic mission, defines the parameters that support the HUP theory.  What follows is his reasoning through the text, which leads to his HUP theory.

After the Resurrection of our Lord, Jesus commissioned His disciples to evangelize the world.   Matthew records this commissioning with these words, "All authority in heaven and on earth has been given to me.  Therefore go and make disciples of all nations . . ."[105]  The HUP theory notes the phrase *ta ethne (nations)* is better rendered "all peoples."[106]   It chooses to

---

[103]  Ibid., 112.

[104]  Ibid., 113.

[105]  Mt. 28:18-19a.

[106] Gibbs points out that the modern tendency is to interpret *ta ethne* as a modern nation, as India, the United States, or China.  However, he along with McGavran and

38

interpret this phrase to mean "class" or "tribe" or "caste". It is explained that the church is to enter into every ethnic unit. The command of Christ is to disciple every ethnic unit of world. In the process of obeying this command, Christianity will assume the color of each group in that local situation. "It becomes indigenous to that unit - that class, or caste, or tribe."[107] Once Christianity has been accepted by a "substantial" part of a peculiar ethnic unity and the Bible has been accepted as their guide for life, then Christ as their Lord will lead them to ". . . purify, and beautify and transform such elements of that culture as they themselves perceive the need to be transformed."[108] The distinction is one of seeing a people group as the target of evangelism as opposed to single individual persons.[109]

Combining this understanding of *ta ethne* with an illustration of India's culture[110], the HUP theory pursues a

---

Arn maintain that *ethne* means castes, tribes, peoples, ethnic units of mankind. Hence, missionary strategy falsely assumes that territorial expansion is successful when in fact it should spread through cultural layers. For a further discussion see "The Spread of the Gospel through Homogeneous Units," 94-97 in Gibbs, I Believe, 1981.

[107] McGavran, Ethnic Realities, 21

[108] Ibid.

[109] McGavran elaborates, "Today we are very likely to think in terms of evangelizing nation-states . . . [but the] New Testament is very clear that the segments of society, the pieces of the mosaic, are to be evangelized." (McGavran, Effective Evangelism, 110)

[110] McGavran illustrates out of the Indian culture the unique challenge to the Gospel of caste even in contrast to racism. Christianity can stand clearly against racist ideologies in South Africa and the United States, but has a much more difficult time formulating a strategy of evangelism in a society like India where the caste system is the culture, the matrix in which the church grows. For a further discussion see "The Matrix - The Caste System," 17-22 in McGavran Ethnic Realities, 1979.

concept of the church which is represented in the following: ". . . All I plead for here is that, as in India the Church presses on to this goal, she offer all communities the option of becoming Christian in their normal ethnic groupings."[111] Both the Biblical understanding of *ethne* and how the Church in India pursues the evangelistic mandate, supports the HUP theory in following the most natural way toward church growth.

A strong emphasis of the HUP theory is finding a meaning of brotherhood while not destroying ethnic culture. It is argued that the fulfillment of the Great Commission is not tantamount to an instruction to eliminate *ta ethne*. Rather the church is to disciple *ta ethne*. ". . . it is not the Church's business to destroy all languages but one, encourage interracial and intercaste marriages, and create a tribeless, casteless, raceless world."[112] From a practical perspective, the HUP theory urges caution when the Gospel is brought into a foreign environment. The Gospel must be communicated but not destroy essentials (such as language) in a different culture.

At the heart of this strategy is the realization that millions more need to be converted to Christianity. That observation calls for thousands of new churches to be formed in addition to the ones that currently exist. McGavran illustrates this perspective by applying the HUP theory to ethnic groups in

---

[111] McGavran, Ethnic Realities, 112.

40

America[113] as one way to generate effective evangelism for the millions who are unchurched.

## The 12: An Example of Jesus and the HUP Theory

The HUP theory does not rest only on an Old Testament argument in favor of its perspective. Rather, it sees it as theologically consistent with the New Testament pattern. For example, it is interpreted that Jesus' selection of His 12 disciples demonstrates the HUP theory. The closest companions of the Lord did not include a Gentile, Samaritan, Idumean or even a Hellenist Jew. Instead, He chose eleven Galileans all who spoke the Aramaic language. The one exception is Judas, a Judean, but who was later replaced by Matthias, a Galilean.

## Parable of the Sower: An Illustration of Strategy

The HUP theory understands that the parable of the sower teaches lessons on evangelism technique. For example, if a congregation in India ignores the forces involved in the caste system and only perceives an Indian as an Indian and does

---

[112] Ibid., 125.

[113] Based on the two sociological facts that most Protestant congregations are English-speaking, middle-class people and that 60 million ethnic Americans of numerous ethnic units will not become members of these established congregations, the suggestion is made to develop homogeneous unit churches. For a further discussion see chapter VI, "Reaching People through New Congregations," 99-120, in McGavran and Hunter, Church Growth: Strategies, 1980.

nothing to discriminate in its evangelistic methodology it will in effect eliminate several groups from potentially responding to the Gospel. "Unwittingly, yet deliberately, he sows seed on the path and in the brambles and the thin soil."[114] It would be far better and more effective if a Christian could recognize his own kind of people, adjust his presentation to suit that situation, and then sow the seed on soil that he knows well. "Widespread blind sowing does - by accident - deposit some seed in good soil. But why sow blindly?"[115] In other words this parable advises that the consequences of indiscriminate sowing of the Gospel will in effect waste a great deal of effort. Since this lesson shows that there are three areas of bad sowing, then, the church should isolate those aspects in contemporary strategies, avoid them, and concentrate on finding good soil in which to promote the Gospel.

## The Demoniac of the Gadarenes

In the Gospels another example that is selected to argue in favor of the HUP theory is Jesus' healing of the demoniac of the Gadarenes.[116] After the demoniac man was healed, he begged Jesus to let him follow Him; but, Jesus would not let him.

---

[114] McGavran, Ethnic Realities, 90,91.
[115] Ibid.
[116] Mk. 5.

Instead, the Lord directed the man to return to his home to report what had happened to him.  It was the cultural difference between Galilee and Gerasenes that was behind Jesus' decision to deny the former demoniac's request.  Healed of demonism, this man naturally desired to express his gratitude through service to Jesus, who had healed him.  But, it is analyzed by the HUP theory that this man was a Gadarene and the disciples of Jesus were all Galileans ". . . two different homogeneous units."[117]  Jesus could have demonstrated visible unity among Christians at this moment by including him as a disciple but that was not the case.  Instead, ". . . Jesus, on his way to Galilee, knew that the Gadarene's witness would be much more effective among his own homogeneous unit than among Aramaic-speaking Galileans, so he turned him down."[118]  Here, then, Jesus demonstrates the importance of applying the HUP theory by sending a new convert back into his own homogeneous unit.  His effectiveness as a witness is argued to be potentially detrimental in a Jewish context but highly productive within his own context.

---

[117] Wagner, Our Kind, 118.
[118] Ibid.

## Preaching Limitations on the 12:
## A Focus on God's Promises to Israel

In another Gospels event, the commissioning of the 12 to preach in Matthew 10 is pinpointed as additional support for the HUP theory. The instructions given by Jesus to his twelve apostles are described as specifically in keeping with the homogeneous unit principle. Jesus told the 12 to go only to the lost sheep of Israel. They were not to go to the Gentiles or the Samaritans.[119] This priority of observing homogeneous associations is observed as a consistent pattern in the guidance of the apostles' and Jesus' ministries of influencing the lives of people. It was not only effective but it was also an expression of the desire of Christ.

## The Syrophoenician Woman

Another suggested example of the HUP theory being applied in the ministry of Jesus Christ is seen when He entered into Tyre and was confronted by a Greek Syrophoenician woman[120]. Initially, Jesus refused to render her any aid. But, she persisted and won His assistance. This shift in Jesus' response is illustrative of the HUP theory. His strategy was to ground the movement ". . . solidly among Aramaic-speaking

---

[119] Ibid., 118.

44

Jews, his own homogeneous unit . . ."[121]  A firm base of operations here would then lend to the strengthening of a future spread of the Gospel to similar groups, then to distant groups, and on to the end of the earth as described in Acts 1:8.  The exception of Jesus healing the Syrophoenician woman's daughter is explained as an expression of Jesus' own personal compassion.  This exception is taught as a reminder that racism must never be the product of the HUP theory.  Remaining "people-conscious" is a priority but not a reason to be negative towards others of a different group.  It is made clear, however, that after this lesson on an exception Jesus ". . . went on his own agenda of proclaiming his message among Galileans."[122]  The pattern of Jesus with the Syrophoenician woman is the same as His pattern in dealing with the demoniac of the Gadarenes. Generally, He followed the HUP theory in dealing with people groups.  However, once that priority was clearly established (as in His initial refusal to grant this woman's request), He would act out of compassion for an individual.  This act of compassion was an exception to the HUP theory standard.

---

[120] Mk. 7:26.
[121] Wagner, Our Kind, 119.
[122] Ibid.

## Acts 6: Church Unity Not Separation

Another New Testament text that is used to describe the HUP theory is Acts 6:1. Hellenist and Hebrew believers were in conflict over the fair distribution of resources among widows in the church. The former group realized that their widows were being neglected by comparison with the widows of the latter group. It is suggested that the eventual outcome or solution to this problem is supportive of the HUP theory. In this explanation an emphasis on cultural differences is made.

Several items noted are that the Hellenists spoke their own provincial language, worshipped in synagogues, used the Septuagint, felt culturally superior, and regarded themselves as fully Jewish. They were economically superior and were bothered by the church leadership being in the hands of the Galileans. It is suggested that this tension is the issue that led the church to divide into two groups. Resolution of the tension was found in selecting Hellenists to serve alongside of the Hebrew leaders.

These observations are combined to argue for several conclusions. First, this is the point where the Hellenist believers were distinguished as a group separate from the Hebrew believers. Acts 8:1 is cited as proof of this separation. Persecution was directed against the church in Jerusalem but it excluded the apostles (the Hebrew believers) a division along

46

homogeneous lines in the mixed church of Jerusalem. Second, this separation of two groups was a kind of "liberation" for the minority Hellenists. Third, with the two groups distinct from each other the result was not only growth but also rapid growth.[123]


## The Church at Antioch: A Heterogeneous Unity

Another New Testament event is used to describe the use of the HUP theory, the ministry in Antioch. Does the Biblical evidence support the concept that this 1$^{st}$ century ministry developed on the basis of a homogeneous pattern? The HUP theory explains that Antioch was developed by a two-prong approach. First, the Hellenistic believers who were scattered as a result of Stephen's martyrdom had a part in its development. Second, a missionary thrust from Cyprus and Cyrene played a part in Antioch as with a cross-cultural intent. With these observations properly emphasized, the following conclusion is reached: ". . . there is no reason to assume that the second group of missionaries had anything to do directly with the congregations of Jewish believers already established."[124] Furthermore, it is postulated, ". . . a cluster of house churches with Gentile membership was established quite separately from

---

[123] Ibid., 123.
[124] Ibid., 124.

the Jewish groups . . ."[125]  Thus, there were two clusters of house churches that existed at the beginning stages of the Antioch church.[126]  And, since there is insufficient evidence to assume a singular unified or joint effort to reach Antioch by Hellenist and Hebrew believers, there is even less evidence to presume a separate effort.

**The Jerusalem Council and the HUP Theory**

It is natural to carry the argument on to the Jerusalem Council at this point.  First, as an illustration and point of description, it is reasoned that an Indian caste should be allowed to become Christian while "remaining themselves." If this is allowed then, evidence suggests that a Christian movement within that group would prosper.  This advice is supported by an explanation of the Jerusalem Council in A.D. 52.  Gentile converts are not required to become Jews when they become Christians.  They can come to Christ ". . . without taking on themselves the whole Jewish law - including, one would think, the endogamy within the Jewish group, whereby all who became Jews thenceforth married Jews rather than their own people."[127] The church in India is called to follow this conciliatory ruling and encourage the growth of the church to follow evangelistic patterns that   ". . . arise in natural ethnic groupings, practicing

---

[125]  Ibid.
[126]  Ibid., 125.

their own endogamy."[128]   Hence, the great decision at the Jerusalem Council is described as being based upon the HUP theory.   No cultural group was required to adopt the Jewish culture upon becoming Christian, but, instead was encouraged to continue following their own cultural milieu.

## Neither Jew nor Greek: A Higher Level of Interrelationships for All Christians

In another New Testament discussion the HUP theory presents its interpretation of the phrase "neither Jew nor Greek" from Galatians 3:28. This text is viewed as essentially similar to Ephesians 2[129] and Colossians 3:11; hence, the discussion of these texts are considered together. The view of the HUP theory in connection with these three texts is that Paul supported pluralism and liberty.

---

[127]  McGavran, Ethnic Realities, 116.

[128]  Ibid.

[129]  The text that is pertinent to this discussion is Ephesians 2:11-22.  In particular the meaning of verses 14-16 is debated: "For he himself is our peace, who has made the two one and has destroyed the barrier, the dividing wall of hostility, by abolishing in his flesh the law with its commandments and regulations.  His purpose was to create in himself one new man out of the two, thus making peace, and in this one body to reconcile both of them to God through the cross, by which he put to death their hostility." (NIV) The HUP theory has a view that integrates an explanation of Ephesians 2: " . . . since Christ does break down the wall of hostility among those  who become His people, bringing them to Christ in their ethnic units will, with the blessing of the Holy Spirit, bring in ever increasing measures of brotherhood." (Wagner, Our Kind, 117)

It is practically argued that Paul applied this attitude of pluralism and liberty by being opposed to Gentile assimilation into Jewish culture. "Paul believed that Gentiles could be Christians in the Gentile way, while Jews could and should be followers of the Messiah in the Jewish way . . ."[130] At the same time Paul is interpreted to be against forced integration and opposed to assimilation. The position of Paul is explained as a defender of an oppressed spiritual minority. Jewish leadership is identified as the oppressive element in the mother church of Jerusalem.

This point of interpretation emphasizes what is perceived to be in the Apostle Paul's mind while dealing with the early churches in these regions. It is argued that the ". . . issue of whether or not a local congregation ought to strive to mix people of different homogeneous units . . ." was not even a consideration.[131] The early church apostles operated from a Homogenous Unit mind-set, therefore, their instructions cannot refer to mixing different homogeneous units but must instruct believers to follow the opposite concept; namely, keep each identifiable homogeneous unit together with its own kith and kin. This togetherness of Christians with their own Homogenous

---

[130] Wagner, Our Kind, 128.
[131] Ibid., 129.

Unit provided the kind of unity[132] that the church was intended to demonstrate to the world.

## Galatians 3:28 and the HUP Theory

Addressing the exhortation to unity in Galatians 3:28, the HUP theory reasons as follows: "The Church of Jesus Christ is One: in the Church there is neither Jew nor Greek, slave nor free, laborer nor bishop nor commoner. All these affirmations are biblical and true. They tell us what the Church is in God's sight."[133] Acknowledging this interpretation, it is then qualified as an "ideal" for the Church. The "real" Church is in the process of developing. It is comprised of people who are still dealing with their sin. They are "on their way to Zion" but they have not yet arrived. The Church is described as a combination of a theological dimension and a "sociological structure."[134]

---

[132] When the HUP theory interprets the problems of division and disorder in the church at Corinth it sees a pattern consistent with the HUP theory: " . . . the sin of the Corinthians was not their decentralized church structure, because for Christians to meet in separate churches was the normal New Testament pattern. Their sin was that cliques had become enemies and rivals because of their carnality. What needed changing were attitudes, not necessarily structures . . . Thus, whenever Paul speaks of Christian believers being `all one in Christ,' he is referring not to a normative pattern for local congregations, but rather to the supracongregational relationship of believers in the total Christian body over which Christ himself is the head (Eph. 1:22-23)." (Wagner, Our Kind, 132.)

[133] Ibid., 31.

[134] Ibid.

The HUP theory believes that in many respects the problem of how Christian diversity can be related to Christian unity is the key theological issue in the homogeneous unit debate. He accepts brotherhood and reconciliation between hostile groups as universally accepted. But how these two crucial matters are accomplished is the issue. If one group must sacrifice its identity to accomplish either or both then the HUP theory believes that the cost is too high.

## *Practical Suggestions in Making the HUP Theory Operative*

The HUP theory has been defined, its philosophy has been elaborated, its Biblical argument has been traced, and its functional application to the church or the practical theology of its concept will now be reviewed. Predominantly, this covers the outworking of evangelism by the church.

## The HUP Theory's suggested Future Pattern for Church Growth

On the topic of church growth, the HUP theory describes what it believes to be the likely pattern for church development as it fulfills the mission of the church. First, faith spreads naturally within the parameters of a particular ethnic unit. This new faith is encouraged to "preserve its own cultural and ethnic identity."[135] As a result, convenient locations for worship arise spontaneously. And house churches form and fulfill the major role of Christian gatherings. Finally, "occasional joint services of worship"[136] will be organized. This is the probable pattern of future church growth. There is a pattern where evangelism takes place in the context of smaller intimate groups. Yet, the larger scale times of worship and celebration[137] will provide the expression of Christian unity.

## Group Conversions

The HUP theory reasons that if there is a celebration for each and every conversion to Christianity, then, it is reasonable to suggest that group conversions warrant even more enthusiastic celebrations. A point is made in support of this by contrasting the traditional mission station effectiveness with a "more Indian way" of responding to the Gospel. Rather than individual conversions being the strategy, which frequently subjected the new Christian to "severe ostracism" and

---

[135] McGavran, Ethnic Realities, 117.

[136] Ibid.

[137] Part of the formula for Church Growth deals with the relationship among three aspects of the church, namely, celebration, congregation, and cell. These three decrease in numerical size but increase in intimacy. The higher the intimacy, hence the smaller cell groups, also has the greater effectiveness in evangelism. For a further discussion see chapter 7 "Celebration + Congregation + Cell = Church", 97-109 in

separation from their "native stock," families from the same caste or group converted to Christianity. These initial conversions resulted in movements of Christian faith that moved throughout a single caste. However, two factors stifled this new growth pattern. First, the prevailing pattern was "one by one". This growth phenomenon by families was not quickly accepted. Second, internal caste resistance against such family movements surfaced.[138] Thus, Church Growth concludes that the limited success of the early foreign mission philosophy of evangelizing through a mission station not only points to the need for a better strategy, it also uncovered the potential of people groups responding to the Gospel en masse.

## People Movements and Cultural Phenomena

The development of the idea of "people movements" is a crucial feature in the Church Growth philosophy and a means of realizing the HUP theory potential. Yet, their potential for large scale effective evangelism requires precise timing and careful attention or the opportunity may be lost. A people movement must be quickly recognized and encouraged to grow for it is in a vulnerable and fragile state particularly where the evangelistic pattern is "one by one." Such movements must be prayed for,

Wagner, Your Church, 1976.
[138] McGavran, Ethnic Realities, 80.

54

gently nurtured in order to prevent stumping their growth for ". . . they very frequently stop after a few dozen or a few hundred have become Christian."[139]  Applying the HUP theory to such a potential situation insures that there will be an environment that will enable the delicate ethnic features of any people group to respond positively to the Gospel.

The HUP theory advocates the consistency of people group conversions with Biblical priorities: "The people movement to Christ is a thoroughly biblical way of coming to salvation.  It was the way the Jews, the Samaritans, and the synagogue communities around the Great Sea came to Christian conviction."[140]  Group dynamics, those features involved with ethnicity and culture, are so strong that if the Gospel is presented contextually within that framework, these same features can be a significant part in the attractive nature of the Gospel.  But, if this dynamic turns instead to offense then, the receptivity of a particular people group could actually be retarded.

**Individual Conversion and a Responsibility to One's Caste**

Keeping the concept of people group conversions in mind, Church Growth believes that effective evangelism must

---

[139] Ibid., 80.

think beyond the individual. With the goal to fulfill the church's mission to the world's 3 billion non-Christian population[141], the HUP theory points to the potential of many more conversions if a single response is utilized to spread the Gospel to the people group represented by that one individual. Notice the following probe: "The reasons for low evangelistic potential are clear and have a great deal to do with the relation of individual Christians and the congregations they form to the society in which they live."[142] In other words, the church must evaluate the perception that society has on Christianity. And it must do some self-evaluation, considering what it perceives about its surrounding society. Also, it must identify what societal changes are necessary to become a convert to Christianity. "[The] structure out of which conversion to Christ and His Church is taking place is of enormous importance. Does the convert leave that structure or remain a part of it?"[143] The community opinion of Christians does affect evangelism effectiveness. Vital to the church's mission is making sure that the community likes what it sees. If that community feels threatened by the church mission, then the church must reconsider its appearances.

---

[140] Ibid., 232.

[141] For a further discussion of the world population analyzed according to Christian and unreached categories please see Donald Hoke, "The Revolutionary Implications of the Unreached Peoples Concept" in Missions Frontiers, Bulletin of the U.S. Center for World Mission, vol. 12, numbers 6-10, June-October 1990 (39-42).

[142] McGavran, Ethnic Realities, 166.

[143] Ibid.

## Open to All

Dealing with the biases and prejudices of unconverted and converted people is not an easy task. While the ideal church that does not give regard to race or ethnicity is everyone's desire, the HUP theory acknowledges that it may not be immediately possible. Hence, its solution that maximizes the evangelistic potential in spite of these existing feelings is finding a welcomed hearing. Nevertheless, it is clear that the HUP theory itself urges universal openness to any who desire to unite with any church. McGavran states it clearly: "All church buildings would be open to all men, Christians and non-Christians alike."[144] However, while universal openness is taught, it is also recognized that certain people groups tend to cluster together due to convenience of residence, education, or language. Such separations are to be acknowledged.

## *Theological Issues*

The HUP theory has been defined, explained, reviewed according to its Biblical support, and summarized in its practical theology. Now, various theological issues of the HUP theory will be perused. Few of the Church Growth proponents claim theology as a first discipline. However, their interest and commitment to the advancement of the church necessitates some theological development. In many ways the HUP theory has been grown in a seed-bed of practical means of putting theology to work. As such it has determined that it has valid theological roots[145] and has addressed several issues related to important theological discussions.

## The Purpose of the Church: Growth

The HUP theory finds support in considering the purpose of the church. It is suggested that the church's purpose is best fulfilled in a Homogeneous Unit church. Generally, the church is described as a fellowship of redeemed individuals. It is a gathering of believers into a community of those who are committed to their Lord as disciples. Their reason for existence

---

[144] Wagner, Our Kind, 117.

[145] McGavran describes the beginnings of his Church Growth concepts in terms of three rivers of theological thought. First, is his commitment to Biblical authority. If this was not respected, then, he saw " . . . no reason at all for missionary labors." (McGavran, Effective Evangelism, 57.) Second, is his commitment to *knowing* as much as possible about the society or people to whom one is bringing the Gospel. This familiarity would increase effective proclamation. Third, is his commitment to an accurate accounting of the church's growth rate and observing patterns of churches that were growing. This was an essential expression of stewardship. For a further discussion on this see "The Rise of the Church Growth Movement" chapter 6, 53-63 in McGavran, Effective Evangelism, 1988.

Arthur Glasser mirrors McGavran's theological commitment. He explains that it is God's will for the church to grow "through deliberate multiplications of vast numbers of new congregations" (Arthur Glasser, "Church Growth and Theology", in Alan Tippett, God, Man and Church Growth [Grand Rapids: Wm. B. Eerdmans Pub. Co., 1975], 52) and if a church is not growing it is out of the will of God. This precept is founded upon a theological base that adheres to the authority of the Scriptures and Christ, the apostolic example of church mission to their own culture as well as to others, and that, as co-laborers with God, men are free to utilize the social sciences as helpful tools in advancing the mission of the church. For a further discussion see

58

has two purposes according to Church Growth, an internal and an external purpose. The internal purpose is ". . . to provide for the Christian growth and mutual care of its members."[146] The external purpose is ". . . to communicate God's redemptive work to fellow human beings and to society as a whole."[147] This external purpose is the mission of the church. Fulfillment of this evangelistic mission is the purpose of the church and is best suited by the HUP theory as a methodological strategy to achieve it.

## Priority of Evangelism

Evangelism is identified as the primary means to fulfill this purpose of growth in the church and therefore has the place of supreme importance for the church. While many churches are theologically sound and biblically astute they are also noticeably quiet in an evangelistic or missions outreach. Complementary to the importance of evangelism is its urgency, even to the point of reevaluating the effort placed on edification: "Fully granting the urgent need to instruct and nurture, one must nevertheless say that stopping to consolidate is always a mistake."[148] Converts must be quickly assimilated and the

---

Glasser, "Church Growth and Theology," 52-68.

[146] Wagner, Our Kind, 17.

[147] Ibid.

[148] Ibid., 115.

evangelistic focus must never be lost. Theologically, then, the church must grow. It grows by fulfilling its evangelistic mission. And the HUP theory believes that it is the strategy best suited to this priority.

The fulfillment of this evangelistic mandate is the basis for the HUP theory. As evangelism occurs, Biblical mandates[149] that are "barriers" to conversion must be confronted by those outside of Christ. But, no human or cultural ones extraneous from Biblical demands must be required as a prerequisite to conversion. Setting aside racial prejudice or ethnic biases is not a condition for salvation.[150]

## The HUP Theory and the Unconverted

McGavran's purpose in advocating the homogeneous unit principle has a consistent emphasis. He desires to bring non-Christians into the Church. This transformation will not only fulfill the church's mission but it will also help to turn the world away from racism and prejudice.[151] Once converted, there is a clearly stated expectation that any tendency toward a sinful expression of bias will be eliminated.

---

[149] McGavran identifies three Biblical mandates that are barriers that must be faced and crossed by those desiring to be baptized into Christ. They are the acknowledgement of one's sinful state, repentance from sin, and public confession of Christ. (McGavran, Understanding, 3rd ed., 168.)

[150] Ibid., 168-169.

[151] Wagner, Our Kind, 32.

60

To further address pertinent theological issues, the mandate from the Lausanne Conference of 1974 is reviewed. The massive number of unevangelized people in the world is presented as a basis to reach them by a pragmatic means. It is reasoned: ". . . since men like to become Christians without crossing barriers . . . the first task among the two billion [yet to be evangelized] is an evangelism designed to multiply churches in each new piece of the magnificent mosaic."[152] The HUP theory argues that since the unevangelized prefer to be with their own kith and kin, then a church strategy should be designed which utilizes this preference because it will work. The clear motive behind the HUP theory endeavor is evangelism and concern for the unconverted.

Next, the HUP theory points out the limited perception of those who are culture-bound. In their individualism their ability to evaluate the logic of this matter is biased. They assume that those from a different culture will respond as they do. However, in comparing Western-thinking Christians to non-Western unconverted the HUP theory notes that ". . . non-Western peoples will not and cannot become Christians in an individualistic, Western way."[153]

This kind of group identity is perceived by the HUP theory in a positive light. Distinctions between peoples are seen

---

[152] Ibid., 21.

". . . not as social defects, but as social dynamics to be used to accomplish the mission of the church."[154]   According to HUP theory, it is useless to say that tribal people ought not to have racial prejudice.  Instead, this prejudice ought to be made an aid to Christianization.[155]


**A Matter of Choice**

The theological option of a choice is clearly acknowledged by the HUP theory.  To select it or some form of a heterogeneous option is in itself amoral.  The question is not a matter of correctness but one of effectiveness and efficiency.  Although both may be legitimate, which one works better?  It is stated: "Christians . . . are free to group themselves in churches in whatever way they wish along homogeneous or heterogeneous lines.  Both are good Christian options, but the decision should be made intelligently, and the consequences of each option weighted."[156]

If an heterogeneous option is chosen, several characteristic features become apparent.  These features are as follows: (1) It allows Christians to feel good about breaking barriers as race and class. (2) Participants are enriched with

---

[153]  Ibid., 21.
[154]  Ibid., 21.
[155]  Ibid.

62

cross-cultural exposure. Yet, the HUP theory also warns that ". . . few non-Christians from outside the congregation are likely to be attracted to such a heterogeneous community."[157]

The sense of choice between amoral options implies that there are pros and cons of either or any selection. These matters once weighed can give strength to one's choice. In this light the HUP theory says that, "If the option of maintaining a homogeneous congregation is chosen, the direct benefit of close intercultural relationships will be sacrificed, but in all probability the evangelistic potential of the congregation will be higher."[158] And should this be the direction of choice by a church, the evangelistic affect on its group is predicted to be higher. Hence, in the comparison of pluses and minuses, the HUP theory advances the thought that its benefits outweigh its detriments.

## The *Imago Dei*

Another crucial theological issue that is germane to the discussion of the HUP theory is the *Imago Dei*. This issue gives theological meaning to human culture. The image of God gives every human the ability to learn a culture. "Belonging to a homogeneous unit that shares a culture and that has a 'we' identity, therefore, is not to be regarded as a human deficiency .

---

[156] Ibid., 33.
[157] Ibid.
[158] Ibid., 35.

. . rather, a positive human characteristic that should be respected and not destroyed."[159]

Continuing along this reasoning the HUP theory appeals to natural law suggesting that pluralism is declared as a part of God's plan by citing two sources and pointing to creation's diversity. This perspective is supported by the following thought: ". . . as a result of God's creation, men and women are individuals, they are family members, and they are also participants in some broader social unit where families relate to other families who share the same social system and cultural values."[160] Thus, culture is directly linked to God's creative act and as such, a theological priority is required to respect the matters related to human culture.


## Liberation Theology

Neither the HUP theory nor Church Growth has a theology from which they spring. However, in the course of ideas formulating and concepts maturing, an identification with the Liberation Theology has been entertained and explored. In constructing a theology that can effectively operate in a pluralistic environment liberation is raised as a feature that must be emphasized. Liberation Theology emphasizes an advocacy

---

[159] Ibid., 97.

on behalf of the oppressed: the poor, the outcast, and the racially discriminated. God is on their side. And Wagner finds this appealing in finding a theology consistent with the goals of the HUP theory.[161] The HUP theory expands the tenets of Liberation Theology to include several channels of theological exploration on its own. This expansion is called ethnic theology.

The purpose of the ethnic theology of liberation is encapsulated in the following statement: "Ethnic theology of liberation is now determined to make Americans of all groups recognize such religious cultural chauvinism for what it is, not only in the remote mission fields of the world, but specifically right here in America."[162] High on the agenda of the HUP theory is the hope to elevate other non-American cultures to a position of parity in the eyes of the American church. Paternalistic attitudes have long influenced missions around the world, especially when missionary influence has originated out of the West.

The HUP theory in part hopes to raise the awareness of the need for cultural respect among churches in the West and particularly in America. For example Church Growth believes that for the majority of white Americans there must be a realization that ". . . a black man can truly be 'redeemed' only

---

[160] Ibid., 106.
[161] Ibid.
[162] Ibid., 82.

when he knows that his blackness is acceptable to God, for his blackness is an essential component of his being-in-the-world."[163]    This statement suggests that the position of the theologians in the 1960's needs to be reevaluated.  It claims that those theologians who were calling for mixed congregations in the 1960's were in fact advocating an end of American ethnic groups and the promotion of the Anglo-American culture.[164] Furthermore, it surmises that ethnic groups (not Homogeneous Units) feel that as Israel had to be redeemed out of Egypt before God established His covenant so minority groups still feel they are in Egypt while Anglo-Americans find themselves in the Promised Land.[165]

Furthermore, whether the discussion of liberation is with a broader ethnic group or more defined Homogeneous Unit, the fact remains that the Gospel must be presented in the context[166] of those intended to be converted.  This concept is explained: "In accepting a theology of liberation, each homogeneous unit must

---

[163]   Donald G. Shockley, Free, White, and Christian (Nashville: Abingdon, 1975), 66,67; quoted in Wagner, Our Kind, 82.
[164]   Wagner, Our Kind, 83.
[165]   Ibid., 84.
[166]   Contextualization recognizes the need to transcend culture in order to bring the Gospel into another culture according to its interpretive traditions.  Yet, any messenger cannot totally separate himself from his cultural links.  While a balance is necessary, it is recognized that even the Biblical writers were culturally influenced: " . . . none of the recipients of God's revelation have understood God's truth apart from concrete historical situations. . . . They . . . were always people-in-culture . . . those who wrote the Scriptures used language, thought forms, proverbs, idioms, and cultural assumptions that made what they wrote perfectly intelligible at face value in only one cultural setting at one point in history." (Wagner, Our Kind, 87)

also accept the right and responsibility to contextualize Christian theology, that is, to bring the supracultural principles of God's revelation to bear on its own concrete situation.[167] Wagner is not comfortable with the idea of a universal Christian theology that applies to all people in every ethnic situation. Contextualization calls for the church to responsibly clothe the Gospel in such a way as to be understood and accepted by the homogeneous unit which is receiving it.[168]

Yet, this application is allowed to be a volitional task depending on the ones who perpetuate it: "Of course liberated people are free to abandon their culture and become part of a different group if they wish. But the choice must always be their own, not something overtly or covertly superimposed from outside."[169] Theologically, as a choice can be allowed whether to adopt the HUP theory or some heterogeneous philosophy in communicating the Gospel, so too must any converts be free to choose to continue in their homogeneous unit or to shift in some way. Notice the following: "It is much better to live as a Christian in an open environment where the integrity of different expressions is honored than to live in a society characterized by

---

[167] Wagner, Our Kind, 86.
[168] Ibid.
[169] Ibid., 86.

the theological chauvinism of a dominant group."[170]   Diversity
with equality is the balance.


## *Conclusion*

      The HUP theory sees the world as billions of people yet
to be converted to Christianity.  Through these eyes, eager to
fulfill Christ's mandate to the church, the earth's population is
seen as a vast mosaic.  It is this analogy that describes all of
humanity according to the HUP theory.   Both in the Old
Testament with the references to peoples and tribes and in the
days of our Lord with Levites careful to marry Levites the
segmental feature of humanity is illustrated.

      When the Gospel is injected into this environment, the
segments remain intact.  The individual Christians are all equal
but they remain in their distinctive and ethnic groups.  McGavran
summarizes that as the church fulfills its mission it will become
more and more comprised of many "Christianized segments."
Their Christianity will make much of the growth similar.  Yet,
their individualized culture with variations in language and
economics will account for many differences.  This dual portrait
is    the    suggested    pattern    for    the    church's    mission.

---

[170]  Ibid., 87.

"Congregations ought to be multiplied in each piece of the mosaic."[171]

A typical city population in the U.S.A. is comprised of people with varying economic, educational, and cultural ties. The HUP theory acknowledges these social dynamics and works with them in an effort to attract as many as possible to Christ. If these features are not observed then the consequence will be the driving away of potential Christian converts instead of winning them to Christianity. McGavran warns, "Each segment must be won to Christ on its own level. If it is invited to join a church composed of people living on a different level, it will reject Christ very largely because the Savior is obscured by His congregation."[172]

And while the HUP theory acknowledges these social symptoms of human preference, it does not assert that the formation of a new humanity in Christ will be secular, humanistic, or immoral. Rather, as new Christian converts are made in every piece of the world's mosaic, the rule of brotherhood will be the goal of each people group.[173] This similarity within each group is equally shared by all and is unity

---

[171] McGavran, Effective Evangelism, 113.
[172] Ibid., 112.
[173] Ibid., 115.

of Christ which will ultimately be demonstrated before the throne of the Lamb.[174]

The HUP theory is emphatic about its perspective of mankind seen as a mosaic. And each part of the mosaic must be targeted for the Gospel. There will be no melting of all pieces into one. Rather, ". . . the red will remain red, the white will remain white, the purple will remain purple. But in each of the thousands of ethnic units societies of the redeemed will multiply."

[175] McGavran, Effective Evangelism, 116.

---

[174] Revelation 7:9.

CHAPTER II

**THINKING THROUGH THE HISTORICAL DEBATE**
**Can the ethnic tensions in the church find redemption?**


### *Introduction*

   While those who have developed the concept of the HUP theory have introduced and presented their viewpoint with growing popularity, it has also been successfully challenged in several significant areas. These issues of disagreement have been articulated during the past twenty years[175] in a number of arenas of discussion, particularly in areas relating to missionary strategy and ethnic churches[176]. Three groups[177] emerged from the debate

---

[175] Even though the main issues involved in the HUP theory were begun with McGavran's The Bridges of God in 1955, Glasser suggests that the movement of Church Growth actually began in 1961. See Glasser, "Church Growth," 403.

[176] Ethnic churches and their Biblical right to exist has been a major point of discussion and concern for all Christians in North America who happen to be of an ethnic minority group. For a flavor of this interest see John Stott, "Reaching Unreached People: An Evaluation and a Challenge," in Chinese Around the World (Hong Kong: Chinese Coordination Center of World Evangelism for Western Churches, May 1988), 1-4. and William Wan, "A Vision for a Multicultural Church," in Chinese Around the World (Hong Kong: Chinese Coordination Center of World Evangelism for Western Churches, December 1989), 1-3.

and can be identified today[178]. The first group consists of those who embrace the HUP theory as a Biblical strategy for evangelism and basis for planning church growth. Characteristic of this position is an optimism over the growing number of its adherents and a shift from a defensive posture to one of confidence. The second group is comprised of those who have been introduced to the HUP theory, perceive some pragmatic benefit, but have yet to be convinced that it is a valid approach. They are in a dilemma. On the one hand they are uncertain about its legitimacy but on the other hand they are intrigued by the practical results of the position. The third group is made up of those who advocate a model of evangelism and a strategy of church maturation that by Biblical precept is unable to accept the HUP theory as a legitimate option for the church. They contest the validity of the proposition from many different backgrounds and on many different issues.

---

[177] Plaisted has identified three groups in the HUP theory debate. He refers to the three groups as the "Scandalized", the "Skeptical", and the "Supportive". The "Scandalized" are the "vociferous opponents" that do not see the application of the HUP theory as legitimate. The "Skeptical" are not yet convinced of the strategy but are attracted to it. And the "Supportive" are those who were once not part of the HUP theory camp but now enthusiastically support it. (Robert Plaisted, "The Homogeneous Unit Debate: Its Value Orientations and Changes," The Evangelical Quarterly 87:3 [1987], 217)

[178] It should be noted that while there are differences of opinion on whether to accept the HUP theory, there is also general agreement by disagreeing sides on fundamental topics as a commitment to the Lord Jesus Christ, the supreme authority of the Bible, and the primacy of world-wide evangelism. Also, there is agreement that dialogue seasoned with openness, grace, and love are paramount to providing any helpful strategy for church development. (The Pasadena Consultation - Homogeneous Unit, Lausanne Occasional Papers No. 1, [London: Lausanne Committee for World Evangelization Archives, 1978], 2.)

## *The Essential Distinction*

The debate over the validity of the HUP theory has been encumbered with a number of spurious topics and distracting issues.[179] Some of these are due to a misunderstanding of the HUP theory and what its ramifications actually are. Once these are effectively set aside, other issues that are germane to the debate such as culture, Biblical interpretation and Theological application can be properly considered.

For those who embrace the HUP theory, culture is considered the central issue.[180] The following observation is noted: "One persistently divisive issue in this debate is cultural, not theological. That is, much discussion turns on whether people attribute positive or negative value to cultural diversity, or if their world-view even acknowledges the significance of the matter."[181] Culture is argued to possess inherent qualities of diversity. From the beginning of man's time on earth the issue of culture has been established by God. And man, being a social creature, organized

---

[179] Harvie Conn notes two unfair criticisms against the HUP theory. They are the accusation that Church Growth is overly concerned with numerical results and quality of Christian maturation can be sacrificed for the sake of quantitative achievement. McGavran intends neither of these matters. (Harvie Conn, "Reactions and Guidelines: The Praxis of a Covenant Ethnos", Consultation on the Homogeneous Unit Principle [Wheaton: Lausanne Theology and Education Group, 1977], 5.)

[180] From the standpoint of human practice, there has been a fundamentally assumed difference between "Us and Them". Whether subtle or overt, these differences are basic to human relations. (Plaisted, "Debate," 215-233.)

[181] Plaisted, "Debate", 216. It is also suggested that "Biblical" objections against the HUP theory are often cultural expressions rather than real Biblical ideas. And that values of those involved in the discussions often change further substantiating the culture-over-Biblical-interpretation comment.

himself into various types of social structures, including families, clans, tribes, countries and united federations. It is emphasized that the pattern of diversity is irrefutable in human history. Focusing on this emphasis of cultural diversity, the distinction made by the HUP theory is as follows: " . . . [the] debate in the church has centered less around the *fact* of such cultural diversity than around the *value* assigned to it."[182] This distinction is related to McGavran's key observation: "Men like to become Christians without crossing racial, linguistic, or class barriers."[183] It is not argued that non-Christians are living correctly when they function according to this statement; rather, it is simply an observation of their normal behavior.[184]

However, culture[185] is not the exclusive area of discussion within the HUP theory debate. For instance some who follow a different model of evangelism and church maturation have

---

[182] Plaisted, "Debate," 216.

[183] McGavran, <u>Understanding</u>, revised, 223.

[184] Wagner notes that critics have attempted to disprove this statement for over two decades but have failed to amass any empirical evidence to the contrary. Instead, proponents have continued to find more and more evidence in support of this concept. (Wagner, <u>Whole Gospel</u>, 167) Plaisted further emphasizes the point that the HUP theory rests on nearly a half of a century of research, applied to many different Christian populations around the world. His comment is indicative of the accumulated evidence: "People *would* rather become Christians without crossing cultural barriers than bear the pain of crossing them, if they are given that option." (Plaisted, "Debate", 217.)

[185] Regarding the matter of culture, there is a large measure of agreement among those who have debated the HUP theory. It is mutually recognized that the rich variety of culture should be respected not altered or abandoned because of the Gospel. Any attitude of superiority by one culture over another during the presentation of the Gospel is cultural imperialism and is disdained by all. This effort to give a high regard for all cultures no matter how different or how limited in population size honors God, respects

tenaciously challenged the New Testament validity of the HUP theory. They maintain that the work of Christ has laid the foundation for the church that is in sharp contrast to the principles advanced by the HUP theory. And along with this hermeneutic challenge has arisen further questions regarding the adequacy of the HUP theory in at least two significant theological areas: an ethical responsibility for moral change or sanctification and a theological pattern for church activity and organization or ecclesiastical application, particularly in regard to ethnic churches.

In light of these matters the following questions have been raised in the debate over the validity of the HUP theory: Even though non-Christians like to become Christians without crossing their sociologically defined barriers, what changes occur, as a result of their conversion to Christianity, which nullify their pre-Christian preferences? And is the organizing of Christians in a local area to be founded upon pre-Christian preferences? Furthermore, is the HUP theory, when applied to congregations, inadequate in light of what the New Testament teaches about sanctification? Is the issue of concern only that of evangelism technique? If the premise of the HUP theory can be accepted as a biblically viable strategy, then does this automatically validate the existence of Homogeneous Churches?[186] These questions are

all peoples, and aids in successful evangelism. (Pasadena Consultation, 3.)

[186] It is granted that certain types of Homogeneous Churches are bound to exist. For example, it is expected that Chinese churches will be in China or Romanian churches will be in Romania or Spanish speaking churches will be in Mexico. But, in a pluralistic

the essence of the dialogue that has surrounded the debate of the HUP theory.

## *Lausanne and the Pasadena Consultation*

One of the high points in the history of the debate over the HUP theory was the first "Occasional Paper" produced by the Lausanne Theology and Education group. This paper highlights the issues related to this debate. In 1977 eleven church leaders met to dialogue over the matter, John R. W. Stott moderated while five representatives, referred by McGavran as the "Fuller Team"[187], presented the case for the HUP theory and five world church leaders responded.

### Methodological Implications

The first area of discussion centered on the methodological matters relating to the HUP theory. Donald McGavran[188] proposed that the HUP theory is an idea based upon Biblical authority. He argues that while unity in churches is a reality, it is necessary for churches to make room for another reality, ethnic

---

society such as the United Kingdom, the United States of America, or Canada should ethnic groups deliberately group themselves together into their own local churches? The author is indebted to Patrick Sookhdeo for this emphasis during a personal interview at St. Andrew's Center, London, 1989.

[187] McGavran, "Genesis," 10.

[188] The bulk of McGavran's argument in favor of the HUP theory is presented in Chapter 1; therefore, what is represented here is a flavor of his specific tone in the

diversity. Social structures are not the enemy and can exist in the framework of the church's unity. His idea is to have the church enter into each HU, convert them in the context of whatever identifies their HU, and thereby convert the entire world to Christianity.[189]

Harvie Conn responds to the methodology presentation by McGavran. Conn's paper is characterized by a lengthy section graciously and discreetly removing spurious and unfair criticisms leveled against the HUP theory. With these effectively eliminated, he then raises four legitimate questions that test this strategy in the area of general methodology.[190] These questions point to what he finds as acceptable ideas presented by McGavran but also draws attention to what he observes as inadequacies of the

---

context of the Lausanne Consultation.

[189] In his position paper McGavran defines an HU. It moves away from seeing the world from the standpoint of nationalistic groups or people within a national border. Instead, they are an identifiable group of people on a more manageable scale linked to each other in a way to attach an evangelistic strategy to them. Also, HU churches are a viable consideration since such groupings tend to develop their own type of religious affinity as well. Another feature in this paper is that McGavran identifies HU's as a basic building block for the church. For a further discussion of McGavran's position see McGavran, "Genesis," 1977.

[190] First, Conn notes the importance of McGavran's distinction of the terms "discipling" and "perfecting" drawn from Matthew 28. He questions whether the dichotomy that results from this distinction inappropriately divides the essence of the Gospel from the subsequent process of maturation. Second, while McGavran has thoroughly elaborated on the benefits of the HUP theory, he has not adequately addressed the potential dangers inherent in this evangelistic strategy: tribalism, regionalism, or syncretism. Third, in his effort to demonstrate the church's diversity, McGavran has not adequately explained how diverse the church can become before it loses its essential feature of being one church. And fourth, Conn suggests that for all that a HU is, whatever the core cohesiveness includes, the concept of homogeneity may not be the best term to describe it. For a further discussion of this see Conn, "Covenant Ethos," 1977.

term and concept, Homogeneous Unit. From here Conn moves
on to suggest a personal alternative to the HUP theory, Covenant
Ethnos. Significant in this Covenant Ethnos is the reality that there
exists in the normal forming of HU's a thirst for God. There is a
necessity to reveal the Savior to a people group who are without
Him and who form around a bond that exists because of His
absence.[191]

## Anthropological Implications

The second area discussed in relation to the HUP theory
was anthropology. Charles Kraft presented a paper where he
identified HU's as a fact of human groupness. He explains that
whether a person likes HU's or not is beside the point. They exist
and must be dealt with as a part of human existence not treated as
an option. Kraft suggests that the importance (one's attitude[192]

---

[191] Conn also notes that it is insufficient to suggest that Christian decisions should
primarily be based upon the resulting benefit for a particular culture's church growth. If
such were the case, then, Dietrich Bonhoeffer would have been in error with his
political criticisms and prophetic statements with the backdrop of the German church.
Similarly, Beyers Naude would have been silent instead of joining his fellows in
standing courageously and alone. Included in the calling of following Christ is the
reality of suffering for Him at the hands of family, friends, and one's own cultural
adherents. For a further discussion see Conn, "Covenant Ethos," 1977.

[192] Kraft categorizes five attitudes toward cultural diversity and homogeneity. The
melting pot attitude views the many HU's in the same country as bad and something
bad, something to be eliminated by striving for a single national or ecclesiastical
identity. The laissez faire attitude also sees the many HU's in the same country as bad
but chooses to leave them alone. Left to themselves cultural processes will blend
these HU's into one group. The tourist attitude is an arrogant position which perceives
diversity as a way of identifying those who are different from one's own group. It is a
convenient way to leave other groups alone. The reactionary attitude elevates diversity

78

toward them) that is placed on HU's is the heart of the matter, not whether homogeneity or HU churches are accepted. From here three anthropological insights are applied to the debate on the HUP theory. The first deals with the problem of ethnocentrism. He treats the discussion as a Euro American issue, noting that several cultural features of this stance affect the HUP theory discussion. For example he takes note of two cultural attitudes: the diversity in language and culture is bad and a mental penchant that bigger is better. Power and influence are dominant pursuits of the Euro American culture, especially a sense of controlling social development as effectively as controlling technology. The second addresses the proper focus on the usage of homogeneity. Here Kraft explains that culture, while still an imprecise subject due to both its broad features as well as its specific nature, can be evaluated according to a number of different perspectives[193]. The

---

to a level of purpose and meaning. Efforts to preserve this diversity is a priority. And finally, the realist attitude is Kraft's preferred choice. It is the transcending position. It accepts diversity in varying HU's and works in light of their reality. Kraft also believes that God worked through HU's throughout the Scriptures. For a further discussion of this see Charles H. Kraft, "Anthropological Perspectives on the Homogeneous Unit Principle", Consultation on the Homogeneous Unit Principle (Wheaton: Lausanne Theology and Education Group Archives, 1977), 1-4.

[193] There are four perspectives relating to cultural analysis that are listed by Kraft: forms, functions, meanings, and usage. Forms refers to the observable features of a culture. These include items such as an axe, house or clothing. Function identifies how a form is used in a culture. For example, an axe is tool for chopping wood or it may be a symbol of power and status. Meaning speaks of the perception by members of a culture regarding toward a particular form. For example, marriage may mean adulthood, freedom, or prosperity in a particular culture. Usage addresses a culture's display of a form to communicate a certain message. For example, a marriage ceremony may be used by a wealthy family to display wealth but for a family with a modest income to simply plan a family reunion.     For a further discussion see Kraft,

third anthropological insight that Kraft gives deals with cultural change and how this kind of change relates to the HUP theory. Kraft notes that all cultures change; therefore, all HU's change as well. The responsibility of missions and the church is to assist such changes and thereby enhance the cause of Christ.[194]

Robert Ramseyer responds to Kraft's paper by expressing a reluctance to accept the HUP theory as an appropriately labeled attempt for the evangelistic responsibility of the church. He does, however, acknowledge the benefit of perceiving society as a mosaic, which in turn can be used for more effective evangelistic and mission planning.[195] Yet, he notes the assumption that the characteristics of an HU are only observations of amoral differences is naive. For social groups also are identified by animosity and biases that need reconciliation.[196]

---

"Anthropological Perspectives," 8-11.

[194] For a further discussion of this see Kraft, "Anthropological Perspectives," 11-14.

[195] Granting the concept of a mosaic society, Ramseyer notes that the issue of culture is not necessarily determinative for church development. For if a church becomes too closely identified with a particular HU that also is an identifiable social group, the Gospel may be associated with that group and consequently spurned by unevangelized groups. For a further discussion of this see Robert L. Ramseyer, "Anthropological Perspectives on the Homogeneous Unit Principle, II", Consultation on the Homogeneous Unit Principle (Wheaton: Lausanne Theology and Education Group, 1977), 4-6.

[196] Ramseyer explains that the church, as the new people of God, is a community marked by love toward one another as God has loved each individual. Thus, human culture does not determine the boundaries of Christian behavior but the Scriptures do. With this in mind McGavran's idea of endogamy cannot be accepted; namely, " . . . that the Bible sanctions the church making as one of its criteria for Christian obedience the practice of someone else's endogamy." (Ramseyer, "Anthropological Perspectives," 8.

## Historical Implications

The third area of discussion was historical. Ralph D. Winter presented the historical case in favor of the HUP theory. His argument begins with an acknowledgement of two historically observed phenomena: assimilation and dissimilation.[197] He suggests: " . . . there is probably more sympathy today than ever before toward the possibility of enduring diversity within the human family . . . "[198] This is a result of the historical phenomenon of uniformity.[199] He suggests that this same attitude exists in a latent form today, a disguised ethnocentric superiority - an assumption that everyone will become White, Anglo-Saxon and Protestant. When this same perspective is translated into Christian missions, there is an expectation that there should be just one national church in a country.[200] Instead, Winter argues for a church that

---

[197] The first term traces the gradual but constant change in language and culture of any people group. The latter term describes the process which detects the conscious and unconscious desire of a people to remain different from other groups. Winter writes that scientists have observed an increase in individual and group identity that is just as closely linked with the process of dissimulation as it is assimilation. (Ralph D. Winter, "The Homogeneous Unit Principle in Historical Perspective," Consultation on the Homogeneous Unit Principle [Wheaton: Lausanne Theology and Education Group Archives, 1977], 1.

[198] Winter, "Historical Perspective," 2.

[199] Winter uses this term to describe the attitude of social groups to see their own way as normative when compared and contrasted with others. He also notes that a basic feature of primitive groups is the intolerance of internal diversity and of other groups that are different than they are. For a further discussion of this see Winter, "Historical Perspective," 2-5.

[200] Winter perceives the churches in America as practicing this type of uniformitarianism which expects all non-Anglo Christians to become Anglo and join their churches. He evaluates this disposition as an infringement on the Christian liberty of other groups to have their own God-given identity. To sacrifice this would be an unhealthy form of Christian unity. He uses the Brahmin caste as an example. When

acknowledges and accepts people-group differences and churches that reflect those same differences: non-assimilative integration.[201]

Victor Hayward responds to Winter's presentation of the historical implications of the HUP theory. Hayward contends that while it is possible to become a Christian without crossing racial, linguistic or class barriers, it is in the crossing of these barriers that the " . . . true nature of the Christian Church and the Christian mission is revealed."[202] From the historical perspective of Pauline instruction in the early church, Hayward believes that Paul desired to both integrate Christians from different backgrounds as well as to highlight the social concept of equality with diversity[203]. He further suggests that a functional decision to separate a church for evangelistic or linguistic purposes does not necessarily superimpose any implication on the nature of the church.[204] In

---

they are successfully converted and encouraged to begin a Brahmin congregation, Winter suggests that this is not condoning segregation but an inclusion of Brahmins into the church of Christ. (Winter, "Historical Perspective," 5-8.)

[201] Far from encouraging racism and segregation, Winter suggests that the HUP theory believes that conversion via true evangelism is the answer to world prejudice. He calls this "culturally sensitive evangelism." (Winter, "Historical Perspective," 8,9)

[202] Victor E. Hayward, "The Homogeneous Unit Principle and the Record of Worldwide Missionary Expansion," Consultation on the Homogeneous Unit Principle (Wheaton: Lausanne Theology and Education Group Archives, 1977), 1.

[203] Once practical reasons as meaningful communication are noted, Hayward argues that the essence of the Christian witness calls for every Christian congregation to display the universality of the Church. (Hayward, "Missionary Expansion," 3.)

[204] Hayward explains that the Christian community has a nature of unity that is universal. It is a feature that surpasses any national, cultural, social or sexual difference. Nevertheless, he maintains that from an organizational perspective, it is " . . . legitimate to take positive account of whatever enables people to worship most truly, as well as to witness and evangelize most effectively - provided the universal nature of

82

concluding his response Hayward refers to two concepts. First, he urges the church to firmly portray the heart of Christ, namely, the unity He brought to all who are a part of His church. That is a direction that is known. The church should not attempt to go too far beyond that and dangerously attempt to control the outcome of the future by using history as a defense for its grand ideas.[205] Second, he argues from the standpoint of priorities. The unity and universality of the Gospel are so important that they must be at the forefront of Christian mission.[206] Matters like culture must be placed in a secondary position by comparison for they are not only complex but they are also unpredictable. History has shown that religious progress has even demonstrated that it can begin to flourish only after a culture has begun to disintegrate.[207] Ultimately, then, Hayward advises that it is faith that must direct the missionary calling, not science. Utilize science in the planning but depend upon the Spirit.[208]

---

the Church is denied neither virtually nor by implication." (Hayward, "Missionary Expansion", 3.)

[205] This concept is derived from Herbert Butterfield in Christianity and History. (Hayward, "Missionary Expansion," 3-5.)

[206] Hayward places the priority on unity: "Only after the universal nature of the Church has been demonstrated, only after the Gospel has been brought, more or less simultaneously, to several different homogenous units within a given locality, is it safe to utilize the insights of the homogeneous unit principle for rapid growth without compromising the very nature of the Church itself. And even then, every opportunity of making manifest the fundamental unity and universality of the Church must be deliberately seized." This idea is derived from H. G. Wood's Hulsean Lectures delivered at the Divinity School at Cambridge in 1933. (Hayward, "Missionary Expansion," 5-7.)

[207] Hayward, "Missionary Expansion," 8.

[208] Ibid., 8.

**Ethical Implications**

The fourth topic addresses the area of ethical implications. Peter Wagner, representing the supportive position, notes that the HUP theory has stimulated concern over a return to blatant racism and support for apartheid. At the same time he believes that the "vast majority" of churches throughout the world are culturally homogeneous.[209] Wagner describes two characteristics that must be in place before he will condone[210] a HU church. First, a culturally homogeneous church must be formed voluntarily. Second, it must be open to all who wish to become a member.[211] When these elements are present, then there is the greatest demonstration of Christian love possible from a church.[212] An HU

---

[209] Wagner admits that there is no statistic available to support this contention. Nevertheless, he maintains that the percentage of HU churches in the world could be as high as 95-98%. He also believes that the early church was also homogeneous. (Peter Wagner, "How Ethical is the Homogeneous Unit Principle?" Consultation on the Homogeneous Unit Principle [Wheaton: Lausanne Theology and Education Group Archives, 1977], 1.)

[210] An HU church which conforms to Wagner's standards, is according to Wagner's estimation, a Biblical church, a congregation that will better demonstrate the power of Christ, a people group that celebrates God's gift of culture, and fully realizes all that the church should be. (Wagner, "How Ethical", 2.)

[211] Wagner, "How Ethical," 2,3.

[212] Wagner lists seven ways in which HU churches are a more effective way to display the love of God. First, he writes that human culture is a part of God's creation design; therefore, it must be considered good. And just as important as culture itself is culture's diversity. Second, celebrating culture protects human dignity. He views it as very unloving to expect a people to adopt the culture of another people-group. Third, he advocates the importance of peoplehood. This is the importance of someone's roots and personal identity. Fourth, HU churches are better in evangelizing because culturally bound non-Christians will be more inclined to listen to the Gospel from their own group of people. Fifth, no barriers to conversion should be constructed. Wagner distinguishes between preaching and teaching here. When the Gospel is preached, the ethical issues that must be confronted are those sensed by the hearer not those imposed on the hearer by the preconceptions of the preacher. Sixth, theological

84

church is to balance the two ethical issues of unity and peoplehood by taking its cue from its surrounding community.[213]

John H. Yoder writes a response to Wagner's paper on ethics. In evaluating the ethical implications (Yoder takes a broader view of ethics than Wagner.[214]) of the HUP theory, Yoder questions that validity of the postponement of an ethical awareness. He is not satisfied that the problems of racism and prejudice would be "later" resolved by proper discipline. To him the nature of regeneration calls for a greater and more immediate change. The Gospel carries with it a moral dimension that cannot be left up to the choice of the sinner.[215] Yoder's understanding of missions is for the missionary[216] to identify themselves deeply with

---

integrity must be maintained. That is, new converts to Christianity must learn to express the "supracultural" principles of theology in their own cultural context. Seventh, brotherhood should be advanced by the introduction of the Gospel to any new people. He explains that HU churches contribute to a better understanding of group identity and thus, enhance brotherhood. (For a further discussion see Wagner, "How Ethical", 3-13) Much of Wagner's views on the HUP Theory are incorporated in chapter 1 (see 28ff).

[213] "The local congregation in a given community should be as integrated as are the families and other primary groups in the community, while intercongregational activities and relationships should be as integrated as are the secondary social groups in the community or society as a whole." (Wagner, "How Ethical", 13.)

[214] Yoder perceived Wagner to use "ethics" to refer to making moral judgments on some specific type of action. Yoder's interests are broader. It includes determining the desire of an individual or a group of people as it relates to the identity they wish to obtain. Also, it addresses the problem of the church's make-up. How should it be organized? And lastly, the issue of obedience must be addressed as a pre-requisite for conversion or as consequence of it. (For a further discussion see John H. Yoder, "The Homogeneous Unit Concept in Ethical Perspective", Consultation on the Homogeneous Unit Principle [Wheaton: Lausanne Theology and Education Group Archives, 1977], 1-4.)

[215] Yoder, "Ethical Perspective," 7.

[216] Yoder identifies the problem of relegating the Gospel and mission to the professional missionary specialist. Instead, every Christian should be a participant in

the culture to which they bring the Gospel, a responsibility for all Christians.

## *Biblical/Theological implications*

Arthur Glasser presented the Fuller position on this topic. He builds an argument first from the Old Testament, pointing to the divine origin of unity in the human race. But, he also addresses the importance of the divine intent of cultural pluralism. This diversity is a reality and will always be a part of human existence, and part of the divine plan; therefore, it must be accepted but with mutuality. From the New Testament he argues that Jesus commissioned all His followers to deliberately make disciples of the world's different ethnic and cultural groupings.[217] He also relates the apostolic writings as emphasizing the great unity in Christ but also that that unity is reflected in diversity. Using the body as an illustration, Glasser suggests that there is an unmistakable presence of the church's diversity that is part of the apostolic focus.[218] And lastly, Glasser refers to the apostolic

---

changing his cultural habits in order to identify with another for the purpose of communicating the Gospel. For a further discussion see Yoder, "Ethical Perspective", 15,16.

[217] This is represented in the HUP theory's understanding of *ta ethne*. While the Great Commission has a focus on the individual it also takes into perspective a person's ethnic and collective identity. For a further discussion see Arthur F. Glasser, "How Biblical is the Homogeneous Unit Principle?" Consultation on the Homogeneous Unit Principle (Wheaton: Lausanne Theology and Education Group, 1977), 7-9.

[218] He explains it as a realistic difference of cultural backgrounds that works itself out in visible unity. Matters such as race, culture, and sex remain; but, as one in Christ

pattern of HU evangelism.[219] That is, Glasser contends that the house church concept was largely a collection of HU's.

Rene Padilla responded to Glasser's position paper. His response is developed in three sections. First, he examines God's purpose in uniting all things in Jesus Christ. All men in Adam are part of a solidarity that is under judgment.[220] In contrast to this, all who are in Christ share a oneness with each other that transcends all external appearances and earthly values. Each one has been incorporated into a new humanity.[221] Second, the early church strategy is examined. Padilla sees that the habit of Jesus and the apostles was the same. Those who were converted set aside normal patterns of selective association and entered house churches that were just the opposite of their previous homogenous tendencies.[222] Lastly, Padilla evaluates the HUP theory in light of

there is a new oneness that is displayed as the essential of the Christian mission. Glasser, "How Biblical", 9-11.

[219] This refers to the supposition that the early church was founded upon an evangelistic pattern that worked through people movements. And people movements is founded upon the concept of the HUP theory. (Glasser, "How Biblical", 12.)

[220] Padilla draws upon Paul's explanation of man's circumstance in Romans 1-3. While man has the law of God, he will not be able to find acceptance before God through it. As a result, all of humanity is unified in sin and death. (C. Rene Padilla, "The Unity of the Church and the Homogeneous Unit Principle," Consultation on the Homogeneous Unit Principle [Wheaton: Lausanne Theology and Education Group Archives, 1977], 1.)

[221] Padilla describes this as part of being under the lordship of Christ. Personal preferences are no longer determinative regarding association. For the same act of divine reconciliation that brought a converted Christian into fellowship with God simultaneously places that same person into the Christian community where individuals now find their identity in Christ not in race, culture, or class. (Padilla, "Unity of the Church," 3.)

[222] Padilla writes, "All the New Testament evidence points in the opposite direction, namely, in the direction of an apostolic practice whose aim was the formation of

his understanding of the New Testament evidence. Here he suggests that the real question is not what people like to do regarding their own conversion but whether the HUP theory is essential for the mission of the church to be fulfilled. He reasons[223] that the HUP theory is not essential and that it does not rest on a sound Biblical basis.

## Evaluation of the Consultation

Three helpful themes emerged from the Consultation[224] on the HUP theory. First, regarding culture, all agree that there is

churches that would live out the unity of the new humanity in Jesus Christ." (Padilla, "Unity of the Church," 10.)

[223] In addition to his analysis of the apostolic pattern he adds the following five observations: (1) Often Jews and Gentiles heard the Gospel while they were together. (2) The breaking down of barriers which separate people has been historically considered an essential part of the Gospel. (3) The early church experienced growth that spread indiscriminately across cultural barriers. (4) Inter-church relationships does not have the historical evidence to support it as an apostolic intent. Instead, each assembly of believers was to portray the unity that they had in Christ regardless of the variety of their racial, linguistic, or class backgrounds. (5) There is no evidence that the apostles approved a Christian who purposefully compromised some feature of his faith in order to avoided family or tribe rejection due to his Christian conversion. (Padilla, "Unity of the Church," 13, 14)

[224] The Lausanne Committee for World Evangelization has identified the common ground between those who embrace the HUP theory and those who practice a universal acceptance priority regarding the appropriation of Ephesians 2 to the church. Four points of agreement were noted: First, all agree that there is no room for any animosity between Christians because there exists a difference of background. Such is inconsistent with the reconciling work already achieved by Christ. Due to the work of Christ active hatred, disdain, or ill-feeling has been obliterated. But, more than this, the basis of such animosity has also been abolished. Second, all people, regardless of their ethnic heritage, once they become Christians become part of a great mystery; they are "joint heirs, joint members of the same body and joint partakers of the

beauty and goodness in culture, but also, that due to man's sin, culture must be tested and judged by Scripture. In fact some of the reasons which identify a particular HU might be essentially evil[225] and therefore must be opposed. At the same time all acknowledged that culture is constantly changing. Part of that change is that conversion brings a new homogeneity, namely, a common identity now found in Christ.[226] Second, the issue of lordship is raised. All found agreement in the essentials of "lordship salvation"; that is, that when Christ is presented in the Gospel, His lordship should also be included, since it is His lordship that gives Him the authority to grant salvation. The two issues of conversion and nurture cannot be separated. They belong together. Hence, conversion calls for a radical change, a pattern of maturation that must follow one's initial declaration of loyalty to Christ. Last, based upon the eschatological hope revealed in John's vision[227] the present diversity of man will be

---

promise." Third, while it is clear that in the early church there were homogeneous Jewish churches and Gentile churches, there were also mixed assemblies of Jews and Gentiles as well. The apostle Paul's admonition to them all was that they belonged to each other and must welcome each other just as they were welcomed by Christ. Fourth, all agree that a homogeneous church can be an authentic church. But, it can never be complete nor mature in isolation with itself. An HU church must actively pursue means of incorporating itself with the wider body of Christ. (Pasadena Consultation, 4-5.)

[225] A few such intolerable evils are cannibalism, racism, crime, prostitution, and wealthy oppression. (Pasadena Consultation, 6.)

[226] Ibid., 6.

[227] Revelation 7:9, 10 and 21:26; 22:2. For a discussion see J. A. Seiss, The Apocalypse: Lectures on the Book of Revelation (Grand Rapids: Zondervan Pub. House, 1977), 170-176, 500-501; John Walvoord, The Revelation of Jesus Christ (Chicago: Moody Press, 1966), 144, 327-328; 329-331; David Hocking, The Coming

forever a part of eternity. And this diversity will enhance the magnificence of heaven's heterogeneous fellowship. Thus, the church as an eschatological fellowship of Christians, is called to display in an anticipation manner the cultural diversity in harmony that is to come.[228]

Two important issues arise from this interaction at the Lausanne Consultation and still remain as points of interest. They are sanctification, as it relates to the moral and ethical change that occurs in a new convert to Christianity, and ecclesiology, as it relates to the existence and perpetuation of ethnic churches. First, the issue of sanctification is at the forefront of evaluating the validity of the HUP theory. For instance some, who routinely utilize an evangelism strategy and church development pattern that is in contrast to the HUP theory, advocate that Christians must reflect a unity that was accomplished by Christ's work. They have observed that following the HUP theory according to its fullest extent leads to a violation of this New Testament mandate. This work of Christ is not merely an abstract hope; rather, it is a decisive fact that must order the lives of all Christians.[229]   A

---

World Leader: Understanding the Book of Revelation (Portland: Multnomah Press, 1988), 144-147, 303-305.

[228] Pasadena Consultation, 7.

[229] Rene Padilla argues this point from a number of New Testament references. In 1 Peter 2:9 he points out that the only concept of peoplehood that has validity in relating individuals to the church is one where ethnically distinctive groups like Jews and Gentiles relate to one another as they are but are now equally part of a third group (see 1 Corinthians 10:32). Then, in Galatians 3:28 he points out that Paul is not arguing that Jews must become Gentiles or that males must become females in order to receive full Gospel blessings. Rather, he is advocating that in Christ something new has been

modified use of ideas incorporated in the HUP theory seems to be an agreeable solution. Respondents at the Lausanne Consultation agree that the Gospel must be presented in the context of a recipient's culture and ethnic milieu. Then, with a positive response of faith and conversion of an individual to Christianity comes a simultaneous capacity for ethical and moral change. But, the evangelistic process and strategy to implement such ideas does not necessarily demand that churches organize themselves around the same type of guidelines as the HUP theory suggests. This leads to the other important feature that results from the Lausanne Consultation, namely, the church.

The church, particularly ethnic churches, is the second item of importance that must be considered. From an examination of the HUP theory an assumption is uncovered; that is, principles that govern effective evangelism also determine local church operations.[230] Yet, such a blending is not necessarily valid. For evangelism primarily deals with Christians relating to non-

---

achieved. A togetherness based on him now exists. The normal barriers of separation in the non-Christian world do not apply any longer. Colossians 3:11 further elaborates this same principle. Christians have been incorporated into a new humanity because of the work of Christ. The previous divisions in the lifestyle of their old humanity are no longer relevant. (Rene Padilla, "The Unity of the Church and the Homogeneous Unit Principle," in Exploring Church Growth, ed. Wilbert Shenk [Grand Rapids: Wm. B. Eerdmans Pub. Co., 1983], 286-287)

[230] In determining the parameters of the debate regarding the HUP theory Wagner does not limit the discussion only to evangelism (Christian to non-Christian relationships) but includes local church organizing and congregational grouping (Christian to Christian relationships). He asks the following questions: "Is it *right* and *good* for Christians intentionally to group themselves into congregations that generally reflect the culture and life-style of just one kind of people? Can a culturally homogeneous church be justified in a pluralistic society?" (Wagner, Our Kind, 1)

Christians while local church operations deal with Christians relating to Christians. The pattern seems to be that a given HU in a designated area will best be converted if there is a local church that is compatible with that HU's characteristics. Yet, the initial conversion of Christians was not always accomplished by members of that HU, but often by a missionary of a completely different background racially, linguistically, and according to class status. Now, realistically, in a multi-ethnic country like the United States of America ethnic churches do exist and will continue to do so as a result of the sociological phenomena already discussed. But, since their limitations have been mutually acknowledged through the Lausanne Consultation and since a more accurate local church perception has been also mutually acknowledged, perhaps then, church leaders should be encouraging an advanced and more fully complete type of heterogeneous church model for the currently existing HU churches to eventually copy.


## *Current Debate Status*

The thorough discussion at the Lausanne Consultation might lead one to expect a greater effort in working together on a common evangelistic strategy and a modification of the HUP theory in its application. Careful agreement in the final Occasional Paper by the Lausanne Committee shed a great deal of light on the inadequacies of the HUP theory as well as on the areas of mutual agreement maintained by both the adherents and the respondents. But, the subsequent climate surrounding the debate has not historically demonstrated a move toward adjustment but a seemingly unaltered position by its adherents.

Ten years after the Lausanne Consultation, Plaisted gives an overview of the debate in its most recent form and takes a position in favor of the HUP theory that reveals little change from the original presentation of the Fuller Team. He describes those who embrace the HUP theory as "products of value change."[231] There was once a time when they adhered to another concept of evangelism and church growth. Now, as a result of the work of Pickett and McGavran, they have convictions that follow in line with the HUP theory. The world of missions was entrenched in thinking of evangelism exclusively as a one-by-one conversion schedule. McGavran was interested in thinking about "people movements" as the necessary means for reaching large scale evangelism[232] and rapid church growth. He identified Western culture's individualistic perspective for the shortcoming of a

---

[231] Plaisted, "Debate", 221.
[232] McGavran developed the HUP theory out of a context of **deep concern for evangelism. He observed that the reasons that** prevented more individuals from converting to Christianity were more sociological than theological. The validity of the Gospel was the issue but there was a sense where the subsequent life of a Christian struck them as too alien. The frequent response to the Gospel was a reticence resulting from a fear of renouncing their own culture and of betraying their own people. (Pasadena Consultation, 3.)

missionary consideration of group processes and decisions in human life.[233]

McGavran's solution to the problem of shifting away from the traditional mission stations to people movement strategies appeals to this group.[234] The former method may have had measurable results in economic or health matters; but, consequential evangelistic conversions were consistently minimal.[235] In contrast to this, a people movement philosophy reemphasized the primacy of evangelism not only as the focus of missionary effort but also as the most important result of the missions endeavor. Part of enacting this people movement

---

[233] Plaisted, "Debate", 221.

[234] A people movement does not identify a large group of people converting to Christianity although it can include that phenomenon. Nor does it emphasize conversion at the expense of postbaptismal care. Neither is it a reference to any sort of mass movement. Rather, it refers to " . . . a tribe, a caste, or any homogenous unit where marriage and intimate life take place only within the society. . . . a tightly knit segment of any society. [Also a] . . . people movement results from the joint decision of a number of individuals all from the same people group, which enables them to become Christians without social dislocation, while remaining in full contact with their non-Christian relatives, thus enabling other segments of that people group, across the years, after suitable instruction, to come to similar decisions and form Christian churches made up exclusively of members of that people." (McGavran, Understanding, 3rd ed., 222-223.) For a further discussion of people movements see chapters 17 "People Movements" and 18 "Kinds of People Movements and Their Care" in McGavran, Understanding, 3rd ed., 221-249.

[235] It was frustrating for McGavran to see large quantities of financial support and administrative effort being poured into foreign mission fields for medical, educational, economic reasons but having little effect on conversion results. He perceived that the mission station approach would attract occasional indigenous persons and may even see them converted but not to the great numbers necessary to make a mark on the unconverted billions left in the world. He writes, "The era has come when Christian Missions should hold lightly all mission station work, which cannot be proved to nurture growing churches, and should support the Christward movements within the Peoples as long as they continue to grow at the rate of 50 percent per decade or more. This is today's strategy." (McGavran, Bridges, 1955)

94

approach calls for church planters to find ways that enable these people groups to become Christians without having to cross barriers that would be offensive to their cultural identity.[236]  This application and respect for culture is the essence of the HUP theory, when properly understood.

Those who embrace the HUP theory strategy explain the legitimacy of their position by using Novak's concept of the "unmeltable ethnics."  He argues that in a multi-ethnic country like the United States each ethnic group has the right to remain itself. This identity should be allowed to remain intact even after adopting Christianity.  The cultural barriers that are erected by each group are a part of defining its identity.  As such, they are not viewed as improper or as matters to be altered but are accepted as normal and desirable.[237]  The blending of the world's myriad of ethnic groups is described as a vast mosaic[238].  The goal of the HUP

---

[236] People live their non-Christian lives in cultural settings.  Their dress, conversation, mores and customs give them identity and distinctiveness from other people groups. Such distinctions are not evil but in fact are good.  McGavran writes, "Human beings do build barriers around their own societies.  More exactly we may say that the ways in which each society lives and speaks, dresses and works, of necessity wet it off from other societies.  Mankind is a mosaic and each piece has a separate life of its own which seems strange and often unlovely to men and women of other pieces." (McGavran, Understanding, 163)

[237] For a further discussion see Michael Novak, The Rise of the Unmeltable Ethnics, New York: MacMillan, 1971.  Also, in this discussion three countries are used to illustrate the reality of "unmeltable ethnics": The United States, India and Afghanistan. Characteristic of such "unmeltable" groups in India are sociological features as endogamy, education, political power, languages and customs. (McGavran, Understanding, 163-164.)

[238] A qualification is placed upon using the mosaic figure of speech.  While the countless pieces of a mosaic never change shape or color, the human mosaic is different.  "Its pieces are constantly changing, merging with,  swallowing, and being

theory is to construct a strategy that spreads the Gospel from one piece of the mosaic to the next very different piece[239].

India still serves as a key illustration for the HUP theory. Due to the domination of caste in that society, no significant Christian movement has occurred in that society either in size or impact except along homogeneous unit/caste line.[240] This emphasis, however, has generated some alarm. For example, criticism has been raised against the HUP theory for its potential in justifying racism or segregation. Wagner acknowledges that there is a danger in this but at the same time condemns such an application.[241] Instead, he suggests a much more preferred balance; namely, to recognize the social dynamics that already

---

swallowed by other pieces . . . Their cultures change radically. In view of this great readiness to change should we think of the propagation of the gospel as a process of change by which all peoples and cultures are gradually transformed into a new and beautiful Christian culture? Or, does the Christian faith enter each changing, yeasting culture and transform it from within while it yet remains itself, and separate from other cultures that have become Christian?" (McGavran, Understanding, 164.)

[239] The oneness of Christians is acknowledged and explained along side of the reality of human diversity: "The biblical teaching is plain that in Christ two peoples become one. Christian Jews and Gentiles become one new people of God, parts of the one body of Christ. But the one body is complex. Since both peoples continue to speak separate languages, does not the oneness cover a vast and continuing diversity?" (McGavran, Understanding, 164.)

[240] Plaisted, "Debate", 222. This concept is the essential theme of McGavran's Ethnic Realities (1979). The nine Christian groups in India are evaluated, found to be non-growing except when the HUP theory is being followed. This leads Plaisted to conclude that the HUP theory is the "only strategy" that will enable the Indian church to grow in the near future.

[241] Wagner explains that there is no intention built into the HUP theory to support racist or segregationist ideals. He admits that the potential exists but calls such an application an abuse. There is in his mind no legitimate connection between the HUP theory and apartheid. For a further discussion of this see C. Peter Wagner, "Recent Developments in Church Growth Understandings", Review and Expositor, 77 Fall 1980.

exists within the thousands of various human groups, predetermine the prohibition of any bigotry, and also to acknowledge that unity does not require uniformity. Instead, the healthy diversity that already exists in human society ought to also be recognized in the "Christian world church."[242]

## Confidence from Trends in the Debate

Four trends are identified by Plaisted as symptoms that the debate is turning in favor of the HUP theory.[243] First, he notes that the participants are now interacting with each other in a helpful dialogue. This is in contrast with the previous use of verbal swipes and mud slinging. Second, he notes that those who have embraced the HUP theory have moved further away from a defensive posture and have portrayed a greater confidence in their view. Also, he is encouraged that "homogeneous-unit-based evangelism" has become part of the pattern for main denominations in church planting efforts. Third, the position of the

---

[242] In Ralph D. Winter's address to the 1974 Lausanne Congress he explained his own discovery of a personal but latent expectation regarding the ethnic diversity of the world and the church. While harboring no biases or bigotries, Winter realized that he was assuming that America's diverse ethnic groups would all eventually come to white churches and practice Christianity his way. For a further discussion on his understanding in this area see Ralph D. Winter, "The New Macedonia: A Revolutionary New Era in Mission Begins," Perspectives on the World Christian Movement (Pasadena, 1981).

[243] From the stand point of tracing a change of opinion supporters of the HUP theory claim significant support in comparison to those in opposition to it. Plaisted argues that value change, the basis for his own change, has been the rule. He states that he knows of no one who has adopted this perspective and who has subsequently been

assimilationist/integrationist is losing supporters. With this trend Wagner's model of seven different ways of dealing with minority culture groups[244] is injected. Both Wagner and Plaisted suggest that the main objection against the HUP theory is couched in the assimilationist racist mentality. It has disguised itself as an integration idealism in the past but has since been exposed by its failure to apply a form of subtle ethnocide on non-white cultures.[245] Fourth, the debate has not disproved the hypothesis[246] of the HUP theory. Plaisted suggests that there is a stalemate in the debate at best. According to his evaluation the problem stems from two different foundations. Those who embrace the HUP theory start by analyzing what strategy appears to produce the best measurable results while those who do not accept the HUP theory as valid begin from a theological basis. David Wasdell concludes that since pragmatic results affirm the HUP theory and theological criticism does not alter those results, then, the latter is spurious to the issue.[247] Plaisted joins in Wasdell's argument reasoning that biblical exposition fails to be convincing unless it first engages in " . . . what is known about social reality."[248]

---

disillusioned enough to abandon it. (Plaisted, "Debate", 224.)

[244] The seven ways of relating to minority cultural groups that Wagner suggests are genocide, deportation, apartheid, structural racism, assimilationist racism, open society, and secession. For a further discussion on this see Wagner, Whole Gospel.

[245] Wagner, Whole Gospel, 175-178.

[246] Wagner refers to the HUP theory as a hypothesis. (Wagner, Our Kind, 4).

[247] David Wasdell, "HUP: A Defense Against Anxiety", Global Church Growth Bulletin 17, January - February 1980, 1.

[248] The suggestion of this pragmatic demand is a severe one as noted in the following statement: "Those who criticize such approaches at least must demonstrate that they

## The Position of Those Who are Uncertain

Not everyone who is introduced to the HUP theory embraces it or rejects it. Some see attractive features in it yet express a reticence to adopt it. This hesitation is a result of a number of varying reasons. Some are culture bound and only feel comfortable in the kind of religious environment that is consistent with their own background. Others are sincerely at a loss to justify such a perspective with the clear mandate of Scripture. And yet, others are well aware of the dangers of any new idea that seemingly allows for an old problem in religion, namely, racism.

Plaisted identifies Martin Marty as one of those in this category. He is noted for his dialogue with C. Peter Wagner over the validity of the theory. In his dialogue[249] with Wagner Marty identifies himself as one who is emerging from a "strong loyalty to the crumbling fortress of classical 1960's liberal integrationist Protestant dogma."[250]

---

are aware of the empirical world of human affairs, and of how the church <u>actually</u> works." (Plaisted, "Debate", 227.)

[249] Marty describes his personal dilemma in his dialogue with Wagner. He is torn between "some convincing and some tantalizing arguments" (Marty, "Christian?", 2) presented by Church Growth proponents and his own background as an integration idealist. His assessment of the HUP theory is that it is attempting to "rationalize cultural separation as the Christian model." (Marty, "Christian?", 3) In his dialogue he " . . . questions Wagner's interpretation of the Tower of Babel as an illustration of God's will to cultural diversity, and also his contention that there is more theological integrity in contextualized and ethnic theologies `than in the more nearly universal kinds of thought'." (Plaisted, "Debate", 220.) One of his great concerns is the image that such a strategy may impart to the world. That is, will the world see the church as wishy-washy Christians shift their basic principles. For a further discussion see Martin Marty, "Is Homogeneous Unit Principle of Church Christian?" <u>Context</u>, March 15, 1978.

[250] Plaisted, "Debate," 219.

Marty's concern over the church's reputation if it should do "another flip-flop on basic principle"[251] wins sympathetic approval by those who embrace the HUP theory. Their response is two-fold. First, they point out that it would be just as deplorable if a " . . . rigid adherence to dogmatic consistency in the face of new knowledge . . . "[252] were maintained. Second, it is suggested that there is commendation for " . . . the intellectual courage involved in an honest change of mind."[253] But Marty's perspective was clearly an outgrowth of an integrationist ideal[254], a societal solution to the real problem of racism and segregation. And seems to be an excessive generalization to maintain that reticence to accepting the HUP theory is largely linked to the generally faded integrationist hopes of the 1960's.[255]

Plaisted surmises that a primary reason for the hesitation on the part of the uncertain to accept the HUP theory is due to their integrationist ideals. Marty's position is described as the "fading of the integrationist dream"[256] while he notes that according to John Alexander[257] integration has more than merely

---

[251] Marty, "Christian?" 2,3.

[252] Plaisted, "Debate," 220.

[253] Ibid.

[254] Plaisted assesses Marty's overall disposition as a regret for the "fading of the integrationist dream" (Plaisted, "Debate," 220.)

[255] Plaisted identifies his own past as connected to the dream of integrationism: "Once I was an assimilationist racist disguised as a passionate integrationist . . . . Abandoning my own unconscious `white is right' bias was a painful experiential struggle. I now hope, with many others, for the end of assimilationist/integrationist racism." (Plaisted, "Debate," 226.)

[256] Ibid., 220.

[257] John F. Alexander is associated with the magazine The Other Side. He can be

100

faded, it has failed. This assessment is founded on the premise that behind an integrationist's desires was the assumption of an assimilationist racism, "white is right." From this position the argument moves on to describe the great differences between the culture of blacks and whites. It is this difference, according to Alexander, that governmental integration has failed. White racist attitudes are not the cause of the problem in Alexander's eyes. He then applies his evaluation to the church. Integration in his mind cannot succeed in the church because blacks find white churches "culturally alien" in its singing, style of preaching, and expression of emotional intensity.[258] This assessment, however, as the primary reason for any hesitation in embracing the HUP theory is too general and imprecise.

## Identifying Remaining Issues of Disagreement

While there is a measure of popularity in using the HUP theory in Church Growth contexts and while the historical analysis of the debate has surfaced a good number of areas of agreement and mutually accepted ideas by both those who embrace this strategy and those who prefer an alternate evangelistic method, there yet remain conflicts related to the topic that call for some

---

identified with a 1974 editorial titled, "A Manifesto for White Christians." Beginning as an integrationist publication, this periodical later changed its stance. (Plaisted, "Debate," 220.)

[258] For a further discussion of this see John F. Alexander, "A Manifesto for White Christians," The Other Side, 10, January - February 1974.

modification in the theory. Plaisted generalizes the concerns of those who are outside of the HUP theory camp. He notes their belief: " . . . spontaneous homogeneous grouping may be a fact in the church but it ought not to be!"[259] He describes the biblical and theological objections as detached to the reality of cultural diversity. Also, he understands this position to believe that HU's should not exist in the church and not be used in the church's evangelistic strategies.[260]

The previous overview of the Lausanne Consultation demonstrates that these generalizations are not completely inaccurate. There was consistent agreement by the respondents and in the final Occasional Paper alluding to the reality of HU's in the church and significant acceptance of evangelistic strategies that could utilize these concepts. What appears to be part of the current problem is that some who embrace the HUP theory are looking for full converts to their terminology and techniques and not allowing for similarities in other approaches or adjustments in their own precepts. While there are areas of agreement that have been clarified as a result of the Lausanne Consultation, several areas of concern regarding the validity of the HUP theory remain.

Glasser isolates four areas of agreement between those who embrace the theory and those who do not. First, much can be learned by observing the numerical results of Christian

[259] Plaisted, "Debate," 217.
[260] Ibid., 217-218.

homogeneous unit groupings. Second, there is benefit in aiding church growth through the use of anthropological and sociological tools. Third, an observation of the preparatory work of the Holy Spirit indicates that some HU's are more winnable than others. Fourth, the Gospel must be presented to a person in the context of his culture.[261]

Next, he addresses the matter of HU churches. He on behalf of McGavran argues that a Hindu who wants to become a Christian will not be inclined to do so if he is first required to join a church which includes a people of another HU that he has learned in his culture to despise. Therefore, to increase the likelihood of this person coming to Christ he should be encouraged to do so with people in his own level of society. Once this is allowed then that person can learn to eventually understand that all believers are members of one family. But, to require such understanding before a person is baptized is not acceptable.[262]

Yet, Glasser's summation is not very far removed from the conclusion of the Lausanne Consultation. For Yoder's inquiry regarding the duration of postponing ethical awareness[263] still remains. How long after a person becomes converted to Christianity does the miracle of oneness in Christ take to manifest itself? The New Testament speaks of a newness[264] that results

---

[261] Glasser, "Fuller," 415-416.
[262] Ibid., 416-417.
[263] Yoder, "Ethical Perspective," 4-6.
[264] 2 Cor. 5:17; Eph. 2:15; 4:24. The author is indebted to Samuel Escobar for

from being converted to Christianity. But, if a person can deliberately avoid association with other Christians while joining a church and being baptized and learning about his new faith over an indeterminate length of time, when does the newness begin? And if this newness of sanctification is not an immediate factor in a Christian convert's new ethic but education is, then, why after nearly 2,000 years church history has the church still "tended to grow within particular homogeneous units?"[265] A familiar adage to those who are of a particular racial minority may be appropriate in considering the place of education in relationship to culturally oriented biases: "You can't reason out a person what was not reasoned in."

To further his point on the matter of HU churches Glasser illustrates with the following: "In America no one says that the Chinese in our midst should not have their own churches. Why can't we allow various types of churches to emerge and function within separate language and cultural groups?"[266] His suggestion here, however, is not clear on what he means by "Chinese" who are in America. The generational problem, common among ethnic churches in North America, is not addressed[267], the growing number of ethnic Asians actively practicing their Christianity in

---

stressing this concept in evaluating the HUP theory during a personal interview at Christ's College, University of Edinburgh, 1989.

[265] Glasser, "Fuller," 416.

[266] Ibid., 417.

[267] See Mark Mullins, "The Life-Cycle of Ethnic Churches," Japanese Journal of Religious Studies 14, no. 4 (1987), 321-334.

multi-cultural churches is not addressed, and the reality of Asian-ethnics seeking advanced Bible and theological training in non-cultural Bible Colleges and Seminaries is not addressed. Obviously, then, there are unresolved issues regarding the HUP theory that call for some alteration of its precepts.

## Non-Christian Attitudes Should Not Direct the Church

One of the most dominant positions against the HUP theory has been the attempt to clarify the difference between a Christian attitude in church compared to a non-Christian attitude in church. Those who argue this position admit that there may be validity to the reality of people grouping themselves together with others like themselves but their contention is that it should not be that way. This position understands Christianity as having risen above cultural distinctions and separateness.

Jurgen Moltmann[268] identifies cultural diversity in the church as an "evil remnant" that must pass away. His thinking calls for all separate national, cultural, and religious histories that

---

[268] Wagner says the following: "Moltmann, the theologian of hope, looks forward to a future made up of a new, free humanity. This he sees as a humanity free from racism, injustice, captivity, oppression, prejudice, war, and hate. He interprets the past as being characterized by a pluralism of cultures, nations, religions, and churches, which he regards as evil. His theology of hope embraces a future of the singular: In order to avoid possible extinction, all peoples must participate in one new community, which Moltmann predicts will erase cultural distinctive, racial barriers, and social classes. Churches which continue to allow themselves to be distinct from others are churches of the past. The churches of the future, those which fully participate in the dynamics of Christian hope, will overcome human differences and make the plural singular."

must submit to a new world history.[269]   He further argues that "National churches, racial churches, class churches, middle class churches, are in their practical life heathenish and heretical."[270] The church is the community of God where its members are unlike each other.   There is a mix of education backgrounds, class status, ethnic ancestry, et cetera.   There may very well be a reaction by the Christian's former non-Christian people in perceiving converts traitors, but, the new Christian community provides true hope for the world.[271]

Moltmann has also elaborated on the church's direction. He believes that it cannot organize itself according to the social order that is established by the society in which it is.  Such a social order will lead to churches that are characterized by a certain race, class, sexual preference or nationalistic spirit.   This Christian choice will necessitate a break with the natural human tendency to observe selective association.[272]

The theological contribution of Moltmann cannot be dismissed as mere futuristic musings. Clearly, he has made a very close connection between a Christian's destiny and the initial call

---

(Wagner, Our Kind, 19)

[269]   Jurgen Moltmann, Religion, Revolution, and the Future, M. Douglas Meeks, trans. (New York, 1969), 27.

[270]   The homogeneity of human preference is described by the Aristotelian adage, "Birds of a feather flock together."  Moltmann urges the church to go beyond this. Jurgen Moltmann, The Gospel of Liberation, H. Wayne Pipkin, trans. (Waco, Texas: 1973), 91.

[271]  For a further discussion see Moltmann, The Gospel.

[272]  For a further discussion on this see Jurgen Moltmann, The Church in the Power of the Spirit, Margaret Kohl, trans. (New York, 1977).

106

to conversion. Intertwined together, there is a universality that mitigates against separation or favoritism: "In the New Testament . . . mission and call are directed `without distinction', to Jews and Gentile. The call to hope and to participation in the mission here becomes universal."[273] Thus, the Gospel enters into a fragmented world and gives every individual the equal opportunity to enter a new life that is shared equally with others. He strongly supports the giving of a person his humanity along with Christian theology. This is based upon the creation of man in God's image, the principle of reconciliation through the incarnation, the inevitable conclusion of history by the kingdom of God, and concern for a person's humanity as well as for their rights and duties.

Specifically, the obligation of Christian theology " . . . is grounding fundamental human rights in God's right to - that is, his claim upon - human beings, their human dignity, their fellowship, their rule over the earth, and their future. It is the duty of the Christian faith beyond human rights and duties to stand for the dignity of human beings in their life with God and for God."[274] Such a theological position desires to hand a spiritually converted person not only his eternal life but also his humanity of which his ethnicity is an essential factor. The HUP theory is not adequate in promoting to this extent the resulting sanctification of a newly converted Christian.

---

[273] Jurgen Moltmann, Theology of Hope (London: SCM Press, 1967), 286.
[274] Jurgen Moltmann, On Human Dignity: "Political Theology and Ethics" (London:

## The Church is Not the Curator of Human Culture

Related to this need for a Church development strategy that is more inclusive regarding sanctification, is the necessity to determine the legitimacy of ethnic churches. What should the priority be for the church to preserve a people group's ethnic identity? If this preservation is vital for a church, then to what extent will such efforts be mandated in comparison to the matter of unity?

There is some merit to studying the churches role in preserving ethnicity. Both groups at the Lausanne Consultation agreed to this; but, as Mullins notes such an issue is only part of the complex of understanding ethnic churches: "Few sociologists would deny that religion is often oriented toward the maintenance of ethnicity. The issue, however, is the long-term effectiveness of ethnic churches as agents of cultural preservation."[275] There is a strong sociological preference to view the church not just as a curator of ethnicity but, as in the case of North America, the church is viewed as an adapting organization.

New immigrants to a new land felt the sense of superiority flaunted by every native that they met. This negative influence resulted in immigrants developing a separate identity from their host society. It was an inward turning, emphasizing features that gave them their identity: language and tradition. The new

---

SCM Press, 1984), 20.

[275] Niebuhr, Social Sources, 322.

environment which had not embraced them also represented the influence that threatened these two identity features. "These were both the uniting bonds of the group and the symbols of its social solidarity."[276] But, the immigrants needed organization to gain any kind of success in their community identity. To accomplish this they needed to find a center and leadership to bind individuals together. Religion became the center that provided this leadership. The church or religious center was accessible and provided a natural link to a people group for maintaining their identity.[277]

While this observation is consistent among most ethnic immigrants, it in no way validates this pattern as proper. It only observes a human tendency. However, the very nature of Christianity, especially the operation of sanctification, should expect some alternative behavior. For example, one dynamic that drives immigrants to segregate into their religious havens is a feeling of superiority demonstrated by the natives of the host country. If Christianity is introduced into this scheme, then, native Christians should act differently. Knowing that true Christianity is a life of humility and equality, feelings of superiority would be suppressed. Instead, hospitality and courtesy with the intent of communicating the love of the Gospel would be generously given. Their churches would open their doors to the new immigrants who

---

[276] Ibid., 222.
[277] Ibid., 223.

have become Christians and warmly accept them at the Table of Communion as equals. Feelings of pride have been replaced by humble and loving acceptance.

In a more intense situation, if the culture in which a particular individual were converted was steeped in influence by a religion contrary to the precepts of Christianity, then, the new life of a Christian would leave those cultural features behind. For example, if the caste system of India is rooted in Hinduism and the hope for reincarnation into a higher caste, then, an Indian converted to Christianity would leave that cultural distinctive in his past. He has a new supracultural identity as a result of his conversion. Paul wrote to the Christians at Philippi: " . . . our citizenship is in heaven."[278] And to the Christians at Ephesus he wrote: " . . . you are no longer foreigners and aliens, but fellow citizens with God's people and members of God's household . . . "[279]

## Interracial Marriage

A striking feature in the unfolding of the HUP theory is the frequent[280] reference to the subject of interracial marriage,

---

[278] Phil. 3:20. For a discussion see Jac. J. Muller, The Epistles of Paul to the Philippians and to Philemon (Grand Rapids: Wm. B. Eerdmans Pub. Co., reprint 1978), 133-134 and M. R. Vincent, A Critical and Exegetical Commentary on the Epistles to the Philippians and to Philemon, reprint (Edinburgh: T. & T. Clark, 1976.), 118-120.

[279] Eph. 2:19. For a discussion see Abbott, Ephesians, 68-69; Simpson, Ephesians, 65-66.

[280] For a reference on this issue of interracial marriage, endogamy or related matters raised in the context of the HUP theory see McGavran, Ethnic Realities, 1979. Each

110

endogamy, or some related issue.[281] Ramseyer raised this topic in his response at the Lausanne Consultation. He suggests that if McGavran was referring to Christians marrying only other Christians, then, this point on endogamy would be valid. But, this is not the idea of the HUP theory. Instead, the church is given the prerogative to adopt as part of its criteria for obedience, the responsibility of determining the limits of endogamy on its membership.[282] Several points on this subject must be explored.

First, the apostle's prohibition in 2 Corinthians 6:14-16 is not given because of a fear of losing girls to a non-Christian religion. Rather, he is simply acknowledging that a Christian individual has no ability to enjoy fellowship with a non-Christian. "The most obvious application of such a prohibition would be to intermarriage with the heathen, which was continually forbidden to the chosen people (see Deut. vii.3, Josh. xxiii.12, Ezra ix.2, Neh. xiii.25), and this is probably the main thought here."[283]

---

page represents one paragraph unless otherwise noted: Preface- 7; Introduction- 18, 23, 24, 34, 41, 42; Chapter 1- 56, 57, 58 (2x), 59 (2x), 60 (2x), 64, 67; Chapter 2- 76, 77, 83; Chapter 3- 94 (2x), 115, 116; Chapter 4- 121, 122, 124, 125, 131, 134, 139; Chapter 5- 142, 143, 153; Chapter 6- 164, 165, 166, 167; Chapter 7- 177, 178, 179 (4x), 181 (2x), 182 (2x), 183 (2x), 184; Chapter 8- 208; Appendix- 251, 254, 258 (2x). Also, see note 22.

[281] The HUP theory concept of `ethnic purity' is a misleading idea. It views "ethnic purity" as something to be celebrated and interracial marriage as a threat to "ethnic purity" therefore it must be unacceptable. It is discomforting to wonder if the HUP theory considers interracial marriage equivalent to ethnic impurity. See previous footnote for references.

[282] Ramseyer, "Anthropological Perspectives," 8.

[283] J.H. Bernard, The Second Epistle to the Corinthians, vol. 3 of The Expositor's Greek New Testament, ed. H.C. Nicoll (Grand Rapids, Michigan: William B. Eerdmans Publishing Co., 1974), 79.

Second, the possible conversion of the non-Christian is not the condition that Paul addressed. Rather, no Christian was to marry a non-Christian under any condition, potential or otherwise. Robertson states the matter succinctly (on this issue of being yoked): "In Deut. 22:10 we read: `Thou shalt not plough with an ox and an ass together.' Literally, `Stop becoming . . . unequally yoked with unconverted heathen (unbelievers).' Some were already guilty. Marriage is certainly included . . . ."[284] Clearly, if the reasoning by the HUP theory were applied, then there would definitely be an infraction[285] of the apostolic injunction.

Next, the issue of intermarriage, which is a major topic in the HUP theory, is not tied into the Gospel either as approved or unapproved. The phenomenon of exogamous marriages certainly affects the church. But, this is a sociological phenomenon not a spiritual violation. Mullins explains, "If a significant number of exogamous marriages are integrated into ethnic churches, the most obvious result will be a diminishing sense of ethnic distinctiveness. It seems more probable, however, that

---

[284] A.T. Robertson, The Epistles of Paul, vol. IV, Word Pictures in the New Testament (Nashville: Broadman Press, 1931), 236.

[285] No one will argue against this basic observation of the human nature. Racial segregation is a manifestation of the non-Christian world. It is a capacity prevalent in every person, unregenerate and regenerate alike. Pride and fear perpetuate this phenomenon. But, why does the HUP theory assume that the limitations that exist in the non-Christian world must rule the Church? Furthermore, the fact of interracial marriage is as frequent among the non-Christian world as it is among the Christian world. Since this is an accepted fact, then, perhaps the reasons for its occurrence is not the doing of Christianity, as the HUP theory seems to imply. Perhaps the dynamics of preferred mate-selection are influenced by Christianity; but, they are definitely not promoted by Christianity.

112

exogamous marriages will tend to discourage affiliation and active participation in an ethnic church."[286] Perhaps, then, it is this ethnic distinctiveness that people do not want to lose. And since exogamous marriages are a visible threat to that security, then, it is expedient to resist them. This is a common attitude experienced by Christians who happen to be an ethnic minority in North America.

To this matter one must argue that simply because a theology allows for and recognizes the freedom to intermarry across ethnic and cultural lines, it does not demand that it be observed to prove the genuineness of belief. Also, while a theology treats exogamy as an amoral issue, wisdom[287] also does allow for endogamy in deference to the persistent difficulty of living in a world that does not have the freedom and love of Christian dogma. At the same time the church must be careful not to be unjustly restricting the choice of marriage partners for the purpose of inclusion or exclusion from the Christian fellowship.[288] This observation has a bearing on the critique of the HUP theory in light of a practical theology perspective. For if a major ingredient for establishing ethnic churches is for the purpose of insuring ethnically acceptable marriages then, perhaps such churches should be checked. And then, Christian leaders can pursue the

---

[286] Mullins, "Ethnic Churches," 326.
[287] For a discussion on the matter of wisdom being utilized in amoral decisions see Garry Friesen, Decision Making and the Will of God (Portland: Multnomah Press, 1980).

establishment or reorientation of churches that reflect a community spirit of complete and equal acceptance.

## ta ethne

The HUP theory interpretation of *ta ethne* has been a point of some discussion. This phrase is understood by the HUP theory from a purely ethnological and sociological sense[289]; that is, Jesus had homogeneous " . . . ethnic units of the world . . . "[290] in mind.[291] McGavran suggests that this is a reference to a " . . . class, or caste, or tribe."[292] On occasion the term *ethne* is used to refer to national or possible ethnic distinction as in Matthew 24:14 or Mark 13:10.[293]

However, from a historical perspective, to assume that this is the universal use of *ta ethne* is weak. Very loosely, the term *ethnos* like *goyim* denotes a grouping of people or animals based on some visible association and experience. Nevertheless, there is no evidence that suggests that such terms are linked specifically

---

[288] Ramseyer, "Anthropological Perspectives," 8.

[289] McGavran, Understanding, 3rd ed., 40. McGavran further suggests that *ta ethne* encapsulates the characteristics that give people their authenticity and identity. These sociological features then must be preserved in the evangelistic process. (McGavran, "Genesis," 8.)

[290] McGavran, Ethnic Realities, 21.

[291] David Bosch, "Nothing but a Heresy," in Apartheid is a Heresy, ed. John de Gruchy and Charles Villa-Vicencio (Guildford: Lutterworth Press, 1983), 27.

[292] Ibid.

[293] See Bertram and Schmidt, "ethne," 364-372, Theological Dictionary of the New Testament, vol. 2, 367.

114

or exclusively to political or cultural[294] connections that related people together based on a racial, linguistic or geographical sense.[295] It is not likely that the term *ethne* in Matthew 28:19 was selected to mean tribes or castes.[296] Also, a comparison between Matthew's and Mark's use[297] of the phrase *panta ta ethne* demonstrates that it is parallel with *hole he oikoumene* (the whole inhabited world).[298] These observations lead to an eventual conclusion that the Great Commission does not indicate that evangelization is to be based upon a `people group' basis; rather, it indicates that evangelism was far beyond the limits of its origin,

---

[294] *ethne* is used in certain contexts of the Revelation to refer to nations as a distinguished group of people. Matters as culture, language, geographical boundaries are in mind in such texts. These demonstrate the universal appeal of Christ's Gospel which attracts people of every nation. (Colin Brown, ed., "ethne" in The New International Dictionary of the New Testament Theology, vol. 2, G-Pe [Grand Rapids: Zondervan Pub. House, 1976], 795.)

[295] The New Testament usage of *ethne* consistently points to a Gentile reference. For a further discussion see Georg Betram and Karl Schmidt, "ethnos, ethnikos", 364-372 in Theological Dictionary of the New Testament, Vol. II, ed. G. Kittel, tr. G. W. Bromily (Grand Rapids: Wm. B. Eerdmans Pub. Co., 1964). Padilla summarizes a similar position. He does not see a sociological use of the term but a reference to Gentiles, those who are in contrast to Jews, the chosen people. (Padilla, "Unity of the Church," 4.)

[296] The availability of other terms that are more specific regarding ethnic groups and caste suggests that ethne does not necessarily refer to ethnic groups. The general use of *ethne* in the LXX represents the term *goyim*. Its reference is predominantly used to identify non-Israelite people. *Ethne* refers to Gentiles as distinguished from Israelites in Matthew 4:15, 20:25; Luke 21:24; Acts 4:25; 7:7; 13:19; Romans 1:5; Galatians 3:8; Revelation 10:11; 14:8; 15:3. (Brown, Dictionary, 790-793.) Also, see Smith, "Principles," 26.

[297] Matt. 24:14 and Mk. 13:10

[298] " . . . `panta ta ethne' means essentially the same as `hole he oikoumene' (`the whole inhabited world', Mt. 24:14) or `pasa he ktisis' (`the entire human world as created by God', Mk. 16:15) . . . The issue at stake is theological, not socio-anthropological. `Jew' and `Gentile' were in Matthew's time essentially religious and not ethnic terms." (Bosch, "Heresy," 27.)

even crossing over previously established cultural barriers: Jewish Christians were to take the Gospel to the Gentiles.[299]  It is this wider application of the term that appears to be more consistent with the context of the Great Commission.

Several key concepts must be noted.  First, since it is clear that *ta ethne* does not generally mean caste or tribe or anything that is culturally prominent in this context of the Great Commission, then, the HUP theory's explanation is incorrect here. Christ's commission was for His disciples to carry the Gospel to the Gentile nations[300], emphasizing the breadth of the message beyond the narrow scope of Israel.  Jesus brought His Gospel to the whole world.  Robertson emphasizes the scope of the commission as represented in *ta ethne*: " . . . not just to the Jews scattered among the Gentiles, but the Gentiles themselves in every land."[301]  Also, the mixing of Jew and Gentile is described by Paul in his reference to Timothy, who was of mixed race yet was accepted by both Jewish and Gentile Christians.[302]

Second, when the Gospel is taken to all parts of the world and received, there is no reason to assume that a culture has been destroyed.  Bringing the Gospel as a foreign missionary into

---

[299]  Smith, "Principles," 26.

[300]  This simple use of *ethne* is both a common usage and contextually supported.  For a further discussion see Bertram and Schmidt, "ethne," 369-372.

[301]  A.T. Robertson, Word Pictures in the New Testament, vol. 1, The Gospel According to Matthew (Nashville, Tennessee: Broadman Press, 1930), 245.

[302]  Acts 16:1-5.  For a discussion see F. F. Bruce. Commentary on the Book of the Acts (Grand Rapids: Wm. B. Eerdmans Pub. Co., 1971), 321-324 and John Stott, The Message of Acts: to the Ends of the Earth (Leicester: Inter-Varsity Press, 1990), 254-

116

a different culture is a task that requires wisdom and care. Warneck wrote long ago of the " . . . twofold cultural contest which the mission has to maintain - a struggle against the heathenish uncultured, and a struggle against the Christian overculture - and we suspect that the latter is the more difficult."[303]

Fourth, as Mark records the same commission, there is ample evidence that God's intent is communication not language preservation: "Go into all the world and preach the good news to all creation."[304] Also, when God ministered in a supernatural way at Pentecost, language was certainly varied but another key element was that all understood: "When they heard this sound, a crowd came together in bewilderment, because each one heard them speaking in his own language."[305]

If *ta ethne* is in reference to Gentiles, then, the mission of each individual Christian is to carry the Gospel to whomever. Reaching groups of people is not the issue but, just reaching all people is the key. And when these people are converted, then, they should be organized together into a local church regardless of their pre-conversion associations and incorporated into a fellowship centered around their new identity in Christ.

---

255.

[303] Gustav Warneck, Modern Missions and Culture, Their Mutual Relations (Edinburgh: James Gemmell, 1883.), 372.

[304] Mk. 16:15. The exhortation "to preach" is more specific than Matthew's "to teach" and the destination of "all creatures" broadens Matthew's "all nations." (Alexander Bruce, "The Synoptic Gospels," in The Expositor's Greek Testament, vol. 1, ed. W. Robertson Nicoll, [Grand Rapids: Wm. B. Eerdmans Pub. Co., reprint 1974], 456.)

[305] Acts 2:6.

## Galatians 3:28

Regarding the Galatians 3:28 text, the HUP theory acknowledges that the unity of the Church is taught here but perceives it as an ideal, not real in this life. However, Paul realized that the Church was comprised of "flesh-and-blood human beings" too. The Church must be confronted with the notion that it has been given the ability along with the salvation experience to live in such harmony. Failure to do so may not be a proof of its inaccuracy or idealism but of man's stubbornness and disobedience. The apostle makes a strong point in this single verse: " . . . `in Christ Jesus' race or national distinctions (`neither Jew nor Greek') do not exist, class differences (`neither bond nor free', no proletarianism and no capitalism) vanish, sex rivalry (`no male and female') disappears."[306] This type of concept is radical yet it uncompromisingly reveals the course, which Christianity was to follow "in the sphere (en) and spirit and power of Christ."[307] A New Testament Christianity does not dictate that Gentiles must become Jews to become Christians. Also, accepting Galatians 3 at face value is not tantamount to reversing the decision of the Jerusalem Council, rather it is consistent with it. This text teaches that unity not diversity in Christ will actually be liberating not debilitating.

---

[306] Robertson, Epistles of Paul, vol. 4, 299.
[307] Robertson acknowledges the difficulty and necessity of such a direction: "Candor compels one to confess that this goal has not yet been fully attained. But we are on the road . . . ." (Robertson, Epistles of Paul, vol. 4, 299.)

118

Galatians 3:28 is lifted up to describe that there is no longer any distinction from a spiritual standpoint among Christians who are one in Christ.[308]   Furthermore, it is evident that due to Galatians 3:28 along with Colossians 3:11 and Ephesians 2:11-22 that HU churches, in particular ethnic churches that deliberately remain separate in multi-ethnic regions, are not God's primary intent and that the use of this concept in "growth strategies and evangelistic plans"[309] should be reevaluated.

## Inadequate Concept of Unity

The unity of the Church is basic to Christianity.   Every person who becomes a part of the Body of Christ enjoys an equality designed by God and expected from each and every member.   It is a blessing enjoyed on both levels, human and divine.   However, when interacting with the HUP theory, one could easily misunderstand its emphasis.   It appears that it is ready to accept that unity is sufficient when realized primarily from God's perspective.   Man's individual participation by accepting all whom God has already accepted is not necessarily absolute.

Unity must involve more than just what is in God's mind.   It would be far too easy for man to pay lip service to that

---

[308]   This position is illustrated with the following allusion: "This reaction to McGavran's findings recalls the rage that medieval clergymen directed against Galileo because the universe he saw through his telescope obstinately refused to behave as their dogma said it should." (Plaisted, "Debate," 217-218.)

[309]   Plaisted, "Debate," 218.

transcendent idea and continue to be inhumane to his fellow man. This is not unity. Rather, Christians are called upon to live out what they possess in Christ. Both what God does and what Christians incorporate into their routine are necessary for true unity.[310] Some diversity is obvious in the Church. The New Testament promotes this as well. But, the standard that guides the type of diversity in Christian unity is the key question.

It has been noted that the HUP theory suggests that the broader perspective of unity can be satisfied on an ecclesiastical level through denominational representatives. This concept of unity maintained by the HUP theory is not adequate in light of the meaning of unity. It attempts to broaden the ideas of diversity and unity. To do so, however, requires it to find room for the certainty of Biblical unity to take place. It relegates this duty to a small group of higher echelon representatives found in a manmade scheme of church denominationalism. But, such a position seems to be quantitatively immeasurable.[311] And even if such an

---

[310] Glasser presents *koinonia* as an important "new mark" of the church. He elaborates on the importance of such intimacy. For a further discussion see Glasser, "Fuller," 411-412.

[311] According to this perspective unity is defined in a negative sense. That is, unity is an absence of hostilities. Diversity dominates any actual interaction. Yet, such a divergence between unity and diversity does not seem to be the intent of the New Testament. Instead, unity is the environment of significant fellowship among believers regardless of their human background. There is a oneness that Christians shared that shatters the reasons of their pre-salvation divisions. Christians " . . . are one in Jesus Christ as the one who reconciled them by dying and rising again in their stead. As divided men they first meet in his crucified body, in which their old life is put to death and destroyed. They are reconciled in one body by the cross (Eph. 2:16) . . . But Jesus Christ rose as well as died, and as the Resurrected One he is the one true life of his people (Col. 3:3-4). They thus meet in his risen body, in which they are the one new

assertion as this could be quantified, it is unsatisfactory to declare that good has been accomplished simply by reporting that something bad is not happening. Also, the degree of unity demonstrated at these highly impersonal levels of denominational affiliation does not seem to come very close to fulfilling what has God directed believers to do.[312]

Paul's language in Romans 12:10 is rich. We are to exercise brotherly love with one another. Denney explains this love as the love of children shared with one another as members of the same family. They are fellow Christians together sharing " . . . the mutual affection of the members of the Christian community."[313] As members of the family of God they have strong natural affection toward each other. It is to be "warm, spontaneous, constant."[314] Unity[315], according to the New

---

man." (Walter A. Elwell, ed., Evangelical Dictionary of Theology [Grand Rapids: Baker Book House, 1984], s.v. "Unity," by G. W. Bromley, 1127-1128.)

[312] Paul admonished the Roman Christians: "Be devoted to one another in brotherly love. Honor one another above yourselves . . . . Share with God's people who are in need. Practice hospitality . . . . Live in harmony with one another. Do not be proud, but be willing to associate with people of low position. Do not be conceited." (Rom. 12:10, 13, 16.) For a discussion see John Murray, The Epistle to the Romans, reprint (Grand Rapids: Wm. B. Eerdmans Pub. Co., 1977), 128-137.

[313] James Denney, St. Paul's Epistle to the Romans, vol. 2 of The Expositor's Greek New Testament, ed. W. Robertson Nicoll (Grand Rapids: Wm. B. Eerdmans Pub. Co., 1974), 691-692.

[314] Ibid.

[315] Within Biblical unity diversity exists and operates without favoritism or discrimination by those within the Church. Whether there is a combination of men or women, Caucasian or Asian, employer or employee, there is genuine interaction and fellowship while respecting these differences. Unity is not taught in the Bible as an exclusive quality. " . . . Christian unity is not identical with uniformity. It does not allow division. But it does not exclude variety. The one Spirit gives different gifts (1 Cor. 12:4-5). In the one body of Christ there are many members. The unity grounded in

Testament, must happen by participation not delegation. Historically and practically it is clear that conventions and conferences do not bring Christians together. Some geographical proximity may be shared by a few but fellowship is not perpetuated on any significant level for the vast majority of Christians through these means.

A prominent term describing Christian unity is *koinonia*: "But if we walk in the light, as he is in the light, we have fellowship with one another, and the blood of Jesus, his Son, purifies us from all sin."[316] The very nature of the word *koinonia* denotes active involvement by the participants. In the New Testament the term is used to portray an "active relationship."[317] And it is also worth noting that the word is " . . . used specially of the closest of all human relationships."[318] *Koinonia*[319] denotes personal interaction.

---

Christ leaves scope for diversity of action and function, the only conformity being to the mind of Christ and direction of the Spirit." (Elwell, "Unity," 1127-1128.)

At the same time, diversity cannot be relegated to human preference based on pre-conversion values. Nor can unity be a duty only to be discharged by man's creation of a religious hierarchy in denominationalism. Unity is the responsibility of every believer not a few representatives who meet en masse once or twice a year.

[316] 1 Jn. 1:7. This *koinonia* reflects both a communion with God and with one's fellow Christians. They cannot be separated from each other. The latter is a consequence of the former. (David Smith, "The Epistles of John," in The Expositor's Greek Testament, vol. V, ed. W. Robertson Nicoll [Grand Rapids: Wm. B. Eerdmans Pub. Co., reprint 1974], 171.)

[317] James Moulton and George Milligan, Vocabulary of the Greek Testament, reprint (Grand Rapids: Wm. B. Eerdmans Pub. Co., 1974), 351.

[318] Ibid.

[319] The HUP position is concerned that an overemphasis of *koinonia* can contribute to a neglect of evangelism. Wagner suggests that an "exaggerated" application of koinonia burns up all of the energy of Christians by Christians. For this discussion see Wagner, Leading, 184.

Distant observation or casual acknowledgment are foreign ideas to the term.

This Biblical concept of unity results in community. It produces a community of changed individuals who love people who now love each other instead of hating each other.[320] Essentially, every person who makes a commitment to this Jesus is changed forever. Evidence of that change includes perceiving one's fellow man with a different attitude: " . . . the cross revolutionizes our attitudes to God, to ourselves, to other people both inside and outside the Christian fellowship, and to the grave problems of violence and suffering."[321]

The New Testament resolutely promotes brotherhood not just as a futuristic ideal but as a fact and daily responsibility mandated for all Christians. Paul's theology reflects a church that is not only one but also indivisible. Bosch concludes that it " . . . militates against even the possibility of establishing separate Churches for different cultural groups."[322] All differences are

---

[320] Two fundamental features are integral to fellowship. They are a sense of community and the basis for the existence of that community, namely, the death of Christ on the cross. Stott notes: " . . . the very purpose of his self-giving on the cross was not just to save isolated individuals and so perpetuate their loneliness, but to create a new community whose numbers would belong to him, love one another and eagerly serve the world. This community of Christ would be nothing less than a renewed and reunited humanity, of which he as the second Adam would be head. It would incorporate Jews and Gentiles on equal terms. In fact, it would include representatives from every nation. Christ died in abject aloneness, rejected by his own nation and deserted by his own disciples but lifted up on the cross he would draw all men to himself." (John Stott, The Cross of Christ [Leicester, England: Inter-Varsity Press, 1986], 255.)

[321] Ibid., 256.

[322] Bosch, "Heresy," 29.

transcended. Christianity began as a new citizenship that bound all men and women together as one.[323] It accepted anyone from any nationality or any status in life and gave them equality "in Christ." While the world assumed the distinction of Jew and Gentile, Christianity showed the world what the love of God could do in uniting all people together into one body.

The all-inclusive unity of the Body of Christ is shunned by some as unrealistic. However, such a reaction is premature for it fails to take into account the diversity that the unity also entails. According to the New Testament, it is a mysterious blend but definitely a reality.[324] Therefore, it is presumptuous and even inconsistent for any professing Christian to automatically reject a class or group of fellow believers from fellowship because of a human distinction.

The Church, then, cannot accept the HUP theory as strategy for growth as it stands in its historical form. Rather, it

---

[323] Bosch carefully builds his argument based upon a New Testament premise: "He pleads unceasingly for the unity of the Church made up of both Jews and Gentiles. God has made the two one, `a single new humanity', `a single body' (Eph. 2:14-16) (NEB). This was the mystery revealed to him, `that through the Gospel the Gentiles are heirs together with Israel, members together of one body, and sharers together in the promise in Christ Jesus' (Eph. 3:6) (NIV)." (Bosch, "Heresy," 29.)

[324] Tutu notes, "St. Paul is constantly at pains to assert that through the Holy Spirit divers peoples have been brought into one fellowship. They may have different spiritual gifts, they may carry out different functions, but it is precisely because of their diversity that they can subsist as one body (1 Cor. 12:12-26). Diversity undergirds and leads to unity and interdependence, with the different limbs of the body each needing the others in order to live fully for the good of the whole. No part of the body is self-sufficient. God has created us unable to do everything of ourselves, so that we must depend on others in order to become fully human." (Desmond Tutu, "Apartheid and Christianity," in Apartheid is a Heresy, ed. by John de Gruchy and Charles Villa-

124

must maintain its New Testament and historical tradition of a pursuit that reflects a unified fellowship. All who make a commitment to Christ become one in Christ. This is non-negotiable. Each shares an equality that operates with a new system of values. And each possesses the privilege to show the world what the love of God can do. By demonstrating a love for each other although there are differences that the world cannot reconcile, God makes His message of the Good News known.[325] Therefore, this Christian unity requires intimate participation and non-selective universal acceptance of all whom God has already accepted.

## Concern for the Danger of Misapplying the HUP Theory: Racism

The debate history of the HUP theory has revealed concern by both advocates and opponents regarding the potential misunderstanding of this evangelistic strategy and the problem of racism.[326] Pushed to extremes the HUP theory admittedly can be misunderstood to condone racism or even apartheid.[327] Perhaps

---

Vicencio [Guildford: Lutterworth Press, 1983], 43.)

[325] Jn. 13:34,35.

[326] The preference of people to associate themselves with others like themselves is a sociological reality; but, racism is also a sociological reality as well. The church must address itself to both in its effort to fulfill its mission not just to one. For a flavor of the problem of racism in the church see United Methodist News Service, "Racism: An Open Sore on the Body of Christ," Engage Social Action 15 (1987), 42-43.

[327] Wagner mentions this point in the introduction to his position paper for the

the issue of racism is of a significant enough force to encourage church leaders to modify the HUP theory ideas in order to keep a clear and cautious distance from it.  The following discussion demonstrates the seriousness of racism as it faces the church[328] and the need for the church to clearly stand against it.

The observations by secular sociologists on this matter are intriguing.  In a study of the popular statement that the eleven o'clock Sunday morning service is "the most segregated hour in the country," the following insights were made.  First, with concern three sociologists state that as major denomination groups address the trend of shrinking membership roles, their concerns for survival and recruitment are more pertinent than the issue of segregation. "Many have even adopted `church growth' tenets which suggest that growth comes easier when a congregation focuses on a homogeneous target group.  Thus, blacks and ethnics may be purposely ignored even when they live near a white Anglo church."[329]  In other words for the sake of numerical growth, separation or at least some type of selective outreach can

---

Lausanne Consultation. (Wagner, "How Ethical," 1.)  Also, Knapp acknowledges the problem of the HUP theory allegedly providing "biblical legitimation" for Apartheid in South Africa (Stephen C. Knapp, Penn. to Leighton Ford, N.C., 30 December 1976, Transcript in the hands of the Lausanne Theology and Education Group Archives, HUP, London.)

[328] For a discussion of the seriousness of racism and the part that the church can have in challenging it see John S. Pobee, "Theology and Racism," One World 124 (1987), 4-6.

[329] Kirk Hadaway, David Hackett and James Miller, "The Most Segregated Institution: Correlates of Interracial Church Participation," in Review of Religious Research, 25 (March 1984), 217.

become the procedure. None who lead the way in Church Growth would support this perspective, but, this scientific study is nevertheless, an indication of the potential danger of the misapplication of the HUP theory.

Second, researchers have observed that segregation in American churches is a reflection of the sociological influences of its culture. And when the HUP theory is evaluated in light of this context these three researchers view the application of the HUP theory as a purposeful avoidance of blacks and ethnics by white churches. Their perception is deduced from the observation that racial segregation is still currently prevalent in the church.[330]

Supporters of the HUP theory may respond quickly and list the statistics of integration failure. But, it should be noted that these sociologists are not advocating total integration in response to the data that they have gathered. This is the third helpful insight

---

[330] They have noted five reasons for segregation in the church which is the next insight that they contribute to this discussion. The five reasons are as follows:
1. Members of a church can legally discriminate against other races without government intervention.
2. Most churches are homogeneous with regard to socioeconomic features (Goldschmidt, 1942; Glock et al., 1967:81) and visitors find subtleties that tend to exclude them.
3. Some white churches have self-consciously singled out evangelistic target groups that eliminate black groups in order to achieve faster growth promised by the homogeneous principle (Carroll, 1978).
4. Racial prejudice still exists in many churches (Roozen 1978:43,44).
5. Most churches tend to be residentially influenced with most of their membership drawn from a few miles of the church building (Price, 1980:43).
These five observations must bring every church leader and theologian to a position of wise caution when developing church development schemes that may easily be misapplied by current racial tendencies. Pragmatically, they indicate the danger that the HUP theory presents to justify an already existing non-Christian attitude

that they present: " . . . we recognize the continuing concern of many denominations that prejudice and racial exclusion persist in their churches and that the ideal may not be complete integration, it certainly ought to be openness and concern toward members of any racial group."[331]  In other words it is helpful to develop a response to the problems of racism in the church without feeling forced to either adopt or reject a position like the HUP theory.  The option of finding value in the HUP theory and modifying it or acknowledging some of its features into another scheme is helpful. It is also helpful to consider the concept of integration not just as a failed disguise for assimilation racism but as a general concept for some form of visible equality in the church.[332]  The point seems to be one of emphasis on a system that will insure the priorities of Christian unity as well as enhancing the measure of results in the church's mission.[333]

A fourth insight from this study is perhaps one of the most obvious ones.  The church is a spiritual institution.  If its members adopt a life that portrays the spirituality of Christ, then, prejudice, segregation and discrimination would not be issues: "Findings which suggest lower levels of prejudice among church members

---

in the church.  (Hadaway, "Segregated Institution," 204)

[331]  Ibid., 205.

[332]  Many Christians do view integration as a description of a necessary issue for the Church to consider.  For a further discussion of this see Randall L. Frame, "Race and the Church: A Progress Report," 16-17, Christianity Today, March 4, 1988.)

[333]  This same attitude was conveyed in the words of Stephen C. Knapp:  "I think the real issue is not so much the homogeneous unit principle itself as much as the larger question of discovering and encouraging models or strategies of mission that challenge

who exhibit high levels of church attendance and religious salience lead us to expect that religious activity should be associated with interracial church attendance (Gorsuch and Aleshire, 1974; Roof and Perkins, 1975)."[334] The evidence from this report is consistent with what Christianity claims. Acceptance for others regardless of the differences is basic to an acknowledgment of having already been accepted by a God who is very different from man.

But, far from the ideal many churches appear to be following a pattern of segregation. The theological theory of oneness and unity is clear from the New Testament. However, the difficulty arises with Wagner's observation that most congregations participate in cultural homogeneity. His experience has been that most Christians choose to " . . . worship and fellowship within the basic sociological groupings into which they are born."[335] The HUP theory assumes that "the most segregated hour" phenomenon is true. Furthermore, it speculates in contrast to the original tenet of that statement that the reality of it may not be wrong.

However, evidence indicates that commonly assumed homogeneous church preference might be exaggerated. Hadaway and company have researched the claim and have concluded that the church may not be as segregated as its reputation has been. Their studies reveal that a large portion of

rather than foster social injustice." (Knapp to Ford)

[334] Frame, "Race," 16-17.

whites (38 percent) do attend church with blacks.  Furthermore, in certain populations and locations in the United States that percentage increases past the point of being a majority.   The report concludes: "The extent to which this represents the token presence of a few upwardly mobile blacks among many white churches is not apparent from these data, but even if partially true, the often repeated statement that eleven o'clock on Sunday morning is `the most segregated hour' must be called a gross exaggeration." [336]  It is also important to note that this study dealt primarily with the white-black issue.  If all Homogeneous Units were taken into account, then, the statistics would most likely demonstrate a more favorable heterogeneous pattern among Christians in the United States.

Perhaps what has happened in the lives of many ethnic minorities is a real spiritual change.  Once they were in a world that judged severely according to the color of one's skin, the shape of another's eyes, or the origin of one's ancestors.  Now, after conversion they have a new identity that is common among many others, others whom they once despised or who once despised them.  Such an attitude is not total, however.  Many in the church still hold on to their past.  Because that attitude is prevalent and universally acknowledged as in error, then, perhaps the church would  best be served by a development strategy that challenges

---

[335]  Wagner, Our Kind, 11.
[336]  Hadaway, "Segregated Institution," 215.

racism and encourages an attitude of complete and equal acceptance.

## *A Conclusion from the Lessons Learned from the Debate History*

Reviewing the history of the debate over the HUP theory has highlighted a number of important themes. First, there is large agreement by both sides on shared ideas regarding the priority of evangelism and the degree of creativity that should be allowed for this mission to be carried out. It was not unusual to sense that those who were outside of the Church Growth camp felt that they had more in common with the intent of the HUP theory than differences. The motive of the HUP theory must be praised. Their passion to fulfill the evangelistic mandate is a priority and serves as a motivation for the whole church to emulate. And their willingness to creatively examine alternatives and their courage to abandon ineffective methods must be applauded. The scope of their illustrations is worldwide and demonstrates an excellent example of insightful missionary expertise.

Second, it seemed that proponents of the HUP theory have perhaps been too rigid in expecting Christian leaders to adopt their terms, their definitions and their guidelines of strategy in total without acknowledging that similar procedures are being used by those outside of their camp, albeit not with the name

HUP. Eclectic options did not seem to be favorably received or encouraged by the Fuller Team in the early days of the debate from the Pasadena Consultation by Lausanne to the publication of Ethnic Realities and Our Kind of People. Later discussions as Whole Gospel and Understanding Church Growth 3rd edition have, however, moderated.

Third, an apparent inadequacy that surfaced in the debate is the lack of newness or change expected from a new convert. Once conversion takes place, then an individual because of sanctification, is called upon to demonstrate a life of change more significantly than the HUP theory allows. The concept of mixing different people together in intimate spiritual fellowship is made possible by the wonder of sanctification and the local church is an arena to display it to a watching world.[337] Creative means to demonstrate the reality of Christian love to a watching world must be at least as much a priority of the church as the willingness to alter ineffective methodologies.[338]

Fourth, the issue of existing HU churches is not contested but the ability of an HU church to best fulfill the New Testament purpose of the church is in question. In this regard the solution is neither the extreme of perpetuating ethnic churches (a kind of HU

---

[337] Peters blends the reality of sanctification's potential for international experiences now in light of an eschatological inevitability: "International and interracism were more than an ideal; they became blessed reality in the church. Their full realization is seen in Revelation 5:8-10 where the raptured church before the throne is composed of representatives `of every kindred,and tongue, and people, and nation.'" (George W. Peters, A Biblical Theology of Missions [Chicago: Moody Press, 1972], 156.)

church) or eliminating them. Ethnic churches exist. They cannot be denied. But, should the establishment of new ones be the norm for church development?

Fifth, there is a fundamental agreement that a single harmonious God who has provided one Savior, the Lord Jesus Christ, and given one out-pouring of the Spirit has one and only one church. The unity of the church is undeniable and the responsibility of Christians to preserve and maintain that unity is also universally acknowledged. The challenge is how to reconcile the concept of church unity and the diversity of culture.[339] On the one hand, those who embrace the HUP theory argue that the solution is best solved in HU churches. But, on the other hand, those who advocate a personal evangelism along with a mutual acceptance theology within Christian fellowships find significant limitations for HU churches. What is the Biblical principle for unity among diverse ethnic groups from contrasting cultures?

Sixth, the nature of the church is unclear in this debate. Although it is generally agreed that the church is to celebrate culture as a part of God's creation, the question is one of balancing this effort with the other agreed issue, namely, church unity. The suggestion that more inter-church celebrations be held for mass worship is helpful but not always realistic. In particular the trend among ethnic churches is to remain alone and practically

---

[338] For a further discussion of these points of similarity see Pasadena Consultation, 7.
[339] Pasadena Consultation, 4.

segregated.  Or when mass celebrations do occur the level of fellowship remains limited.

Perhaps the solution in part lies with the understanding that evangelistic strategy does not determine ecclesiastical orientation.  The HUP theory teaches that ethnic churches should be planted for evangelistic advancement.  This may not need to be an absolute.  If the sociological realities of people groups are going to develop these ethnic related churches as they have done in the past, then, could it be that enough effort is already being channeled in their direction?  Is another emphasis necessary to keep the New Testament principles actively directing the church?

# CHAPTER III

## A CHRISTOCENTRIC SOLUTION TO THE HIDDEN HOSTILITIES

**Constructing a growth pattern for the church according to the principles in Ephesians 2:11-22 and a Christocentric Theology**

### Part 1

Formulating a Growth Philosophy for the Church According

to the Principles Outlined in Ephesians 2:11-22 and

a Christocentric Theology

### *Introduction*

   A basic provision, which results from the redemptive work

of Christ, is the union of both Jewish (Hebraic) and Gentile[340]

---

[340] My use of "Gentile" is not a designation of a single or distinct ethnic group by itself. Rather, it is an identification of a group of people (made up of many ethnic groups itself) which is distinct from the Jews, as Paul used the distinction in Ephesians 2.

(Hellenistic) ideas and people into a single Christian church.[341] This international blend of two formerly distinct groups[342] that once thrived on mutual animosity against each other demonstrates the divine intent to formulate a church comprised of a single people. Such singleness is not accomplished by ignoring or depleting cultural, ethnic or other social distinctive. Those features still exist and remain as an important part of a Christian's life. Instead, these two groups now share something in common with each other that surpasses their differences. This common item is something new brought about and made possible by the grace of God.

However, this pursuit of a miraculous and mysterious singleness has not continued to be a priority in the practical relationships among members of today's church. Even though the theological reality of uniting Jew and Gentile into a single visible fellowship is acknowledged as a biblical if not also a spiritual fact, church members of varying ethnic backgrounds are

---

[341] The formation of any church strategy must begin with the precepts that God has outlined when He began the church. Stott explains: " . . . [God's] purpose, through the work of his Son and his Spirit, is to create a new reconciled society in which no curtains, walls or barriers are tolerated, and in which the divisive influences of race, nationality, rank and sex have been destroyed. He means his church to be a sign of his Kingdom, that is, a model of what human community looks like when it comes under his rule of righteousness and peace." (John Stott, Issues Facing Christians Today [Hants: Marshalls, 1984], 101.)

[342] My reference to the Jews and Gentiles as "formerly distinct groups" concerns those who became converted to Christianity. Both designations continued to be distinct outside of the church for both groups.

still at odds with each other, which is evident in varying forms of racial tension.[343] Some critics argue that the church is more known for its racial separation and conformity to society's pattern rather than representing a new way of life, a new order of community, or a new value of equality.[344] But of the elements contributing to this unpleasant reputation, a lack of biblical or spiritual guidance cannot be identified as instrumental in the problem. Quite to the contrary, the New Testament[345] speaks directly to this issue both in quantity and in direct address. It

---

[343] There is a touch of irony in this particularly when a Christian gathering is comprised primarily of converted Gentiles. While the cross of Christ joined two of the world's most antagonistic ethnic groups (Jew and Gentile), the result is a church where many cannot accept one another with equality (Gentile and Gentile).

[344] The concept of pluralism is an expressed desire of the common person. Racial separation is decried if it takes place in public schools, restaurants and neighborhoods but not in churches. Sweet argues, "The spirit of divisiveness and racial tribalism that is abroad in our churches and has ecclesiastical sanction is a heresy of the heart. . . . It is the height of hypocrisy for the church to decry with one breath ethnic minority [institutions] and then, with the next breath, to idealize ethnic minority churches." (Leonard Sweet, "The Rainbow Church," Christian Ministry [November 2, 1988], 7.) For a further discussion of racism and the part that the church can have in addressing the matter see R. Elliot Kendal, Christianity and Race, British Council of Churches (1982); Keith Jenkins, The Closed Door, British Council of Churches (1984); and Alistair G. Hunter and Steven G. Mackie, A National Church in a Multi-Racial Scotland, Scottish Churches Council (1980).

[345] Exploring the New Testament for guidance in the area of racial equality is not unanimously favored. For example, C.F. Sleeper warns that it can be dangerous to hunt for answers in the New Testament that deal with complex questions of social ethics, such as race relations. Sleeper's comment is a precaution growing out of his preference to derive a basis for social ethics from the entire Bible to avoid proof-texting a problem. Yet, if a central text of Scripture makes a clear statement on an issue as race relations, then the onus is on any effort that contradicts it to defend its position first. For a further discussion see C. F. Sleeper, Black Power and Christian Responsibility (New York, 1969).

pointedly declares a kind of unity that is required of all Christians not as an obligation to obtain spiritual merit but as an expression of a spiritual reality already possessed. One of the key passages of Scripture that addresses this tension is Ephesians 2:11-22.[346] Since God has reconciled both Jew[347] and Gentile in the New Testament there are a number of substantial implications for the church in formulating a positive attitude toward race relations, particularly in the area of growth and development.[348]

Part of the problem in applying Scripture to race relations is that culture, which is frequently impregnated with racial biases, influences any discussion of the church and its responsibility

---

[346] C.H. Dodd highly esteems the value of this text in dealing with the issue of race relations. He states, "In its historical aspect it refers to a particular event of considerable importance - the effectual overcoming of a longstanding and deep-rooted enmity, which we may fairly treat as a model of the process of reconciliation between nations." (C. H. Dodd, Christianity and the Reconciliation of the Nations, 25.)

[347] In the discussion of Ephesians 2, as related to the race issue, it is important to note that there is a measure of reluctance on the part of a few to even consider the Jews as a racial group. It is argued that the Jewish people occupy a unique place in history. Also, a case is made in that they are not just one people among many but they are chosen by God. Furthermore, it is said that Israel has not consistently maintained her own understanding of a religious or racial emphasis. Nevertheless, in contrast to such objections, it is apparent in Scripture that Jews are racially distinguished as a group from Gentiles. (1 Cor. 12:13; Gal. 3:28; Col. 3:11.) Also, Israel was chosen to represent all mankind. And whenever Jewish-Gentile relationships are examined, they represent relationships with all other human groups. Lastly, the reconciliation of Jew and Gentile in the church is the first visible step to God's plan to "unite all things in Christ." (Eph. 1:10.) For a further discussion see William Rader, The Church and Racial Hostility: A History of Interpretation of Ephesians 2:11-22 (Tubingen: J. C. B. Mohr [Paul Siebeck]), 2.

[348] Rader, Racial Hostility, 1.

138

toward racial equality.[349] Rader observes that there is substantial information that deals with the problem of racial discrimination and it is readily available to churches; but the material with its insights is from sociology, psychology, and contemporary literature. Very little is from theological or biblical studies.[350] Perhaps this is one of the fundamental reasons that the HUP theory has met such energetic support as well as challenge. Churches with a strong desire to grow but struggle to attain that goal are presented with an appealing growth strategy that is based on a sociological and pragmatic phenomenon. On the surface it appears to be reasonable; but, it fails to adequately address the basic biblical principle stated for example in Ephesians 2 or in a theology that adequately portrays Christ.[351] To properly formulate an accurate growth strategy that church leaders and lay people can implement into their assemblies they must consider its foundation of reasoning. That is, as a first priority, any growth philosophy adopted by the church should be

---

[349] In relationship to his own church's struggle with the white-black issue, William Rader notes, "We had been so accustomed to congregations which reflected the divisions in society that it was difficult to conceive that this might be denial of the very nature of the church." (Rader, Church and Racial, 1.)

[350] Rader, Racial Hostility, 1.

[351] The appearance of our churches is much too homogeneous. The impression that they are so does not make it correct. Sweet explains, "Our churches are too much the same color. We worship with people who look alike, think alike, dress alike and talk alike. Whether we are black, brown or white, we tend to want to worship with `our kind of people'." (Sweet, "Rainbow Church," 7.)

tested against the precepts of the New Testament. A key passage from which a foundation for addressing this issue may be developed from Ephesians 2:11-22.

## A Christian's Past Spiritual Heritage And Present Spiritual Union Cannot Be Separated. - Ephesians 2:11-13

Paul begins this text with a strong reminder of the Gentiles' past relationship with God. It was no relationship at all. The inferential particle (dio) is the strongest that Paul could have used to portray this contrast of past and present. What follows is indicated to be a personal and ethical application of Paul's previous discussion, that is, Gentile Christians should automatically turn their attention to their desperate past from which God has graciously delivered them.[352] This emphasis on divine mercy would prompt them to express their gratitude for the wonder of their salvation.[353]

---

[352] Simpson and Bruce observe the significance of Paul's point: "The full recognition of the glory of that grace whereof they have been made partners is not brought home to these Gentile fledglings by reverting afresh to their unregenerate days. Nothing is so apt to promote gratitude as a retrospective glance fixed on the hole of the pit from whence we have been dug out." (Simpson and Bruce, Ephesians and Colossians, 58.)

[353] Salmond explains the significance of Paul's focus on this contrast: " . . . great things done for them by God's grace should incline them to think of the past from which they have been delivered. The remembrance of that past will make them more thankful for their present privilege, and more careful to walk in good works which God has in view for them." (Salmond, Ephesians, 291.)

140

To enhance this contrast even further, Gentile believers are commanded never to forget their pre-salvation condition.[354] The contrast between their pre-conversion state and their consequential state as converted Christians was intentionally raised to indicate the value of their current state. As Gentiles by birth are called the "uncircumcision" by the Jews, their physical separation was the reason for Jewish disparagement.[355] This physical difference was symbolic of a completely separate way of life.[356] What once began as a symbol for spiritual loyalty eroded into an ugly racial tension. Consequently, both socially and spiritually a wall of separation[357] existed between them. If what

---

[354] Salmond provides a helpful statement in this regard: "The term [sarki] also is to be taken literally, not as referring to the former unregenerate life, but . . . in the sense of flesh to which circumcision is applicable. They are reminded that they belonged to the class of the Gentiles, their bodies proclaiming their heathen character." (Salmond, Ephesians, 291.)

[355] Salmond explains: "The point seems to be that the inferiority in which they were held, and which was expressed by the contemptuous name Uncircumcision, meant all the more as it was fastened on them by those to whom, while proudly calling themselves the Circumcision, the distinction was nothing more than an outward manual act performed on their bodies." (Salmond, Ephesians, 291.)

[356] Moule describes the intensity of this physical mark of distinction: "The lack of the bodily mark was the condemning, and characteristic, thing, supplying a short expression for a state of entire difference and alienation." (H. C. G. Moule, Studies in Ephesians [Grand Rapids: Kregel Publications, 1977], 75.)

[357] A practical benefit of remembering one's past is the resulting contrast that drives one to appreciate the benefits of grace. Bruce notes, "It is salutary from time to time to be reminded of what we were apart from God's grace, in order that we may the better appreciate the riches of His grace and be armed against the temptation of having high thoughts of ourselves." (F.F. Bruce, The Epistle to the Ephesians [London: Pickering & Inglis Ltd., 1961], 52-53)

was symbolized by this physical mark were fleshed out in daily living, then, God's chosen people, the Jews, would not mix at all with Gentiles.[358]

Because the Gentiles lacked the physical circumcision or the sign of being of God's chosen people, they also lacked three privileges[359] that God had given exclusively to Israel. The Jews took great pride in relishing these advantages. And every Gentile who crossed the path of a Jew would quickly be educated. First, they were "separate from Christ."[360] That is, they were without Christ sharing in a personal relationship and they had no Messianic hope as a people belonging to God's nation.[361]

---

[358] Harold W. Hoehner, Ephesians, The Bible Knowledge Commentary:New Testament edition, ed. John F. Walvoord and Roy B. Zuck (Wheaton, Illinois: Victor Books, 1983), 625.

[359] Simpson and Bruce describe the Jewish advantage that the Gentiles did not have: "The Hebrew theocracy, despite its decadence, abode the pharos of the world's illumination, and to be remote from its beacon-gleam was to dwell in darkness or be mocked by tantalizing wild-fires. Substance, solidity, satisfaction, the cults of heathendom had none to proffer. Their forlorn plight is delineated in three sable strokes as Christless, Godless, hopeless." (Simpson and Bruce, Ephesians and Colossians, 59.)

[360] Some might point out that Israel was not always faithful to her Messiah, often marking history with acts of disobedience and rebellious moments clearly indicating a lack of faith. However, while acknowledging this, Paxson observes, " . . . there was always a remnant of the true Israel that kept its faith fixed on that Coming One. While the Gentiles were just a race of individual pagans having no essential oneness except in sin. They had no part in the promised Messiah and no claim upon Him." (Ruth Paxson, The Wealth, Walk and Warfare of the Christian, [Old Tappan, New Jersey: Fleming H. Revell Co., 1939], 62.)

[361] Salmon explains the significance of this phrase: " . . . (It) describes their former condition as one in which they had no connection with Christ; in which respect they were in a position sadly inferior to that of the Jews whose attitude was one of hoping

142

Second, they were "excluded from citizenship in Israel."[362]  To be
identified with Israel was to be identified with God.  Theocratically,
Israel's salvation was inseparable from her national blessing from
God.[363]  Even though individual Gentiles could and did become
proselytes, thus adopting the national and theocratic blessing of
Israel, Gentiles as a whole were excluded.  The term "excluded"
is very strong.  The contrast is between one who a total stranger
is compared to one who is at home.[364]  Third, they were
"foreigners to the covenants of the promise."  Israel looked
forward to future glory and blessing as God's chosen people.[365]

---

and waiting for Christ, the Messiah." (Salmond, Ephesians, 292.)

[362]  The Jewish contempt for the Gentile outsiders is sensed by Barclay's
observation: "The Gentiles, said the Jews, were created by God to be fuel for the fires
of Hell.  God, they said, loves only Israel of all the nations He had made.  The best of
the serpents crush, they said, the best of the Gentiles kill.  It was not even lawful to
render help to a Gentile mother in her hour of sorest need, for that would simply be to
bring another Gentile into the world."  (William Barclay, The Letters to the Galatians
and Ephesians [Edinburgh: The Saint Andrew Press, 1964], 125.)

[363]  The concepts of "exclusion" and "citizenship" does not imply that there was once
a previous unity.  Abbott suggests that if a Greek or Roman concept of citizenship
was the Apostle's intent there may be some merit to this idea.  However, " . . . it is the
theocratic constitution from which they were excluded; and the name Israel implies
this, since this was the name of the people in their theocratic relation." (Abbott,
Ephesians, 58.)

[364]  Abbott notes, "The verb always means to estrange; hence therefore `estranged
from' as opposed to `being at home in'." (Abbott, Ephesians, 57.)

[365]  Hope is at the heart of the Jewish faith: "For the Jew history was always going
somewhere; for the Jew, no matter what the present was like, the future was glorious;
for the Jew, all life was an appeal from an impossible present to a radiant future; that
is to say, the Jewish view of history is essentially, inherently, innately optimistic.  On
the other hand, for the Gentile history was going nowhere." (Barclay, Ephesians, 126.)

They counted upon being blessed as a nation. To them they lived for this hope[366] promised to Abraham. But, Gentiles had no such hope.[367]

As a nation, Israel was certain of her future glory. Gentiles could only envy from a distance. Furthermore, Israel could look to the future with optimism. No matter how oppressive their current situation was they had a hope[368] of national redemption. Every Jew took great pride in their faith of a future deliverance. They detested the nations for their oppression of Israel and shunned them as dogs unworthy of Israel's future hope.[369] No Gentile nation could be so optimistic.[370]

---

[366] Abbott observes the strength of anticipation embodied in this nationalistic "hope": "The absence of the article shows that it is not the definite hope of the Messiah that is meant, but hope in the widest sense, so that the expression is so much the stronger, `having no hope.'" (Abbott, Ephesians, 58-59.)

[367] Moule describes the sense of the text: "The deep truth of this is fully attested by classical and other heathen literature, old or modern. Aspiration and conjecture there often was, but no hope, in the Scripture sense; no expectation on a firm basis. A profound uncertainty about the unseen and eternal underlies many of the strongest expressions of the classical poets and philosophers. And in the special reference of `hope' here, hope of a Redeemer and a redeemed inheritance, there was (and is) a total blank, apart from revelation." (Moule, Ephesians, 77.)

[368] "Hope" occurs here as an anarthrous noun, indicating that the hope for Messiah is not Paul's reference. Rather, this is a reference to " . . . hope in the widest sense, so that the expression is so much the stronger, `having no hope.'" (Abbott, Ephesians, 59)

[369] This vast separation between Jew and Gentile was intense as life and death. "If a Jewish girl married a Gentile boy, the funeral of that Jewish boy or girl was carried out. Such contact with a Gentile was the equivalent of death. Even to go into a Gentile house rendered a Jew unclean." (Barclay, Galatians and Ephesians, 125.) In other words, for the Gentile it " . . . is not only that they had not the hope, the Messianic hope was one of the distinctions of the Israelite, but that they were utterly

144

The contrast for the Gentiles that is described here is clearly marked by the terms "formerly" (v.11) and "But now" (v.13). This shift is enhanced further by the contrast of "separate from Christ" (v.12) and "in Christ Jesus." Gentiles in verses 11 and 12 had a past that is no longer valid. Now, they ("you" v.13) are "in Christ." This is a new position for Gentiles that nullifies the woeful state previously described. They have not become Jews.[371] Judaism has not opened up to them. Israel has not granted them citizenship. Circumcision has not been imposed on them. Something far more inclusive than any one or any combination of these has been established.[372]

The Gentiles have gained all that they lacked in comparison to the Jews by means of Christ's sacrificial death. The phrase "brought near by the blood of Christ" has a layered meaning. Bullinger describes the metalepsis in verse 13: " . . . by

---

without hope. Ignorant of the Divine salvation and of Christ in whom it was found, they had nothing to hope for beyond this world." (Salmond, Ephesians, 3:292.)

[370] Hoehner, Ephesians, 625.

[371] The phrase "brought near" (v.13) " . . . is in contrast with the whole previous condition of separation from Christ, with all that that meant with regard to the commonwealth of Israel, the covenants, hope, and God. It is probably to be taken, therefore, in the large sense of being brought into the Kingdom of God, made near to God Himself and so brought to hope and privilege." (Salmond, Ephesians, 3:293.) Barclay notes, "When the Rabbis spoke about accepting a convert into Judaism, they said that the proselyte to the faith had been `brought near.'" (Barclay, Ephesians, 130.)

[372] Hoehner, Ephesians, 625.

His death, not by His life: yet not by His death alone, but by the atonement made in His obedient act in dying for His people."[373] By the blood of Christ Gentiles now enjoy all that Israel does regarding a future hope and present meaning in life. Sin had caused a separation between God and man. This barrier of separation was removed by Jesus' atonement.

At this point some could stop their analysis and declare that all believers share a common relationship as individuals to God. But, this would only emphasize the breaking of the barrier between men and God. The pietists, Rationalists and mystics were caught up in this shortcoming. Instead, the thought must be continued to acknowledge that human groups have a new relationship to one another as a result of the Gospel as well.[374]

### *All Christians Share in a Common Horizontal and Vertical Peace - Ephesians 2:14-18*

Paul has made it clear that because of Christ's redeeming work Jews and Gentiles are now joined together in a union. What that union involves is now addressed by the Apostle. Primarily this union consists of the issue of peace.[375] It is a peace that now

---

[373] E.W. Bullinger, Figures of Speech Used in the Bible (Grand Rapids, Michigan: Baker Book House, 1968), 610.

[374] Rader, Racial Hostilities, 251.

[375] The peace that now exists between Jew and Gentile believers is Christ Himself.

146

exists between Jew and Gentile in the horizontal plane and also between God and those who have put their faith in Him on the vertical level.[376]

Jesus did not amalgamate one into the other but He created something completely new. To accomplish this new man, the barrier, the dividing wall of hostility, was destroyed. The "and" that introduces the phrase "has destroyed the barrier" is epexegetical giving it the meaning "in that." Thus, the new man was made by the destroying of the barrier.[377] And, it should be noted that the barrier that was destroyed was not fully erected by the Jews who despised Gentiles. Rather, the hostilities were mutually shared.[378] These hostilities by the Jews and the

---

"Christ is he who has made something new of the two: the near and the far, the insiders and the outsiders. `In Christ those afar have become such that are near' (2:13). Christ is that reconciliation which is greater and stronger than the hostility of either or of both. He is not what a Christian can give to others. He is the gift of God to both. If he `is peace' (2:14), then he is by nature a social, even a political event, which marks the overcoming and ending of barriers however deeply founded and highly constructed these appear to be." (Markus Barth, The Broken Wall: A Study of the Epistle to the Ephesians [London: Collins, 1960], 39.)

[376] There is great emphasis in the construction "he himself" (v.14). At its very least it means that Christ Himself is our peace and perhaps with the abstract "peace" (v.14) could emphasize that it " . . . is not only that the peace was made by Christ and ranks as His achievement, but that it is so identified with Him that were He away it would also fail, - so dependent on Him that apart from Him we cannot have it. . . . [This feat was accomplished by making two groups one.] "The sing. neut. [hen] (=one thing, one organism) expresses the idea of the unity, the new unity which the two long separate and antagonistic parties became . . . " (Rader, Racial Hostilities, 294.)

[377] Rader, Racial Hostilities, 294.

[378] Barclay notes, "The Greek called any man a barbarian if he could not speak Greek, and they despised the barbarians and put up the barriers against them. When

147

Gentiles were destroyed by Christ. All who are in Him have only His peace, and the human walls of separation for those in the church have ended.

This argument does not make Jesus guilty of ethnocide because He overrode Judaism or ignored the vast cultural variations of the Gentiles. He gave both something better. Without destroying what they possessed culturally, racially, or linguistically, Christ gave every converted Jew and Gentile a new citizenship that enabled them to fellowship equally with one another in the church while preserving their ethnicity to mingle among those in the world for the purpose of evangelism. Surely, if Jesus, who is the head of the church, provided a commonness for all men of conflicting cultures as Jew and Gentile to enjoy mutual fellowship, then there must be something to this "newness" that the church is obligated to perpetuate. What Jesus initiated in the church demands that there be a visible unity regardless of race, language or culture. The world, which is steeped in prejudice and bigotry, needs to see a contrast. When the church is comprised of different classes and races living in equality and harmony, then, the world will take notice and the effect of Christ's new commandment will began to be realized.[379]

---

Aristotle is discussing bestiality, he says: It is found most frequently among barbarians, and by barbarians he simply meant non-Greeks." (Barclay, Ephesians, 132.)

[379] John 13:34, 35.

The "dividing wall," which is mentioned exclusively here in the New Testament, has been interpreted in a number of different ways. One view identifies the "dividing wall" as the wall in the Temple at Jerusalem that separated the Court of the Jews from the Court of the Gentiles. This wall kept Gentile visitors away from Jewish worshippers and branded pagans as "those afar." However, this particular notion has a weakness in that contextually Paul does not make any reference to the Jerusalem Temple.[380] And furthermore, the wall separating the Courts of the Jews and Gentiles may very well have still been standing when Ephesians was written or at least when Pentecost occurred in Acts 2.[381]

Another view is that Paul may have been referring to the curtain or veil that separated the holy of holies from the holy place in the Jerusalem Temple. Then, according to Mark 15:38 at the hour of Christ's death the curtain was completely torn. Hebrews 10:19f explicitly alludes to this access as a result of Christ's death. Yet, the inconsistency of calling a veil a "wall" makes this possibility unlikely.[382]

---

[380]  Barth explains: " . . . 2:14–15 indicates that the wall was separating men from men (i.e. Gentiles from Jews), according to 2:16 the same wall means enmity between man (both Jew and Gentile) and God. The wall in the Temple, around Jerusalem, or around the Promised Land, therefore cannot exhaust what the author had in mind." (Barth, Broken Wall, 34.)

[381]  Barth, Broken Wall, 34.  For an alternate view see Abbott, Ephesians, 61 and Moule, Ephesians, 79.

[382]  Rader, Racial Hostilities, 294.

Then, another suggestion is that the Rabbinic tradition of a "fence" around the Law is referred to here. That is, this partition is a "hedge" around Old Israel, a reference to Isaiah 5:2. It has the purpose of keeping the nation secluded from the rest of the world.[383] However, this teaching referred more to the protection of the Law rather than to the hostility that is in this context. And, it is a cumbersome and narrow explanation of what appears to be much more simple and broad.[384]

A fourth view suggests evidence that the "dividing wall" does not refer to an actual physical barrier. Instead, it appears to represent the enmity that exists between Jews and Gentiles.[385] What separated Jew and Gentile in history was far more than a physical barrier and the admonition by the Apostle for succeeding generations seems to include more than historical symbols. For those who become part of the community of Christians leave behind the hostile attitudes that now are non-essential issues in light of a newness in Christ.[386]

---

[383] Rader explains the meaning behind this perspective of the barrier: " . . . what Paul really expresses then is the fact that the legal system, which was meant primarily to protect the Jewish people against the corruption of heathen idolatry, became the bitter root of Jewish exclusiveness in relation to the Gentiles. This is to give the [phragmou] here the sense of something that fences in or encloses . . . " (Rader, Racial Hostilities, 294.) For a further discussion see Moule, Ephesians, 79.

[384] Rader, Racial Hostilities, 294.

[385] Hoehner, Ephesians, 625.

[386] Marcus Barth summarizes this study well when he writes, "The great variety of meanings entitles and indeed compels the reader of Ephesians not to limit the
150

The text gives a clear basis for discounting any reason for hostilities between men of different races. Notice that since the "hostility" (v.15) is in antithesis to the "peace" (v.14), "hostility" should also be taken in an abstract sense. This "hostility" seems to be between Jew and Gentile not between God and man.[387] Consequently, if the animosity has been destroyed by Christ, then, Jew and Gentile believers are forbidden to be hostile toward one another.

The reason for and the matriculation of ending this enmity is now explained. The animosity between Jew and Gentile believers ended because of Christ's death. This reference to Christ's physical death, implied by the phrase "in His flesh," portrays a death of the hostilities between Jew and Gentile. Since the Jews preserved their segregation from Gentiles in an effort to abide by the Law, the removal of the Law's presence would consequently remove the reason for separation. The Gentiles had no concern over the commandments and regulations whereas the Jews meticulously obeyed them. This difference

---

meaning of the broken 'wall' only to the realm of the religious. Political and cosmic, moral and righteous, intellectual and psychological, physical and metaphysical distinctions and divisions must also be thought of when Eph. 2:14 is read. To put it in more modern terms: this verse says that Jesus Christ has to do with whatever divisions exist between races and nations, between science and morals, natural and legislated laws, primitive and progressive peoples, outsiders and insiders. The witness of Ephesians to Christ is that Christ has broken down every division and frontier between men. And even more, Ephesians adds that Christ has reconciled men with God!" (Barth, Broken Wall, 37.)

[387] Salmond, Ephesians, 3:295.

was like a wall between their lives. In this situation Jesus removed the wall, hence, Jewish-Gentile hostility was gone. It is also worth noting that the Law was not the enmity but it certainly was the cause of it.[388]

Even though a Jew was still a Jew and a Gentile still a Gentile, they were also much more. Because of Christ they now share something in common that is greater than their ethnicity.[389] Yet, within the church racial hostilities among human groups who share a greater spiritual affinity with each are still heated and show little evidence of abating. The ugliness of human bigotry is clear. Man-made taboos are designed to keep a psychological and sociological distance between groups. Especially when a narrow geographical area exists with members of at least two groups intermingling, law and custom arise to keep a separation. Along with the segregation comes stereotyped thinking, mistrust, and scapegoating. The solution for some is to say that there is no significance at all to racial, cultural, or linguistic differences. In the "new man" they argue, Jews cease to be Jews and the same with Gentiles. Yet, racial, cultural and linguistic distinctions obviously

---

[388] Hoehner, Ephesians, 626.

[389] Salmond explains: "What was contemplated, too, was not simply the making of one man [hena anthropon] where formerly there were two, but the making of one new [kainou] man. The result was not that, though the separation between them was removed, the Jew still remained Jew and the Gentile still Gentile. It was something new, the old distinctions between Jew and Gentile being lost in a third order of `man'- the Christian man." (Salmond, Ephesians, 3:296.)

152

continue after conversion.[390] Something was destroyed by Christ's death, but what was it? Certainly, something significant ended. What it was is clearly evident in His purpose for dying.

Christ had two reasons for ending the hostility. First, He wanted to make peace and did so by making one new man out of the two. The "newness" of this "new man" is not a reference to recent time (*neos*) but rather to a freshness in character or quality (*kainon*). It would be appropriate to describe this "new man" as a "new creation"[391] or "one body" as it is done in verse 16, referring to the church. In Christ's church Jews do not become Gentiles nor do Gentiles become Jews. Instead both Gentiles and Jews become believers, Christians, which is a new creation.

Second, Christ destroyed the enmity in order that He could reconcile both Jew and Gentile believer to Himself in one body. By His death on the cross He killed the enmity that existed between God and men. As He was put to death, He put to death the Jewish-Gentile hostility. Reconciliation with God is now raised but within the context of the already accomplished reconciliation of Jew and Gentile.[392] Thus, in verse 14 reconciliation happened

---

[390]  Rader, <u>Racial Hostilities</u>, 252.

[391]  2 Cor. 5:17.

[392]  Barclay explains: "The work of Jesus is to show all men that God is their friend, and because God is their friend, that they must be friends with each other. Reconciliation with God involves and necessitates reconciliation with man." (Barclay, <u>Ephesians</u>, 137.)

153

between Jew and Gentile and in verse 16 God and man are reconciled.  It is also from this text that the term reconciliation is elucidated.  An emphasis is made, indicating that it has a special feature, namely, the removal of enmity.[393]

There is a clear grammatical link between verse 14 and 17.  This seventeenth verse begins with an untranslated "and" (*kai*).  In particular the text indicates that Christ is  not only "our peace" but He also preached peace.  "Not only did Christ effect the reconciliation, but He also came and preached the glad tidings of it, and that not to one class but to both."[394]  A mystery is apparent at this point for Christ preached almost exclusively to Jews.  But it is probable that this is a reference to the apostles' preaching, since these "sent ones" were appointed by Christ and given the message to preach by Him as well.  Also, the message of peace was based upon Christ's death not His life on earth.  Jew and Gentile alike receive this peace.  Gentiles are described as the ones "who were far away" (v.17) since they were without a Messiah and alienated from Israel's covenants.  Jews are the ones who "were near" (v.17); that is, their covenants and Law put them in closer proximity to God from a relationship standpoint.

---

[393]  Barclay observes: "He had first to kill this enmity between the two before He could bring them both into right relations to God in the way indicated, viz., in one body, as one great, united whole." (Barclay, Ephesians, 137.)

[394]  Ibid.

With possession of the peace, all believers enjoy a benefit of "access" (v.18) to the Father. Some consider this "access" to be an introduction but the context indicates instead that Christ gives believers access. Thus, believers can approach the Father whether Jew or Gentile through the Holy Spirit because Christ's work on the cross achieved reconciliation.

These amazing spiritual advantages make one wonder why racial hostility has been a factor in church history. For the faith outlined thus far should have been perceived as something much stronger than the bonds of race and culture and language. Yet, tracing back through history it is worthy to note that since Constantine, Christianity was assumed to be a birthright; therefore, it was difficult to accept a Jew or Turk as a real believer resulting in Jewish and Turkish believers. Rader observes that the ". . . factor of natural heritage was regarded as more important than the factor of common faith."[395]

The union of Jew and Gentile is emphasized in several ways. From verse 14 it is stated that "the two" are made "one." Also, in verse 15 the "one new man" is created "out of the two". Then, in verse 16 "in this one body . . . both" are reconciled. And finally, "both" have equal priority to enjoy access by the Spirit into the Father's presence. The oneness from the redemptive work of Christ that is described here challenges many of the limits

---

[395] Rader, Racial Hostilities, 250.

observed in Christian circles.  While the intent of such limits may be positive they may in fact be a violation of the very reason that brings them together.  Thus, Christian fellowships that segregate groups due to sex, race, and economic status should be reevaluated in light of the Ephesians 2 principle.  The peace that Christ brought must result in a new man that challenges previous schemes of "insiders" and "outsiders" and live in mutual acceptance of each other.  A history of selectivity is replaced by oneness in Christ and a new history of brotherhood of inclusiveness is displayed.[396]

---

[396] How these observations from Ephesians 2 affect the practical ministry of the church is stated by Marcus Barth.  "In the light of Eph. 2:13-18, the continuing existence of `Christian men's and women's clubs, of `Christian' managers' and laborer's associations, of suburbanite and colored churches, of American and indigenous congregations overseas, of communities for the educated and for those less sophisticated are nothing less than a repudiation of Christ.  When no tensions are confronted and overcome, because insiders or outsiders of a certain class or group meet happily among themselves, then the one new thing, peace, and the one new man created by Christ, are missing; then no faith, no church, no Christ is found or confessed.  For if the attribute `Christian' can be given sense from Eph. 2, then it means reconciled and reconciling, triumphant over walls and removing the debris, showing solidarity with the `enemy' and promoting not one's own peace of mind, but `our peace.'  If preaching the Gospel (evangelizing) is what its name suggests, then it is exactly the same as it was in Galilee, on Golgotha, and in the apostolic Church after Pentecost: `He came and proclaimed peace to those who are far and peace to those near.' (2:17)." (Barth, Broken Wall, 39.)

156

## The Union that Christ Established for Jew and Gentile has Specific Consequences - Ephesians 2:19-22

As a result of Christ's unifying work, Gentiles can shed the stigma of being foreigners and aliens. Believing Gentiles become "fellow citizens with God's people and members of God's household." They join in the company of all who are the redeemed.[397] This new man which Christ created, however, does not necessarily mean that the church inherits all of Israel's blessings.

Three observations are pertinent to this point. First, the new union was not a blending of the Gentiles into the Jews but both groups formed into a new humanity. Second, the language of the text is specific. The Gentiles were incorporated "with God's people" and are in "God's household." The name "Israel" is not used. And third, it was at Pentecost when the "one new man" began. This is clear from the fact that the new union is "built on the foundation of the apostles and prophets with Christ Jesus Himself as the chief Cornerstone" (v.20). For the Gentiles become a part of the redeemed of all ages but their entrance into the one new man is not begun in the Old Testament but at

---

[397] Those who are called "God's people", then,
". . . are not the Jews, nor specially the patriarchs or Old Testament saints . . . as Chrysostom says, nor the angels, as some other commentators. Nor, again, does the word mean `holy men of all times and places'. The word does not refer to personal holiness, but to membership of the spiritual commonwealth to which Jewish and Gentile Christians alike belong." (Abbott, Ephesians, 69.)

Pentecost.[398]  This "new creation" or "new humanity" that Christ established for people of all ethnic groups is described as a building, a holy temple in which God dwells, an Old Testament figure.   The figure is described in three parts:   the building's foundation, formation, and function.

Fellow citizenship can be claimed by the Gentiles because they are built on the foundation of the apostles and prophets. Since the term prophets follows apostles, it is likely that these individuals are of the New Testament era not the Old Testament. Notice that this sequential pattern is repeated in 3:5 and 4:11. Very likely, these New Testament prophets received the mystery of the church in the post-Christ days, a mystery that was hidden in the past.[399]

There are several possibilities in interpreting the phrase "the foundation of the apostles and prophets."  It could mean that the foundation of the church was built by them.  Or it could mean that these individuals were the source from which the church originated.  As well, it could be conceived that the foundation was owned by them.  But, most likely it appears that these individuals themselves were the foundation.  This choice is substantiated by a comparison with 4:11 where these apostles and prophets were gifted people given to the church as its "foundation."  Also, since

---

[398]  Ibid.

[399]  Hoehner, Ephesians, 626.

Christ Himself was the chief Cornerstone[400], that is, part of the foundation, all of the apostles and prophets were to be aligned first with Him. All other believers who are added to the church follow suit and align their lives with Christ.[401]

It is clear from this text that segregation in the church is an indefensible position. As well, genocide is equally an unacceptable extreme. Nor is there an allowance made for some kind of delayed post-salvation union with the new humanity. Instead, at the point of conversion there is a new level of spiritual being where all men with their differences are elevated into a common brotherhood. Therefore, it seems highly contradictory to build churches on the principle of racial, cultural or linguistic differences and hope that they will later on convert into the picture of unity that Christ completed at the cross.

Next, the formation of the superstructure on a firm foundation is laid out. The phrase: "In Christ the whole building is joined together," emphasizes a single superstructure rather than its several parts. This singleness is emphasized further by Paul's use of a synecdoche[402]. There is no careless construction but

---

[400] Abbott makes an important point regarding the figure of Christ being the `chief Cornerstone'. "The figure of the corner-stone as uniting the two walls is pressed Theodoret as referring to the union of Jews and Gentiles; and many expositors have followed him. but this is not only to press the figure unduly, it is also unsuitable. For the point is that Jews and Gentiles now indifferently are built into the one building, not as if the Jews were one wall and the Gentiles another." (Abbott, Ephesians, 71.)

[401] Ibid.

[402] Bullinger explains, "Syndoche of the whole is when the whole is put for a part.

one that is planned and deliberate. "The image is that of an extensive pile of buildings in process of construction at different points on a common plan. The several parts are adjusted to each other so as to preserve the unity of design."[403] This structure "rises to become a holy temple in the Lord." Therefore, as new people are converted they are included in the one superstructure, the one new man. Jew and Gentile alike are joined together into this one organism. "That is what the church should be like. Its unity comes not from organization, or ritual, or liturgy, or worship. Its unity comes from Christ."[404]

Lastly, the superstructure[405] designed by God has a specific function. As God places individual believers into the structure, He is building a dwelling place for His Spirit to live.[406] In the past God lived in the Temple. His glory there represented His

---

This is a closer connection than that of mere genus or species. It is when the one is not merely of the same kind as the other, but actually a part or member of it . . . the 'whole building' [pasa oikodoma], every being put for every part of it." (Bullinger, Figures of Speech, 636.)

[403] Abbott, Ephesians, 75.

[404] Barclay, Ephesians, 139.

[405] Moule elaborates on the significance of this structure illustration: "The idea is not a completed but of a progressive work, a 'framing together' of the structure ever more closely and firmly. The building shrinks into greater solidity, binds itself into more intense coherence, as it grows. The spiritual union of the saints needs but to be more believed and realized to tell more on their actual closeness of connection." (Moule, Ephesians, 85.)

[406] Simpson and Bruce, Ephesians, 68.

presence with the people. Now, God lives in His new temple built not by the hands of men but by Him, not with earthly materials but with living beings. It should be noted that the references to the Spirit indwelling individual believers[407] here in Ephesians 2 seems to refer to the Spirit's corporate "dwelling." Thus, this new dwelling is the composition of all Jewish and Gentile believers, " . . . every believer has his own niche to fill."[408]

### *Conclusion of Chapter III, Part 1*

Before the church adopts a growth philosophy that addresses the issue of race and class it must first articulate the New Testament foundation of the church's existence. Included in that explanation of its existence are two essentials: unity and fellowship. They are more than pleasant expressions or hopeful ideals, they are basic to the Gospel and priorities for the church. Along this line, several helpful observations can be made from an analysis Ephesians 2:11-22.

First, this text deals with the concrete fellowship between Jew and Gentile in the church. There is harmony without the elimination of differences. "Christianity was neither a Jewish sect nor a Hellenistic cultic community but a <u>tertium quid</u>. It was

---

[407] Rom. 5:5; 8:9,11; 1 Cor.2:12; Gal. 3:2; 4:6; 1 Jn. 3:24; 4:13. For a discussion see Murray, <u>Romans</u>, 164-165; Hodge, <u>Romans</u>, 135.

[408] Simpson and Bruce, <u>Ephesians</u>, 68.

organized as a voluntary fellowship without regard to the distinction of religion, race, class, nation, or gender, that divided the ancient world."[409] When this text is compared to Galatians 3:28, Colossians 3:11, and 1 Corinthians 12:13, unity with diversity is the emphasis that prevails. Any notion that Paul is describing a total dissolution of human distinctions among believers is extreme and not permissible. There is sufficient evidence of Paul continuing to address specific groups as Jews, Gentiles, husbands, or wives to indicate this. But, granting differences, Paul is advocating a commonness among Christians, a reason for those who were once at odds with each other to now live together in mutual acceptance.[410]

Second, it is the visible unity of the church that this text is emphasizing. This visible unity is a symptom of the reconciling work of God. On the one hand, if there is no reconciliation between Jew and Gentile, then no reconciliation between man

---

[409] Moltmann, "Life Signs," 38.

[410] Barth explains this new humanity: "Abolition and peace - these great words will keep us from dreaming of, or scoffing at, a sexless, raceless, homeless, neuter superman, whom Christianity allegedly out to promote or to produce. The words `neither Jew nor Greek, neither slave nor free man, neither male nor female; you are all one in Christ Jesus' (Gal. 3:28; Col. 3:11; 1 Cor. 12:13) by which Paul describes Christ's work, do by no means wipe out or deny distinctions between nations, sexes, classes and occupations. Otherwise Paul would not have included in his letters special exhortations for Jews and Greeks (Rom. 2:17ff.; 11:13ff.), husbands and wives (Eph. 5:22ff., Col. 3:18ff.), slaves and masters (Eph. 6:5ff.), etc. But, faith in Christ, even Christ himself, means that the two - whatever their distinctions are - can and do live together: those who were formerly opposed, mutually exclusive, separated by what seemed to be an insurmountable wall. To say `Christ' means to say community, co-existence, a new life, peace (2:14)." (Barth, Broken Wall, 38.)

162

and God can be claimed.  On the other hand, since reconciliation has been accomplished, then divine power has molded " . . . all these incongruous  elements into one consistent whole, stamped with one  regenerate likeness . . .."[411]

Third, certainly if the intense hostility between Jew and Gentile was made impotent by the death of Christ, then, it is presumptuous of the church to cater to lessor sociological phenomena as in the case of white versus all others, wealth versus poor, or caste versus caste.  The significance of displaying this genuine internal change is a part of the church's mission and purpose.  Essential to the Gospel is its proclamation.  Part of that proclamation is the display of this oneness begun by Christ and carried out by His followers.[412]

Fourth, if churches adopt the attitude that involvement in race relations will distract from its primary calling of preaching the Gospel and observing the ordinances, then it has in fact denied the Gospel which is concerned with bringing peace and did so between two of humanities most ardent foes.  The peace that

---

[411]  Simpson and Bruce, Ephesians, 68.

[412]  Paxson observes the vital nature of this public display of Christian reality in uniting people together: "Here is a oneness that is inward and vital.  A new start has been made from a new center.  Here is no camouflage of a patched-up, man-made peace, but a divine reality in a positive brotherhood of goodwill and love, born out of true family relationship established by life in Christ." (Paxson, Wealth, Walk, 65.)

Christ provided affects every human dimension including national, social, and economic boundaries.[413]

Finally, the church must follow the early church's example. It preached the Gospel to Jew and Gentile. The early church overcame the initial temptation to be only a Jewish sect.[414] Their fellowships demonstrated a visible unity not an invisible one. This is demanded from the very nature of what it means to confess Christ. A true confession must mean to affirm the end of all division and hostility, separation and segregation, enmity and contempt, prejudice and bigotry. "It does no good to call Christ "Lord, Lord" unless we mean by `Christ' even this new man, the end of divisions, `one new thing made of both,' `one new man,' `one body' instead of two which formerly were antagonists of God (2:14-16)."[415]

According to Ephesians 2:11-22 the church must organize itself and operate with a priority of unity achieved through mutual acceptance. The church was founded upon the basic principle

---

[413] Barth notes, "When this peace is deprived of its social, national, or economic dimensions, when it is distorted or emasculated so much that only `peace of mind' enjoyed by saintly individuals is left - then Jesus Christ is being flatly denied. To propose in the name of Christianity, neutrality or unconcern on questions of international, racial, or economic peace - this amounts to using Christ's name in vain. On the other hand, if true evangelism is carried out, it not only will involve some social action, but will be from beginning to end even that social, reconciling, uniting action with which Christ is identified when he is called `our peace.'" (Barth, Broken Wall, 40.)

[414] I am grateful to Ainslie Walton for this idea.

[415] Barth, Broken Wall, 38.

164

that all dividing walls have been destroyed by Christ's death. They continue to exist in the non-Christian world but among the fellowship of believers such distinctions have no place. The racial conflict between Jew and Gentile was notorious in its day. Nevertheless, God through the sacrifice of Jesus, overcame that enmity which was a demonstration of the power of the Gospel. That same power is present in the church today. "Only `the immeasurable greatness of God's power,' exhibited in the resurrection of Christ, could break down `the dividing wall of hostility' and unite Jew and Gentile `in one body.' It was miraculous. So is the overcoming of the barriers of race and rank today."[416]

Proponents of the HUP theory claim to have a case when they assert that their strategy for church growth causes greater growth-results than the orthodox methods of Christian missions. But, it is possible that the orthodox methods of church history have not been completely faithful to the principle of a visible unity described here in Ephesians 2:11-22. Has the church really lived up to its "newness" in Christ with the oneness of all men in the church? What effect would the church have on the world if in great contrast to the habit of racial segregation congregations displayed a unity of its members from all different backgrounds sharing in a common worship around the Table of Communion?

---

[416] Stott, Guilty Silence, 75.

Would not the world which sees no possible solution to the race problems sit up and take note? Would they not ask how the church manages such a feat? And would not the church then have the opportunity of pointing the world to Christ?

## Part 2
## Formulating a Growth Philosophy for the Church According to a Christocentric Biblical Theology

### *Introduction*

The construction of a plan for church development must include some means of addressing the practical issue of Christian fellowship. With the success of missionary endeavors and evangelistic thrusts converts will enter the church from many different backgrounds. They will have a habit of life that is still present in their lives. Some will have a background disposition that has not accepted people who are different from themselves. Or a new Christian's background may be so unique that he may feel out of place in any culture that is foreign to what he or she has been familiar for a lifetime. How can Christians who are so different operate together in unity? When the Gospel is introduced to a community that is already homogeneous, that is one thing. But, when the Gospel is introduced to a heterogeneous community that is in many cases socially fragmented, what posture should the resulting church assume?

With regard to the issue of developing a consistent, practical theology for the church that addresses the problem of racial and ethnic tensions in the church three important topics must be discussed. These three topics are an adequate view of a functioning sanctification[417], a balanced view of pragmatism in culture, and a caution with regard to civil religion[418].

## *Sanctification*

The HUP theory, as it applies to HU churches, does not have an adequate explanation of how sanctification[419] operates in

---

[417] I am reluctant to qualify the term sanctification with the term "functioning" for fear of being redundant. However, the practical problem of sanctification in the church is that what may be adhered to by confession is not carried out in practice. When the doctrine of sanctification is examined apart from the issue of race, it is clear that something new has begun with Christian conversion. A new capacity for righteous living is initiated. When this is applied to the problems of race in the church, Christians are pressed to realize a need to freely accept all other believers regardless of ethnic background, language, or class.

[418] Closely linked with this matter of civil religion is a theological dualism. For a discussion of this see James Torrance, "The Covenant Concept in Scottish Theology and Politics and its Legacy," the Inaugural Lecture, delivered on October 20, 1977 in King's College, University of Aberdeen, transcript available from King's College library. Also, see James Torrance, "The Contribution of McLeod Campbell to Scottish Theology," in The Scottish Journal of Theology, 26, no. 3, August 1973.

[419] Yoder referred to this as a "postponement of ethical awareness." (Yoder,

the lives of Christians. In considering the issue of the local church[420] the commonness shared in Christ by all Christians assumes the existence of a universal fellowship. This doctrine addresses the practical lifestyle of Christians as a result of their conversion and the capacity to enact it. It addresses the practical nature of Christian living. Its focus is on this earthly life in contrast with a distant heavenly future. A natural expression of a newly converted Christian[421] is the inquiry of how he may best live out this new life. Sanctification deals with this search and desire.[422]

On the subject of racial tensions, assurances that proper teaching would eventually eliminate this do not seem to be satisfactory. There is no practical timetable for its occurrence.

---

"Ethical Perspective," 4.)

[420] I understand a "local church" to be an assembly of a geographically identified body of Christians. They profess their faith in Christ, are baptized, worship together, and observe the ordinances of the faith.

[421] Non-Christian spiritual perceptions are limited. For example, can a non-Christian really perceive becoming righteous in God's sight as a real possibility? The topic of sanctification is therefore, limited only to Christians. (Rom. 1:18-20. For a discussion see Charles Hodge, Commentary on the Epistle to the Romans, reprint [Grand Rapids: Wm. B. Eerdmans Pub. Co., 1972], 34-38. Denney makes the helpful explanation of New Testament truth being moral not speculative, hence, concludes that Paul is referring to those who do not yet possess truth. [Denney, Romans, 592.])

[422] Anderson describes the practical feature of sanctification not as a pursuit or even a struggle to become what he is not. Rather it is simply to realize what he is as a consequence of redemption. He states the following: "He does not live righteously in order to become justified, but because he has been justified; neither does he live holily in order to become sanctified, but because he has been sanctified." For a further discussion see Robert Anderson, Redemption Truths (Grand Rapids: Kregel Pub., 1980), 87.

Nor is there any guideline as to how an attitude as racism in any degree can continue to operate in the Christian life while growing out of it. Christians are beneficiaries of the reconciliation work of a gracious God. This same reconciliation is to be expressed by every believer toward his fellow believer. Christians are obligated to be peacemakers. Neither compromise nor appeasement are options. God secures a peace for Christians that came at great cost, the blood of Christ on the cross. Stott reasons, "To reconcile himself to us, and us to himself, and Jews, Gentiles and other hostile groups to each other, cost him nothing less than the painful shame of the cross. We have no right to expect, therefore, that we shall be able to engage in conciliation work at no cost to ourselves, whether our involvement in the dispute is as the offending or offended party, or as a third part anxious to help enemies to became friends again."[423]

There is no debate related to the HUP theory over what causes conversion, only what occurs once conversion has taken place. Are those who profess Christianity required to act uniformly as a result of their conversion? And does this uniformity of behavior include a specific enough scope to call the HUP theory into abeyance when new converts face pre-conversion biases of association? More specifically, does the reality of sanctification call for immediate changes of mutual acceptance in

---

[423] Stott, Cross of Christ, 296.

a meaningful *koinonia* of all other Christians regardless of their past racial, linguistic, or class identities? On a practical note the issue of segregation in the church or separate ethnic churches must be discussed further. Is it acceptable to place a Christian in a homogeneous environment where pre-conversion racial or social biases can be conveniently hidden or even condoned because they are in an environment where they are not confronted?

**Various Views of Sanctification**

Addressing the doctrine of sanctification is difficult in that there are many perspectives from which to view this matter. The Wesleyan perspective of "entire sanctification" or the ability to live this life without sin is one distinctive view.[424] Another perspective highlighting the unique role of the Spirit in practical holiness is the Pentecostal view.[425] Its distinctive view indicates that only those

---

[424] For a further discussion see Melvin Dieter, "The Wesleyan Perspective," 11-46, in Five Views on Sanctification (Zondervan Pub. House, 1987) and Laurence Wood, "The Wesleyan View," 95-118, in Christian Spirituality: Five Views of Sanctification (Downers Grove: Inter-Varsity Press, 1988). For an alternate view see the four responses in each of the two volumes named. Also see B. B. Warfield, Perfectionism (Philadelphia: The Presbyterian and Reformed Pub. Co., 1974).

[425] For a discussion see Stanley Horton, "The Pentecostal Perspective," 105-135 in Five Views on Sanctification (Grand Rapids: Zondervan Pub. House, 1987) and Russell Spittler, "The Pentecostal View," 133-154, in Christian Spirituality: Five Views of Sanctification, ed. Donald Alexander (Downers Grove: Inter-Varsity Press, 1988). For an alternate view see four corresponding responses in each of these two volumes.

who have spoken in tongues can be empowered for service through filling of the Spirit. The Lutheran view places great emphasis on "faith alone" as the basis for Christian spirituality.[426] Resting in the fact that a believer stands before God by faith is sufficient for spiritual success. Four other perspectives emphasizing a combination of faith in God's redemption and man's responsible participation (perhaps sharing more in common than in differences) are the Reformed perspective[427], the Keswick perspective[428], the Contemplative perspective[429] and the Augustinian-Dispensational perspective[430].

---

[426] For a further discussion see Gerhard Forde, "The Lutheran View," 13-32, in Christian Spirituality: Five Views of Sanctification, ed. Donald Alexander (Downers Grove: Inter-Varsity Press, 1988). For an alternate view see four corresponding responses in the same volume.

[427] For a discussion see Anthony Hoekema, "The Reformed Perspective," 61-90, in Five Views on Sanctification (Grand Rapids: Zondervan Pub. House, 1987) and Sinclair Ferguson, "The Reformed View," 47-76, in Christian Spirituality: Five Views of Sanctification (Downers Grove: Inter-Varsity Press, 1988). For an alternate view see four corresponding responses in both volumes.

[428] For a discussion see J. Robertson McQuilkin, "The Keswick Perspective," 151-183 in Five Views on Sanctification (Grand Rapids: Zondervan Pub. House, 1987). For an alternate view see the four corresponding responses in the same volume.

[429] Glenn Hinson, "The Contemplative View," 171-189, in Christian Spirituality: Five Views of Sanctification, ed. Donald Alexander (Downers Grove: Inter-Varsity Press, 1988). For an alternate view see four corresponding responses in the same volume.

[430] For a discussion see John Walvoord, "The Augustinian-Dispensational Perspective," 199-226 in Five Views on Sanctification (Grand Rapids: Zondervan Pub. House, 1987). For an alternate view see the four corresponding responses in the same volume.

Despite the various interpretations of how sanctification is accomplished and verified all five positions agree that Christians have had a unique change in their lives, a change that results from Christ's completed work. Also, all agree that all Christians are to express righteousness in their daily life. They are to make choices against evil. And all agree that the prospect of some measure of success is real in this life. It is not merely an ideal reserved for heaven.[431] It is in the spirit of these common features of sanctification that the following discussion commences.

## Essence of Sanctification

Sanctification is in part the continuation of redemption. The connection between these two point to an orderly progression[432]. They complete the final glory for all who are the sons of God. Sanctification, since it is not the beginning of this logical order, presupposes a number of other elements involved in the picture of redemption. Some of these aspects are election[433],

---

[431] Five Views on Sanctification (Grand Rapids: Zondervan Pub. House, 1987), 7-8.

[432] Horne describes sanctification as the most relevant feature of the Ordo Salutis. In the attempt to logically order the activities related to the salvation of the individual, he describes this doctrine as the one which is " . . . the most directly and immediately relevant . . . " (Charles M. Horne, Salvation [Chicago: Moody Press, 1971], 77.)

[433] Some as Murray refer to this as "calling". He describes it as follows: "Calling is addressed to our consciousness and elicits response in our consciousness. . . It is by
172

regeneration, justification and adoption.  Two of these which are particularly pertinent to sanctification are election[434] and regeneration[435].  Both are acts of the Holy Spirit who indwells each Christian and causes each of them to live spiritual lives.  "Sanctification is specifically the *work* of this indwelling and directing Holy Spirit."[436]

The practical implications of this doctrine relate to the effect on sin in a Christian's life due to this election and regeneration.  One of the results of the new life gained through

---

calling that we are united to Christ, and it is this union with Christ which binds the people of God to the efficacy and virtue by which they are sanctified." (John Murray, Redemption: Accomplished and Applied, reprint [Grand Rapids: Wm. B. Eerdmans Pub. Co., 1975], 141.)

[434] I understand election as God's sovereign choice of those whom He lovingly, justly, and graciously grants salvation to whomever He chooses.  It is only part of a broader divine plan.  Mysteriously, it is not equal with fatalism, inconsistent with human freedom nor is it tantamount to making God the author of sin.  Rather, in its Biblical scope election has as its purpose for Christians " . . . service and good works . . . . Its purpose for God is to manifest His glory . . . .  Therefore, the doctrine of election is highly motivating and should never be deadening tone's spiritual life (Col. 3:12)." (Charles C. Ryrie, Basic Theology [Wheaton: Victor Books, 1986], 314.)

[435] Regeneration is the action of God which grants life to a person who expresses faith.  It is equivalent to the John 3 concept of being "born again".  The means of its actualization is based upon God's will, carried out by the Holy Spirit, completed at the time of a person's faith in the Gospel message.  As a result of regeneration, this new life will bear new fruit. (Ryrie, Theology, 325-326.)

[436] Murray, Redemption, 141.  Also, Paul's letter to the Thessalonians illustrates that sanctification was a consistent appeal to these Christians.  Horne notes, "[Paul] had enjoined them to the cultivation of certain graces and the exercise of certain duties and these could only be realized through the work of God upon them. . . . [The] author of this sanctification is God." (Horne, Salvation, 79.)

conversion is righteousness.[437]   A new capacity that enables a Christian not to commit sin is now made possible.[438]   Being called and thus united with Christ also results in the benefit of being dead to sin.[439]   In his analysis of Romans 6:14 Murray comments in light of this discussion, " [Paul] is making an apodictic statement to the effect that sin will not have dominion over the person who is under grace . . . here he is making an emphatic negation - `sin will not have dominion.'"[440]

With the Holy Spirit directing in the life of every Christian, the resulting character is holiness.  This is the essential definition of sanctification.    It means "to make holy."    And "holy" is "separated" or "set apart" not perfect or absolute in purity.  In this regard, Horne makes a helpful distinction between majestic[441] and

---

[437] Anderson describes the link between justification and sanctification: " . . . when the sinner, on his believing on the Lord Jesus Christ, becomes one with Him in His death, `the merits' of that death are his, and he stands before God both righteous and holy in Christ." (Anderson, Redemption, 87-88.)

[438] Ryrie, Theology, 326.

[439] Murray describes this affect: " . . . sin is dethroned in every person who is effectually called and regenerated." (Murray, Redemption, 141.) See 1 Cor. 1:9 and Rom. 6:2-6.

[440] Murray, Redemption, 142.

[441] This aspect of holiness emphasizes the transcendence of God.  It means that God is separate from all creation and His created beings.  The attribute of God that demands this is His infinity, He is exalted above all.  He is completely "other" than His creation. (Horne, Salvation, 78.)

174

ethical[442] holiness.  Both features operate in tandem and in consequence to each other as illustrated in Isaiah 6.  When the majesty of God is perceived, then a consciousness to one's own sinfulness is raised.  Subsequently, the need to respond with a separation from one's sinfulness is clear.  "It is this ethical aspect of God's holiness that provides the basis for our understanding of the doctrine of sanctification."[443]        With the Spirit controlling the life of a believer and holiness being manifested the relationship toward sin must be described since man is still an imperfect creature even after he is redeemed.  Sanctification means at the very least that a Christian cannot sin so as to be lost again.[444]  Once God executes His selection and the Spirit does His indwelling work the result is regeneration.  And far more than being limited to a theoretical or positional reality it is actual and practical ". . . as much as anything comprised in the application of redemption is actual and practical."[445]

---

[442] This feature of God's holiness focuses on God's necessary separation from any kind and every kind of sin.  God acting consistent with His character must demand that all conform to His moral law.  And as a corollary to this, any who would have a relationship with Him must by necessity be separate from sin. (Horne, Salvation, 78.)

[443] Horne, Salvation, 78, 79.

[444] Murray explains that in John's epistle he " . . . speaks of the regenerate person as not doing sin and as unable to sin (1 John 1:8, 5:18).  It is not that he is sinless . . . .  What John is stressing is surely that fact that the regenerate person cannot commit the sin that is unto death (1 John 5:16),  he cannot deny that Jesus is the Son of God and has come in the flesh . . . he cannot abandon himself again to iniquity, he keeps himself and the evil one does not touch him." (Murray, Redemption, 142.)

[445] Murray, Redemption, 142.

Freedom from the power and dominance of sin is not a feature toward which a Christian must progressively work. Rather, this liberty from sin is accomplished instantaneously once one is united with Christ and the regenerating Holy Spirit. Credit for this achievement is not the Christian's but exclusively God's. It is secured by a single act of faith not intense laboring.[446] Once redemption has occurred a permanent separation from the dominion of sin has been accomplished by divine intervention. The converted Christian is now united with Christ and the death of Christ has effected an absolute obliteration of any eternal claim that sin can have on a new Christian. Emancipation from the power of sin has been completely and permanently secured.[447]

**Emphasis of Sanctification**

While a convert to Christianity is delivered from the power of sin as a direct benefit of being united with Christ, there is no absolute separation from sin. There is a remaining sin nature[448]

---

[446] In contrast to this view Murray notes that those who maintain a "perfectionism" position of salvation make three errors in their understanding of sanctification: "(1) They fail to recognize that this victory is the possession of every one who is born again and effectually called. (2) They construe the victory as a blessing separable from the state of justification. (3) They represent it as something very different from what the Scripture represents it to be - they portray it as freedom from sinning or freedom from conscious sin." (Murray, Redemption, 143.)

[447] Murray, Redemption, 143.

[448] For an alternate view in dealing with the concept of a sin nature see David Needham, Birthright (Portland: Multnomah Press, 1979.) in particular chapter 6, 121-176

that continues with a Christian throughout his life. While a believer is united with Christ, he is not completely like Christ. This variation is the precise focus of the doctrine of sanctification; namely, " . . . it has as its aim the elimination of all sin and complete conformation to the image of God's own Son, to be holy as the Lord is holy."[449] Resolving the resulting tension is complicated. For if it is accepted that Christians have real holiness due to their union with Christ yet a sin potential is still present in them, then it must also be concluded that final and complete sanctification will not be realized until the body of the believer is transformed into the likeness of Christ's glory as the apostle described.[450] The interim period of life between conversion and glorification then faces difficulties. It is this difficult situation that can be addressed by spiritual behavior.

First, " [all] sin in the believer is the contradiction of God's holiness."[451] Sin is the same whether a person is or is not a Christian. While a Christian has a new and permanent

---

136. Also, see Anthony Hoekema, "Response to Walvoord," 230-232 and J. Robertson McQuilkin, "Response to Walvoord," 236-237 in Five Views on Sanctification (Grand Rapids: Zondervan Pub. House, 1987.) Both express some reservation to a "two-nature theory" of the sanctified Christian.

[449] Murray, Redemption, 143.

[450] 1 Corinthians 15:35-57. For a discussion see Charles Hodge, An Exposition of 1 and 2 Corinthians (Wilmington, Delaware: Sovereign Grace Pub., 1972), 190-199; F. L. Godet, The First Epistle to the Corinthians, trans. A. Cusin (Grand Rapids: Zondervan Pub. House, 1971), 441-448.

[451] Murray, Redemption, 144.

relationship with God and no eternal condemnation will result from sin, his act of disobedience to the law of God deserves the wrath of God and fatherly chastisement. All sin is a contradiction of God and therefore an affront that is forbidden. Second, "[the] presence of sin in the believer involves conflict in his heart and life."[452] An immediate tension that results from this realization is that conflict[453] with sin is normal for the Christian life. Sanctification injects into this tension the possibility to pursue holiness to such a degree that the more sanctified a Christian is the less he will be involved with sin. The more consistent his contemplation of the majesty of God, the more conscious he will be of the threat of sin. He should also consequently be more repulsed by it.[454] Third, "[there] must be a constant and increasing appreciation that though sin still remains it does not have the mastery."[455] The difference between a life that is ruled by sin and a life that is in conflict with sin is enormous. For the Christian, the Apostle Paul counts the reality of being separated from sin as a fact that simply needs to be realized. Grace has been applied to the Christian's life and sin no longer has

---

[452] Ibid.

[453] I am referring here to the difference caused by conversion itself.

[454] "Truly biblical sanctification has no affinity with the self-complacency which ignores or fails to take into account the sinfulness of every lack of conformity to the image of him who was holy, harmless, and undefiled." (Murray, Redemption, 145.)

[455] Murray, Redemption, 145.

178

dominion.  Murray describes the reality  of  the  Pauline instruction[456]: " . . . the indicative lies at the basis of the imperative and our faith of fact is indispensable to the discharge of duty."[457]

## Divine Agency in Sanctification

A Christian does not sanctify himself.  Rather, it is God that is the cause of sanctification.[458]  More specifically, it is the Holy Spirit who is the agent of sanctification.[459]  This divine supervision in the life of every Christian must be evaluated in the light of two necessary ingredients.

First, when an application of sanctification is made, it must be done with a recognition that the involvement by the Spirit is a mysterious one.  That is, the mode by which sanctification is administered is not fully understandable.  How the Spirit makes

---

[456]  Romans 6:12, 13.  For a discussion see Hodge, Romans, 203-205; Murray, Romans, 226-228.

[457]  Murray also describes the balanced perspective of accepting the fluid nature of sanctification as a developmental and maturing feature: "It is the concern of sanctification that sin be more and more mortified and holiness . . . cultivated." (Murray, Redemption, 146.)

[458]  Horne discusses the cause of sanctification from three perspectives.  He describes the *efficient* cause as the triune God listing Scripture references for each person (the Father in 1 Th. 5:23; 1 Pet. 1:15-16; 5:10), the *moving* cause as the good will of God (1 Th. 4:3) and the *instrumental* cause as the Word and acts of God. (Horne, Salvation, 85.)

[459]  The subject of sanctification emphasizes " . . . the believer being *experientially* set apart unto God by virtue of the ministry of the indwelling Spirit." (Horne, Salvation, 85.)

every Christian to be like image of Christ eludes complete explanation. This however, must be kept in balance with the reality that there is a consciousness regarding the Spirit's influence in a Christian's life. There is conscious activity in which sanctification plays a significant role.[460]

Second, sanctification requires complete dependence upon the Spirit. There is a divine-human interplay in sanctification. As the Apostle described the irony of spiritual living, as being strong when we are weak, so sanctification has this feature of some cooperative activity. Grace directs in the salvation of every Christian both as it has been accomplished and also as it is being accomplished. An awareness of human helplessness is a part of the activity of balancing the Christian's part in realizing the mystery of sanctification.[461]

## Sanctification as a Process

The feature of total dependence upon the Spirit for the achievement of sanctification must be kept in balance with the

---

[460] Walvoord, "Augustinian-Dispensational," 220.

[461] Murray points out the features of humanness and its partnering with divine involvement: "Self-confident moralism promotes pride, and sanctification promotes humility and contrition." (Murray, Redemption, 147.)

reality of the process[462] of spiritual maturation, which requires the believer's conscious participation.[463]

While sanctification is a work of the Spirit, part of its mystery is the active part of each believer who is involved in the process; they are not passive. This dynamic is captured in the Apostle Paul's exhortation for believers to work out their own salvation.[464] The meaning of this admonition is not in reference to the feature of salvation already obtained but of exercising what is already in place. There is no sense of a conditional cooperation here. God will not refuse to do His divine part of sanctification if the Christian fails to do his. A positive perspective is more accurate. That is, a Christian grows in righteousness because God has already done His work. Little distinction can be made regarding willing and doing in this matter. They function together.

---

[462] Horne explains the "process" aspect of sanctification: "The work of regeneration is instantaneous, consisting in one single creative act; hence, it is not subject to degrees. No one is more or less regenerate than another; one is either dead or alive. But sanctification is progressive and admits of degrees; one may be more sanctified than another." (Horne, Salvation, 85-86.)

[463] Murray, Redemption, 148. Horne notes that total involvement is a Christian's part in sanctification: " . . . sanctification includes our whole nature - spirit, soul, and body." (Horne, Salvation, 79.)

[464] Philippians 2:12, 13. For a discussion see Muller, Philippians, 90-92 and Vincent, Philippians, 64-67.

The Apostle Paul identifies the ultimate goal of Christian sanctification as conforming to the image of God's Son.[465] Accompanying instructions and expectations indicate that a believer must be intimately involved in his process toward sanctification.[466] Placement of the effort is critical to understanding this doctrine. Some in the world of religion are attempting to gain something through their efforts. But, the converted Christian enjoys the actual possession of salvation but learns to acknowledge what he has become. Consequently, he actively conforms to what he is.[467] Practically, sanctification calls for a Christian to put off the old man[468] and to put on the new.[469]

---

[465] Romans 8:29. For a discussion see Hodge, Romans, 283-286; Murray, Romans, 315-320.

[466] Phil. 1:9-11. For a discussion see J. B. Lightfoot, Saint Paul's Epistle to the Philippians, (Grand Rapids: Zondervan Pub. House, reprinted 1953), 86-87. 2 Pet. 1:5-8. For a discussion see Charles Erdman, The General Epistles (Philadelphia: The Westminster Press, 1966), 115-117.

[467] Anderson explains the paradoxical nature of sanctification: "The Divine grace which freely justifies a sinner, and then teaches him to live righteously in order to become justified, but because he has been justified; neither does he live holily in order to become sanctified, but because he has been sanctified." (Anderson, Redemption, 87.)

[468] Horne identifies the "old man" as the corrupt nature with which all were born with into the world. Furthermore, he identifies the "putting off" as a reference not to the obliteration of a sinful capacity but a removal of sin's control. The opposite is to "put on" or to function according to the graces that emulate the new nature. He also summarizes how sanctification manifests itself in relationship to God, Christ, the Holy Spirit, sin, others, and to each aspect of the fruit of the Spirit (Gal.5:22-23). (Horne, Salvation, 81-84.)

[469] Eph. 4:22-24. For a discussion see Bruce, Ephesians, 93-95; Moule, Ephesians, 118-121.

## _Implications of Sanctification for the Local Church_

Sanctification calls all believers to a holy life. This holy life is not a demand for "perfection" but life of separation from sin. For every believer their moment of conversion was not the end of the salvation experience but the beginning of God's work in them.[470] It was more than reform; rather, it was a supernatural work by God. Man cannot generate what sanctification achieves. Neither learning nor exposure can account for its results. Such aspects can aid in its purposes but they cannot produce it.[471]

What is definitive about sanctification is its connection with justification. Each Christian is called by God into an eternal union with Christ.[472] This union with Christ connects every believer instantaneously with the death of Christ to sin and to the power of His Resurrection. "When Christ died, He died to sin once for all. And the believer, called into union with Christ, dies with Christ to sin."[473] Thus, it is proper to call for an immediate ethical change

---

[470] Sanctification is the continuation of the salvation experience. (Millard J. Erickson, Salvation: God's Amazing Plan [Wheaton: Victor Books, 1978], 91.)

[471] Erickson, Salvation, 93.

[472] 1 Cor. 1:9. For a discussion see Hodge, 1 Corinthians, 14-15; Archibald Robertson and Alfred Plummer, A Critical and Exegetical Commentary on the First Epistle of St. Paul to the Corinthians, in The International Critical Commentary (Edinburgh: T. & T. Clark, second edition reprint 1975), 8.

[473] John Murray, "Sanctification," in Basic Christian Doctrines, ed. Carl F. Henry (Grand Rapids: Baker Book House, 1962.), 228.

in any area of a Christian's life that is inconsistent with the morals or ethics of a new man. Included in this are a person's past biases and prejudices that limited acceptance based upon language, race, or class. To narrow the scope of this matter even further, every Christian is called into the fellowship of other believers. As he was fully accepted by God, he too becomes fully capable and morally obligated to accept all that God has already accepted, due to the mysterious supernatural phenomenon of sanctification. If Christians are directed into a local church that organizes itself around distinctives related to their pre-converted state, then the breach made with sin by Christ and the newness of life that is a product of salvation are defiled.[474]

The progressive aspect of sanctification also points to an immediate newness in every Christian's life. Mortification, cleansing from sin, is very much an on-going process, especially in light of the sin that resides in the believer.[475] But even more constructively, the believer is to be "transformed."[476] The

---

[474] Murray explains the importance of this separation from sin: "No datum is of more basic importance than the definitive breach with sin and commitment to holiness secured by identification with Christ in His death and resurrection. . . . The breach with sin and the newness of life are as definitive as were the death and resurrection of Christ." (Murray, "Sanctification," 229.)

[475] Rom. 8:29. For a discussion see Hodge, Romans, 283-286; Murray, Romans, 315-320.

[476] Rom. 12:2. Murray notes that believers are to both reflect and behold the glory of Christ in the process of transformation. Consequently, " . . . we become like that in which our interests and ambitions are absorbed." (Murray, "Sanctification," 230.)

progression on this matter is more than an individualized matter. It also must manifest itself to the church and to the members in the church.[477] Thus, a Christian, as a result of His salvation and as an expression of his progressive maturation in holiness, must mortify immoral ill feelings of prejudice against other believers who are in the church. To locate or initiate a church where pre-conversion prejudices can exist in comfort or be ignored is in conflict God's call for a holy life. In this sense, then, ethnic churches in a multi-cultural environment may be sociologically understandable but not theologically expedient.

This reasoning is consistent with my personal experience as a post-immigrant ethnic minority in the United States. The Bible and Theology teach me that I have been reconciled to Christ. Part of my responsibility as one who has responded in faith to the Gospel is to accept others in the church as God accepted me. Yet, the subtle pressure to be identified with a church that is ethnically compatible is ever present. The pressure appears in two forms. First, is the internal pressure. Those who are more closely attached to their ethnic roots either by a closeness to their immigration links or by personal choice urge, admonish and exhort the cultural response in the Christian context. Often, ecclesiastical loyalty is equated with ethnic loyalty. Second, is external pressure. In the majority or host

---

[477] Murray, "Sanctification," 230.

culture of the United States, white Churches are unfamiliar with multi-cultural adaption. Opportunities for service and leadership are noticeably rare.

## *Cultural Pragmatism*

Pragmatism[478] is an essentially American philosophical phenomenon. It is not a theological perspective per se but its principles are ingrained both in American and other Western cultures. As a result, it has seeped into the thinking of many Western church leaders and theologians. While it is appealing in its high profile of productivity, it must be examined in light of theology. Does it remain consistent with the truths of the Christian faith?

## Sorting Out a Proper Theological Starting Point

Dietrich Bonhoeffer advanced the helpful idea of determining a correct theological starting point in order to properly control the resulting emphasis on dogmatics.[479] For Bonhoeffer it

---

[478] For a discussion of the principles of pragmatism see John Dewey, Logic: The Theory of Inquiry (London: George Allen & University Ltd., 1938) and William James, Pragmaticism: The Meaning of Truth (Cambridge: Harvard University Press, 1978).

[479] I am indebted to Professor James B. Torrance for introducing me to this concept during his lectures in Christology given at the University of Aberdeen as part of his course on Dogmatics given in the Spring of 1989.

was the priority of asking the question "Who?" instead of "How?".[480] Whichever question is selected, as the beginning of one's theology, the resulting dogmatics are significantly affected. To begin with the "Who?" question produces a focus on a relationship. To begin with the "What?" question produces a focus on problem-solving.[481]

When this selection scheme is applied to the realm of theology, it reveals what is central to one's dogmatics. If the emphasis is on "Who?", then Christology is at the core of one's dogmatics. However, if the emphasis is on "What?" or "How?", then Soteriology or Anthropology is at the core of one's dogmatics. Essentially, the logical sequence of Christianity in life should be to first know who Christ is then to respond to that knowledge. Instead of concentrating on nurturing the relationship shared with the person of Christ (Christology), the concern of man

---

[480] For a more detailed discussion see Dietrich Bonhoeffer, Christ the Center, trans. Edwin H. Robertson (San Francisco: Harper & Row, Pub., 1978), 27-37.

[481] To discover a proper Christology, one can begin by asking "What is there to know about Christ?" However, this leads to the next logical inquiry of "How can that be possible?" or "How does that relate to me?" Bonhoeffer rejects this beginning point for it will logically dictate where Christ fits into the world. Instead, the proper starting point in a New Testament Christology is the question "Who?" Bonhoeffer explains, "The question `Who?' is the question of transcendence. The question `How?' is the question of immanence. Because the one who is questioned here is the Son, the immanent question cannot grasp him. Not, `How are you possible?' . . . but `Who are you?' The question `Who?' expresses the strangeness and otherness of the encounter and at the same time reveals itself as the question of the very existence of the enquirer himself . . . . In theological terms: man only knows who he is in the light of God." Dietrich Bonhoeffer, Christology (London: Collins, 1966), 30,31.

(soteriology and anthropology) is to solve his problems in the most effective and efficient manner possible.[482]

If anthropology dominates one's dogmatics, then the person of Christ is no longer in the central place. Man usurps this place by default as theologians concentrate on solving man's problems. Christians should be dwelling on who Jesus is. Instead, the church has skewed view. It is distracted. Energies instead focus on how to relieve man's guilt, how to satisfy the mandates of the law, and how to resolve the problem of sin. Man concentrates on how to acquire the benefits of Christ rather than on enjoying Christ for His own sake.

## Apperceptions of the Western Culture

The important question to ask is this: Why does theology slip into a focus on anthropology? In great part, the answer to this question comes from a realization that the Western world is preoccupied with solving problems. Thinkers that developed the American philosophy of pragmatism, Pierce, James, and Dewey have left a lasting impact on Western tendencies. According to the direction given by their reasoning, all things are interpreted by a "means and ends" perspective. The "How?" question pervades every area of consideration. How to solve problems in the most

---

[482] Bonhoeffer, Christ the Center, 37-39.

efficient and effective manner is the conspicuous characteristic of Western pragmatism.[483]

John Macmurray describes a three-fold world view that characterizes the dominate ways that life is seen: apperceptions of life. By apperception he means the different ways of interpreting the same perceived view of the world. Macmurray suggests three apperceptions that flavor a world view. They are an aesthetic, a pragmatic, and a religious apperception. For example, three people could be looking at a tall oak tree and come to three very different conclusions about their observations. One could see the beauty of the tree. He could imagine its growth over the years and the history that has past by it. The strength of its trunk, the breadth of its branches and the countless acorns that shower on to the ground amaze him. Yet, another could see that same tree and conclude that it would be the ideal tree for a room full of oak furniture. He thinks of bringing out a chain saw and cutting it down, trimming the branches and milling the wood into useful shapes and sizes to build a chest of drawers, a dining room table with matching chairs, a china hutch, a serving table, and a roll-top desk. A third could marvel at the evidence of a Creative God. By a single act (ex nihilo) the life of a grand tree

---

[483] A "means and ends" perspective is not to be completely jettisoned. It is an orderly method of functioning productively in the world. However, as Macmurray suggests, it is far more than an objective analysis: "We need wisdom in the selection of ends, so that we do not aim at the wrong things; and we need knowledge in the use of the means at our disposal to enable us to act efficiently in the pursuit of our ends." (John Macmurray, Religion, Art, and Science [Liverpool: University Press, 1961], 45.)

could be called into being.  All three individuals have the same tree in perception but they have very different apperceptions of that tree.  One is aesthetically appreciative of it, another is functionally oriented, and yet a third is religiously awed.  It is not likely that any apperception is exclusively one or the other of these possibilities.  But, for most individuals in the Western world there is a dominant one.[484]

First, Macmurray describes what he calls the aesthetic apperception.[485]  This is described as the contemplative form of viewing the world.  It was dominant in the Hellenic or Greek culture.  Its emphasis flowered in the realm of music and mathematics.  Whatever was beautiful, true, and good were its focus.  Platonic[486] thought pervaded this kind of idea.  This perspective fit in well with a religious system of values for God became the ultimate object of contemplation.  And as seen in later medieval life, via contemplation, the life of Christ was to be imitated by all Christians.

---

[484] Also, there is no effort at this point to value what is necessarily good or bad about any of these.  For all three have important value.  However, when a particular bent influences an individual or society, then, there can be consequences that may not be beneficial particularly in a theological context.

[485] Macmurray also refers to this as the "artistic attitude."  This perspective of common experience " . . . organizes data of experience in terms of their beauty." (John Macmurray, The Structure of Religious Experience, reprint [Archon Books, 1971], 11-12.)

[486] For example, Plato believed that politicians should be motivated by the "good". All the world should be seen with eyes valuing beauty.  I am indebted to Professor J. B. Torrance for this concept.

Death was conveniently dealt with in the aesthetic apperception of life. Since the highest contemplation was God, then death was simply the freeing of the spirit from the body to fully enjoy the ultimate contemplation. Until that time bodily longings were to be denied. This kind of thinking was essentially establishing a false dualism. The body did not matter; only the soul did. The soul was in a bodily prison waiting for death to free it. When this kind of viewpoint is injected into one's ecclesiology, then there is an imbalanced affect. For example, liturgy is good, but if it is dominant then one's view of God is adversely affected.[487] A dualism that is contrary to the New Testament is produced.

Macmurray describes the next apperception as pragmatic[488] or scientific. It was dominant in the Latin or Roman culture. There was a primary focus on "use". The concept of "means and ends" was the basis for accomplishment, productivity, and purpose.[489] Stoic philosophy was behind

---

[487] I am grateful to Professor J. B. Torrance for several personal discussions leading to this analysis of this aesthetic apperceptions.

[488] Bloesch explains, "The pragmatic theory . . . says that truth is a matter of fulfilling genuinely human needs and solving the perplexing problems in life." Truth is relative to meeting man's needs. Trial and error allows man to find what satisfies him and hence, truth. (Donald Bloesch, The Ground of Certainty: Toward an Evangelical Theology of Revelation [Grand Rapids: Wm. B. Eerdmans Pub. Co., 1971], 132.)

[489] Macmurray points to an emphasis on "causal properties and general characteristics" to describe this apperception. Experience is valued according to its utility. (Macmurray, Religious Experience, 10.)

pragmatism. Everything was in flux; therefore, what was right was what was right for the individual involved. Meaning is linked with the way in which purpose is fulfilled. Anthropology, man and the meeting man's needs, is at the core of a pragmatic life.

Lastly, Macmurray describes the religious apperception.[490] This worldview was dominant in the Hebrew-Christian tradition. It was characterized by love and a deep sense of community. Individuals learned to love other people for their own sake. Their sense of community was very strong and at the center of their livelihood community is built on personal relationships. Society, according to Macmurray, was in need of a proper sense of community. And community was a gift of God. Community was at its very core a religious notion. Individuals in a community did not see each other as a means to an end.[491] Instead, community is an emphasis on relationships, a composite of persons. Hence, the unit is not the individual but community. Love prevails in community. No conditions are required to gain love.[492] No contract exists.

---

[490] For a further discussion of this see "The Religious Experience" in Macmurray, Religion, Art, and Science, 45-78.

[491] For example in the religious community women were not viewed just aesthetically or pragmatically. They were more than mere objects of beauty and they were far more than an economic consideration. Women were loved as a "person." (Ibid.)

[492] Marriage, for example, is a covenant of mutual giving and receiving.

## Pragmatism and the Local Church

The Stoics lived by reason. According to their values, nature became the basis of civil law. And it was law that gave guidance for life in a chaotic world. The passions of life were to be shunned. This was the value system adopted by the medieval church of the West. In Latin culture the medieval Roman church was where Christianity adapted itself to the pragmatism of the Latin Roman pragmatic mind. And it produced the terminology "means of grace."

When the focus of theology is on man's problems, then the issue of means and ends results. The consequence is that man becomes the starting point of one's theology. And the person of Jesus Christ is overshadowed by a system of thinking that is arbitrary rather than absolute.

Bloesch notes, "Pragmatism is probably the dominant philosophy in contemporary American culture. Not timeless truth but workable truth is the concern of most Americans. It is not the problem of the One and the Many but the problem of a better life for myself and my neighbor that occupies our attention. The criterion for truth is whether it serves the human enterprise, whether it has beneficial effects upon the human community."[493] The focus is on "end-justifies-means" and it has influenced the church. Advocates of this strategy begin with a problem. They

---

[493] Bloesch, Ground of Certainty, 133.

want to resolve the difficulty of stagnant and shrinking churches. How then, they ask, can the church overcome the problem of losing members? How then, they ask, can the church reach the world's 3 billion non-Christians with the Gospel in the most efficient way? What is the best means to see the grace of God applied to the world at large?

Two problems dominate this kind of thinking. First, there is a passion to fulfill the evangelistic mandate. Church leaders want to take the Gospel of Christ to every creature. This is the command of Christ. Few ministers or serious Christians would fail to list evangelism on their list of most important desires. But the task is massive to say the least. After nearly 2,000 years of attempting to fulfill the great commission, much of the world still does not profess Christ as Savior and Lord. Of the 5 billion people on the earth 3 billion are outside of the Church of Christ. Missionaries on the field of foreign lands are decreasing and the number of workers is in dangerous peril as the main body of current missionaries is reaching retirement age. Problems like this make church leaders scramble for a solution. Yet, the pressure of pragmatism is not just centered here. A second problem causes an increasing strain on seeking a solution. Churches in the Western world are shrinking. Membership roles are declining. How can those who faithfully minister under such conditions even think about reaching the world when all they can do is face the stress of dissolving their own church assembly?

194

When these frustrations plague the church, there is a struggle to find something that "works". Any idea that gives the appearance of "success" is quickly branded as valid. If the end of numerical growth can be assumed, then the means is automatically accepted as Biblical. Consequently, church leaders began to cater to the desires of the people. Every effort is made to give the people what they want in church. The assumption is that if the people who are wanted in the church are given what they want then surely they will come to church. In this context the McGavran idea fits comfortably: "Men like to become Christians without crossing racial, linguistic, or class barriers."[494]

Proponents of the HUP theory argue that their critics have never disproved McGavran's thesis statement. But, the validity of this statement is not the issue.[495] Rather, the issue is whether the statement is at all germane as to how the church ought to operate. It is not. Biblical theology directs the church to operate according to an ecclesiology that centers on who Christ is. The HUP theory can only exist when the church operates according to an ecclesiology that centers on what man wants.

---

[494] McGavran, Church Growth, reprint, 223.

[495] Padilla describes circumstances where Christians could possibly insulate disobedient attitudes of racism, materialism or animosity. They could too easily justify their hidden agendas behind a statement of their "likes" but Padilla responds, " . . . what does that have to do with the gospel concerning Jesus Christ, who came to reconcile us `to God in one body through the cross'?" (Padilla, "Unity," 301.)

## *Civil Religion Is A Theological Contradiction Not An Ecclesiastical Solution*

Another topic of discussion that will guide church development and mutual acceptance is civil religion. This dualism has historically distinguished the matter of nature and grace as it applies to the problems of race. Viewing nature, it has been philosophized that God by nature has assigned people to different races and positions in life. Those divinely appointed positions are to be accepted as God's gracious dealings with mankind. This type of reasoning has invited some to justify racist policies and procedures in some of the world's most Christianized areas.[496]

---

[496] I am indebted to Andrew Konig, Professor of Theology at the University of South Africa for these ideas derived from his lecture, "Why Apartheid is Wrong", delivered at Aberdeen University on 4 November 1988. He made three points of special interest: (1) The government of South Africa is Christian. (2) 77% of the population belong to the church (3) The DRC justified Apartheid. It should be noted that several branches of the DRC would take a similar position. (For a further discussion see W. A. Saayman, "The Case of South Africa: Practice, Context, and Ideology," in Exploring Church Growth, 132-143, edited by Wilbert R. Shenk [Grand Rapids: Wm. B. Eerdmans Pub. Co., 1983]. He identifies two smaller Afrikaans Reformed Churches that also support varying forms of racially separated churches.)

A dualistic theology generates an atmosphere of compromise and conflict. It falsely orders theology at the expense of the Gospel's intent to restore the universal dignity of everyone who responds to its message of grace. An understanding of these three tensions can lead to a correction of the church's theological focus and move it back on track to the practical benefits of the Christian faith, one being racial equality or even more practically, a church that shows no favoritism, a church where anyone is welcome to fellowship because they "feel comfortable" with other Christians whose lives center around the person of Christ.

## Civil Religion Defined

When theology is formulated it requires a place of application not just with individuals but also with groups of people, even entire nations. One historic feature that stands in the way of the issues of true humanity demonstrated by Jesus Christ is the predominance of Civil Religion. This phenomenon of Civil Religion is predominant in the hotbeds of racial and religious unrest today as well as in the past. South Africa's Apartheid policy is a product of Civil Religion. Violence in Northern Ireland is also an example of Civil Religion. Historically, the Nazi oppression of the Jew had its influence stirred by elements of Germany's 1930's Civil Religion. And, of course, the racial tensions in the United States are linked to Civil Religion.[497] This also occurred both during the Civil War over the issue of the rights of slaves and during World War II over the rights of American Japanese. This strange blend of civil law and religious faith must be addressed by a plan which renovates the church's growth philosophy.

A definition of Civil Religion is in order. On the simplest level it is a union between the factors of human government with the precepts accepted by those same people regarding their faith.[498] There are several key factors that relate to the problem of

---

[497] I am grateful to James Torrance for these helpful illustrations.

[498] Moodie elaborates, " . . . [Civil Religion] denotes the religious dimension of the state. As such, it is invariably associated with the exercise of power and with the

Civil Religion. One is the presence of wielding power by a few over the many. This preoccupation of controlling others makes it extremely difficult for theology to correct the situation for power over one's fellow is foreign to the New Testament ideal. Secondly, there is a strong emphasis on the religious aspect to condone or justify the strong hand of the government. Injustice is too often excused by hiding behind an imagined divine scheme of approval.

Civil Religion is generally a blend of three volatile ingredients. First, there is politics or nationalism[499], right or wrong. People are in need of some system of legislation to govern their interaction and a method to enforce the statutes that they formulate. Second, there is an exclusive romantic loyalty to race or nation or class or color. Passion runs high with this element. The exclusiveness is at times a blind loyalty that automatically discriminates against outside intrusion, interpreting

---

constant regeneration of a social order; it provides a transcendent referent for sovereignty within a given territory. The ultimate nature and destiny of political power is thus connoted in the symbols of the civil faith and re-enacted by civil ritual. The origins, the extent and limits, and the final purpose of political sovereignty are all thereby set within the context of ultimate meaning; aspirations to sovereign power and the exercise of sovereignty are given transcendent justification." T. Dunbar Moodie, The Rise of Afrikanerdom: Power, Apartheid, and the Afrikaner Civil Religion (Berkeley: University of California Press, 1975), 296.

[499] Moltmann describes the volatile nature of this dynamic influencing the church: "Nationalism is one of the worst seductions of the people. It is an instrument of the domination of the people with which one people can be incited against another people. It is evil to 'divide and conquer', to play with human anxiety about starvation and with the aggression to which it gives rise." (Moltmann, Open Church, 100-101.)

any disagreement as a threat or interference. Third, there is religion. This is the feature that gives justification to loyalty and the deeds necessary to protect one's race, nation, class or color. If God can somehow be explained as the central figure behind one's biases, then there is a blanket approval of one's deeds, even deeds of violence.[500]

## Two Common Means of Dealing with the Problem

Both civil law and religious faith are important ingredients. Some solution to their relationship must be suggested. Three possibilities may be explored. First, there is Piety. This is a separation of church and state based on the generality of issues. A solution like this assigns the church to deal only with the Gospel. It is admonished to stay out of politics altogether. Social issues as poverty, injustice, unemployment, and racism are left to the state. A pietist solution to the problem of a church and state relationship is exemplified in the Southern Presbyterian Church in the United States during the Civil War. According to them the issue of slavery was an issue for the state to handle not the church.[501]

---

[500] I am grateful to James Torrance for this idea.

[501] For a further discussion see J. D. Douglas, editor, The New International Dictionary of the Christian Church (Grand Rapids: Zondervan Pub. House, 1976), s.v. "Pietism," by Robert Clouse. Also, see Earle Cairns, Christianity Through the Centuries, revised (Grand Rapids: Zondervan Pub. House, 1967), 412-414.

A second possible solution is Erastianism. In this system the state has a certain measure of control over the church. Both coexist in harmony by appearance but the state ultimately determines the course of the nation. For example, in South Africa, during the term of B. John Vorster as Prime Minister, the Dutch Reformed Church issued a statement decrying the policy of Apartheid. Vorster ordered the Dutch Reformed Church to withdraw its statement. And the church obeyed. This Erastian solution is a false synthesis between the church and the state. It cannot be a satisfactory solution for it divorces evangelism from humanization.[502] The headship of Christ cannot be limited to the church for He is head over all.[503]

## Priority of Grace Over Law

A third and more acceptable solution to the problem of Civil Religion is a perspective that properly prioritizes grace over law. The order of grace in relationship to law is crucial. If law is given priority over grace then grace becomes subordinate to it. When Calvin first wrote his Institutes in 1536[504], he followed the

---

[502] I am indebted to Professor J. B. Torrance for this idea and illustration.

[503] 1 Cor. 11:3. For a discussion see David Lowery, "1 Corinthians," in The Bible Knowledge Commentary, New Testament edition, ed. John Walvoord and Roy Zuck (Wheaton: Victor Books, 1983), 528.

[504] James B. Torrance, "The Incarnation and `Limited Atonement,' in The Evangelical Quarterly, 55, no. 2 (April, 1983), 89.

200

order of law first, then grace. However, he inverted this pattern when he clearly saw the priority of grace in the New Testament.[505]

When law is given first priority instead of grace, the practical consequences of the resulting theology are immense. The most notable result of this scheme is the development of separation among races based upon an argument from nature. By the observed laws of nature God has made some white, some black, some Asian, and some Hispanic. The civil government can legitimately exercise segregation as it acknowledges this. Then, grace which according to this view is subsequent to the laws of nature comes to perfect what is already existing. Hence, since God has according to natural law made some black and some white, then there is every reason to believe that separate churches based on color is proper. The church, then, derives its structure from natural law.

There are at least two possible ways to critique this line of reasoning. First, if the approach of the critique is made from the Federal Theology viewpoint, then a challenge is made from the standpoint of natural law. It is argued that God by nature has made all men equal. By the laws of nature all men have the right of life, liberty, and the pursuit of happiness as demonstrated in the American Constitution and Bill of Rights. Yet, when this fact is

---

[505] J. B. Torrance observes, "For Calvin, all God's dealings with men are those of grace, both in Creation and in Redemption." (James B. Torrance, "Covenant or Contract?" in Scottish Journal of Theology, 23, no. 1 (Feb. 1970), 62.

given due consideration, those who argue for segregation based upon natural law are left entrenched in their position because there is merely a difference of opinion on how natural law can be interpreted. For each, the beginning point of their discussion is based on the same principle.

A second alternative may prove to be more effective in countering the racial tension seen in the church. This perspective acknowledges that Jesus Christ is both Creator and Redeemer. Jesus was not merely the Redeemer but He was the Creator as well. It was the Triune God who created Adam. And what was lost in Adam was restored in Christ in whom there is no distinction between Jew or Greek, male or female, black or white. Since there is only one church in Christ; and since that in Christ there is no difference among men, then, there is no basis for separate churches for different races or ethnic groups.[506] The basic precepts of justifying racial separation in the church echo throughout the discussion of Civil Religion. And the problems that arise when elevating natural law above the traditional reformed emphasis on grace are problems intertwined in the application of any type of separation theory. Since much of the McGavran school fundamentals are based on what is observed in nature and

---

[506] Addressing this issue J. B. Torrance explains that God acted out of love both as creator and redeemer: "He is the triune God whose nature is love, and who is in creation . . . what he is in his innermost being, the God who reveals himself in covenant love in Christ, and who brings fulfillment in redemption his purposes in creation. The doctrine of the incarnation and the trinity are our Christian logical starting point." (J. B. Torrance, "The Incarnation," 92-93.)

what differences are noted as preferred by men, the church must formulate a strategy for growth that has a proper theological starting point, one that is true to a Biblical Theology. And, from a historical theological perspective, if the church were to examine its Reformed heritage and reaffirm its commitment to a priority of grace over law, then every Christian church would be as accepting of any Christian who came to be a member and deliberately make a universal appeal in its effort to reach out to its community without regard to race, language, or class.

## The Doctrine of the Image of God Requires Equality Among All Christians

Two doctrinal issues speak specifically to the issue of equality among all mankind. They are the fact that man is created in the image of God and that all of mankind share a universal humanity regardless of race or ethnicity. This equality is shared among all humans in their pre-converted state and continues to dictate the kind of relationship that all mankind must continue to enjoy after conversion. It is especially indicative of the church to visibly portray their humanity as those created in the image of God.

## The Meaning of the Image of God

Genesis 1:26-27 teaches that God created man in His image and according to his likeness. This mysterious image and likeness eludes exact analysis since so little about it is specifically revealed in the Scriptures. However, several observations about the image and likeness are clear. First, the image is transferred from generation to generation, beginning with Adam to his offspring and so on. Thus, all humans have it.[507] Second, the image is of great importance since the murder of a man and the subsequent violation to that image is subject to capital punishment.[508] Third, the issue of headship and the image are closely linked.[509] Fourth, Paul correlates the new man with the image.[510] And fifth, the image is put in partnership with the concept of proper speech.[511]

---

[507] Gen. 5:1, 3. For a discussion see Derek Kidner, Genesis, An Introduction and Commentary (Downers Grove: Inter-Varsity Press, reprint 1972), 79-80; H. C. Leupold, Exposition of Genesis, Vol. 1, reprint (Grand Rapids: Baker Book House, 1972), 230-233.

[508] Gen. 9:6. Kidner, Genesis, 101; Leupold, Genesis, 333-335.

[509] 1 Cor. 11:7. For a discussion see Lowery, "1 Corinthians," 529.

[510] Col. 3:10. For a discussion see Norman Geisler, "Colossians," in The Bible Knowledge Commentary, New Testament edition, ed. John Walvoord and Roy Zuck (Wheaton: Victor Books, 1983), 681.

[511] Jas. 3:9. For a discussion see James Mayor, The Epistle of James, reprint (Minneapolis: Klock & Klock Christian Publishers, 1977), 121-123 and A. T. Robertson, Studies in the Epistle of James, revised and ed. by Heber Peacock (Nashville: Broadman Press), 120-121.

204

The terms for image and likeness both in Hebrew and Greek have been the target of discussion throughout church history. In an attempt to find some specific meaning to the image and likeness of God various concepts have been suggested.[512] The clearest and most faithful interpretation of the available texts may be to acknowledge that perhaps it is a blend of some sort of concrete and abstract representation of God in created man.[513] Erickson concludes that the image is reflected in man's ability to participate and enjoy relationships with God and one another. He concludes that the actual image is a set of qualities that makes these relationships possible.[514]

---

[512] Ryrie summarizes these efforts: "The Greek and Latin fathers distinguished between image and likeness, referring the former to the physical and the latter to the ethical part of God's image. Irenaeus understood the image to refer to man's freedom and reason and likeness to the gift of supernatural communion with God which was lost in the Fall. But such distinctions cannot be substantiated on the basis of the words. Note also that the prepositions are used interchangeably in Genesis 1:26-27 and 5:1-3." Ryrie, Theology, 190.

[513] Ibid.

[514] Erickson explains: "The image itself is that set of qualities that are required for these relationships and this function to take place." Sometimes referred to as communicable attributes, these features (note this is plural not singular) " . . . constitutes personality or selfhood: intelligence, will, emotions." It is this quality in man that enables him to commune with his fellow man and God. (Millard J. Erickson, Christian Theology [Grand Rapids: Baker Book House, 1983], 514.)

## Implications from the Image of God Doctrine

In considering the Biblical and Theological primacy of equality among Christians in the church, the implications of the doctrine of the image of God are significant.  It is closely connected to the practical operation of progressive sanctification.  For a Christian can accept another Christian who is in the image of God, a person he may have once despised because of racial or ethnic differences.  First, the image of God indicates that all people belong to God.  In fact, all humans are related to each other and to God by this image.  And, it is because of the image of God that all humans are equal in value to God and also share an equal responsibility to him.  Their equal standing before God gives all of mankind an equality with each other as interrelated beings.  It can also be argued that if God had intended each nation or group of people to be separate from each other in their churches, then God would have had a multiple of Spirit outpourings.  But there was only one coming of the Spirit.  This single outpouring of the Spirit is indicative of the unity that is intended by God for the church.[515]  If an ecclesiastical policy divides and gives a basis for the operation of inequality, then it cannot be acceptable.  The church must express a theology in her activities that display mutual acceptance, an unbiased equality,

---

[515] I am indebted to Professor Andrew Konig for the thoughts on this topic.

206

and the same kind of unity demonstrated at the outpouring of the Spirit.

Second, the practical outworking of the image of God in Christians is to be patterned after the Lord Jesus Christ, Himself. He is the complete revelation of that image.[516] And it is this same Jesus who left the example of love in the form of a mandate, "Love one another as I have loved you for by this all men will know that you are my disciples."[517] Part of the responsibility that comes from having the image of God is treating other human beings with equality.[518]

Third, man was created in the image of God, a condition that was deeply affected by man's sin. The glory of this original state will not ever be fully realized until man is fully perfected in the presence of God. However, the restoration of the fullness of humanity is begun with a rebirth into a faith relationship with God in this life. It is only with this restored relationship with God that a

---

[516] Erickson notes, "He [Jesus Christ] is the full image of God, and he is the one person whose humanity was never spoiled by sinning (Heb. 4:5). If we wish to know the outworking of the image of God, we can see it in Jesus." Erickson, Christian Theology, 515.

[517] Jn. 13:34,35. For a discussion see Edwin Blum, "John," in The Bible Knowledge Commentary, New Testament edition, ed. John Walvoord and Roy Zuck (Wheaton: Victor Books, 1983), 321-322.

[518] I am indebted to Andrew Konig for pointing out that one of the features that is characteristic of Apartheid is its preoccupation with self-love. It is chiefly concerned with its "own group". This flawed choice means that participants never get around to loving other groups.

person's true humanity can be experienced.[519]   Hence, the Christian endeavor must carry out its mission to evangelize the world, giving all men of every race and ethnic group not only the Good News of eternal life but hope in the fullness of their humanity in Christ shared equally among all Christians.

Fourth, every human is valuable to God.  God forbade murder after the fall.[520]  He did this because every human being possesses the image of God, even those who have not been redeemed.  Thus, it is imperative that violence which results in the murder of one's fellow man never be committed in the name of God.  Racial bigotry and ethnic pride too often lead to this violent conclusion.  Such injustices are condemnable when seen in the light of the doctrine of the image of God.

Fifth, the image of God is a fact for all of mankind. Everyone shares in this common reality of the imprint of the creator in their life.  This single common denominator is greater than the many and varied differences that are present in culture, language, or class.[521]  Segregation based upon race, ethnicity, or

---

[519] Erickson notes, "We experience full humanity only when we are properly related to God.  No matter how cultured and genteel, no one is fully human unless he is a redeemed disciple of God.  This is man's teleos, that for which he was created." Erickson, Christian Theology, 515-516.

[520] Gen. 9:6.

[521] Erickson elaborates on the practical implication of this issue: "Because all are in the image of God, nothing should be done which would encroach upon another's legitimate exercise of dominion." (Erickson, Christian Theology, 517.) The exception to this absolute that Erickson notes is a forfeiture due to personal abuse.  This

208

class will forever violate other human beings created in the image of God from exercising their right to dominion. The extreme of an overt demonstration of limitations backed by force or the subtle prejudices that are socially polite are equally contrary to what God has intended.

## Equal Humanity for All of Mankind

While it is Biblically and Theologically certain that all of mankind shares equally in the image of God and therefore, enjoys equal value before God and one another, there are the obvious differences in appearance of various races and ethnic groups.[522] Through church history there have been periodic attempts to support bizarre notions that some human groups are inferior by God's design. One of the more common efforts has been to put some sort of imagined significance on the account in Genesis 4 claiming that the curse on Canaan is reflected in the dark skin of

---

includes murderers, thieves, traitors, et cetera. Several implications are noted. One is that slavery is not acceptable. Also, any illegal means such as manipulation or intimidation are unacceptable. "Everyone has a right to exercise dominion, a right which ends only at the point of encroaching upon another's right to exercise dominion." (Ibid.)

[522] The Bible is especially instructive of the positive way that God deals with various human groups in the Jewish-Gentile relationships. Erickson elaborates that it may be concluded that divine interests in human activity is limited to Israel since she receives a unique status as God's chosen people. "Yet it is apparent that the Jews were chosen not to be exclusive recipients of the blessing of God, but rather to be recipients and transmitters of that blessing." (Erickson, Christian Theology, 543.)

certain human groups. This unfounded and imaginative argument is better dismantled in other excellent works and is not fully germane to this thesis.

In the less extreme forms of racial prejudice the aim is identical with the excessive forms, namely, they have a " . . . tendency to attribute a lesser human status to the out group."[523] No Biblical evidence exists to support the notion that any human group is inferior or less human than others. In fact, the Bible is significantly positive about the equal treatment of all ethnic groups regardless of cultural identity.[524]

## *Suggested Theological Redirection*

The problems race relations in the church are linked in part to inconsistent applications of traditionally orthodox Biblical principles and Theological patterns. On the one hand, the themes of Biblical thought advocate equality among all who come to Christ. On the other hand, in the development of church policy

---

[523] Erickson, Christian Theology, 543.

[524] Erickson summarizes this point. He notes that the "image of God" in which man has been made is a vast topic with unique implications. It distinguishes man from the rest of creation and is universal among all men. This common "mark" means that all people are equal before God. "The distinctions of race, social status, and sex are of no significance to him (Gal.3:28). Salvation, eternal life, and fellowship with God are available to all persons. And because this is the case, those who are believers should show the same impartial interest in and concern for all humans, regardless of the incidentals of their lives (James 2:9)." (Erickson, Christian Theology, 558.)

and mission philosophy, there is an all-to-frequent separation of race among churches. And nearly as frequent, such separation is justified as a kind of realistic theology. An acknowledgment of the theoretical ideal is given mention, but, it is too often dismissed as something that is "beyond-this-world". This inconsistency between theological principles and pragmatic results requires a review of the church's theological starting point and the subsequent application for the church, especially with regard to the issue of race.

## A Trinitarian View of God and Christ at the Center of Theology

An initial suggestion that could prove helpful to the dilemma of an ecclesiastical tradition that is inconsistent with theological principles is that the church should consider returning to an emphasis on Christology as the center of its theology. As in its historical roots, a proper starting point with Christ allows for all men to stand equal before God and therefore with each other. When anthropology and man's salvation usurp that center, presumption has demonstrated itself to be the norm for man.

For instance, historically, Theology in America has justified separation of the races in worship. It has argued that one group is the preferred, the elect, the blessed. But when this is assumed, how are race relations interpreted? How are blacks and whites, Asian and Caucasian to relate with each other? By default these relationships are no longer interpreted Christologically but by natural law. Natural diversity as seen in different ethnic groups is an accepted emanation from which God now works. Grace does not operate in a mode that will destroy nature but only enhances or perfects it.[525]

In the history of the United States of America, the Civil War, which occurred in 1859-1861, can be analyzed from an ecclesiastical perspective. It was as much a disagreement of theological interpretation as it was a war between the States from ideological or economic reasons. Calvinists were at war against Calvinists. Their point of contrast was different views of natural law. Those in the North believed that God by nature decreed that all men are created equal with the inalienable rights for the pursuit of happiness. Both blacks and whites were equal under God[526]. But those in the South, Dabney, Thornwell, Palmer, responded with a resounding "No!"[527] According to their thinking, God not

---

[525] Torrance develops this concept of grace presupposing nature in his evaluation of Federal Theology. He notes that the assumed separation between Nature and Grace is a " . . . reversion to the pre-Reformation medieval view that . . . *grace perfects nature*." (Torrance, "Covenant or Contract?" 67.) He further notes that the implications of this thinking is a clear departure from the Reformation emphasis that there was nothing logically in advance of grace. (Ibid.)

[526] I am referring to institutionalized attitudes here. I acknowledge that anti-black feelings were present in the North.

[527] For a further discussion of this historical evaluation see E. T. Thompson, The Spirituality of the Church (Richmond: John Knox Press, 1961.)

only made different ethnic groups, but He also made some masters and some servants.[528] Their use of slavery was accepted as consistent with the will of God because they were simply living their life according to the laws of nature that they observed. Hence by appealing to the concept of natural law and orders of creation they found Biblical theological justification for separation based on race and class.

This illustration from history demonstrates the consequences of interpreting Creation non-Christologically. And the reasoning that "Christians" have used to justify Apartheid and slavery in the United States are similar.[529] And the clear danger is that the HUP theory is attempting to introduce itself in this historical context that has been deeply wounded by racial unrest and for which the church is guilty of joint complicity. The theological misapplication of the past and the danger of aligning

---

[528] Torrance explains the reasoning of such theology which maintains that the law of nature is the basis for arranging both social and State practices. And if the law of nature is violated, then there is cause for divine judgment. Flowing from this position are types of justification for racial discrimination and segregation in the church. Torrance elaborates how this kind of theology operates: "God has made men by nature black and white. Grace does not destroy nature but conforms to nature, and so justification has been sought for the fact that black and white Christians should worship apart." (Torrance, "Covenant or Contract?" 67.)

[529] Part of Americana that highlights itself throughout the history of measuring the relationship between the church and the State is the doctrine of the separation imposed between these two institutions. Torrance notes, " . . . a doctrine of separation of nature and grace has been the ground of certain doctrines of `the spirituality of the Church' where it has been argued the Church is concerned with spiritual matters like the preaching of the Gospel but civil matters like civil rights and race relations should be left to the State." (Torrance, "Covenant or Contract?" 67-68.)

the church with another justification for racial preference are sufficient to call for a new direction in the church. Based on the clear Biblical principle of oneness elaborated in Ephesians 2 and the mistake of the church's past, the church should take clear steps to acknowledge past misdeeds and deliberately perpetuate a priority in the church that follows a full and equal acceptance philosophy of all men regardless of race, language or class.

In order to move away from racial injustice and restore a theological integrity that the churches can confidently put into use, church leaders should place Christology back at the center of its doctrine. This particular choice of emphasizing Christ as the center of Theology abandons the historical dualism of grace versus nature. Of the two possible schemes of beginning with the "Who?" question or the "How?" question it is the first that takes precedence. Then, the matter of acting on observed difference will be challenged and abandoned. Instead, as Christ accepted all, then those in the church accept all.

If, however, man's problems and the search for their solutions dominate, then man will make his theology adapt to his quest. What will result will be a theology that becomes a product of seeking a pragmatic solution to difficulties. Theology erodes into a whatever-works system. Christians then develop a mind-set that results in valuing something only when a solution or benefit for man is produced. The person and work of Jesus Christ is seen as a problem-solver of human problems. An inappropriate

214

placement of "sin and need" at the beginning of one's theology produces a "means and end" basis of reasoning. Thus, in the Western Ordo Salutis grace is presented as a solution to man's problems.[530]

There is a danger in such a scheme; namely, that there is far more interest in the blessings of Christ rather than in Christ Himself.[531] Knowing Christ is <u>not</u> just what is gained out of Him. Rather, men must enjoy Christ simply for who He is. It is a priority that theology recognizes that the indicatives of grace are prior to the imperatives of law.[532]

The practical dynamics of this perspective are seen in the Apostle Paul's life, at the time of his conversion and calling into the ministry. Saul of Tarsus was on a reign of terror against the

---

[530] This type of reasoning is parallel to the complications that Torrance describes as the consequences of limited atonement theology. While the emphasis of his discussion in that article vary slightly from the emphasis of this thesis, his observations are instructive. He notes that the loss of Christ's Headship over all creation is implied whenever man and his problems dominate. The solidarity that He has with all men due to the incarnation is lost. This solidarity is the core message of both Ephesians and Colossians and is substantiated by arguments of Irenaeus, Athanasius, the Cappadocians, Calvin, Boyd of Trochig. An interpretive bias is superimposed over whom Christ has a personal relationship and the sad consequence is that the incarnational oneness with Christ is replaced. For a further discussion see Torrance, "Covenant or Contract?" 68. This sense of a historical dualism in theology and its relationship to race relations in the church was reenforced during a personal interview with Professor Torrance in Aberdeen on November 1988.

[531] On this particular topic Professor Torrance made a helpful statement in a personal interview on November 1988 in Aberdeen: "We don't do theology just by dealing with cases."

[532] Torrance, "Covenant or Contract?" 69.

Christians.  He was on his way to Damascus to capture and imprison any followers of the Way.  He is confronted by the Resurrected Jesus Christ who asks him "Saul, Saul, why do you persecute me?"[533]  And the following question is instructive for all theologians to consider, "Who are you, Lord?"[534]  Jesus responds with "I am Jesus, whom you are persecuting."[535]  Then, Paul discovers that he is blind.  He is led in that state to a house in Damascus where the Lord sends Ananias to explain to Saul what Jesus Christ has done to reconcile both Jew and Gentile.  And Saul learns that he is called to be the apostle to the Gentiles. That was a culture shock as enormous as his new spiritual awakening.  Time was necessary for this matter to settle into Saul's own thinking.  Thus, he retreated into the desert to contemplate all that had transpired.[536]

The richness of the doctrine of the Trinity overflows into the practical benefit of the church.  Ryrie elaborates, "Fellowship

---

[533] Acts 9:4.  For a discussion see Bruce, Acts, 194-196 and Stott, Acts, 169-173.

[534] Acts 9:5.  For a further discussion see Bruce, Acts, 194-196; Stott, Acts, 169-173.

[535] Ibid.

[536] Donald K. Campbell, "Galatians," in The Bible Knowledge Commentary, New Testament edition, ed. John Walvoord and Roy Zuck (Wheaton: Victor Books, 1983), 589-590. Also, the author is grateful for an additional insight suggested by Professor Torrance during a personal interview in Aberdeen on November 1988. He suggests that the implication of this time of rethinking in the desert related to race relations, he was contemplating Christ and the reconciling work of Christ.  Christ was desegregating his heart and mind to set him free to be the apostle to the ethne.

and love within the Godhead is only possible in a Trinitarian concept of God, and that fellowship is akin to the believer's fellowship with Christ."[537] And as the Father and the Son share a loving fellowship with each other so that same loving fellowship is shared between God and each Christian. These two relationships then place the responsibility on each and every Christian to be as accepting and loving and forgiving of each other regardless of race, ethnicity, or culture.

## Anthropology Based upon a New Testament Christology

When man is confronted with the redeeming work of Jesus Christ and subsequently called to live out a life that reflects his redemption there is a responsibility to be as forgiving to others as Christ has been to man. Peter faced this enormous struggle when he asked Jesus how many times he was to forgive his brother who has sinned against him. To this Jesus told a parable of the unmerciful servant. He began with the typical formula for introducing a parable:

". . . the kingdom of heaven is like . . . . "[538] Then, the story begins. A king wanted to settle accounts with his servants. One

---

[537] Ryrie, Theology, 59.

[538] For a discussion of the phrase "kingdom of heaven" and "kingdom of God" see J. Dwight Pentecost, The Words and Works of Jesus Christ: A Study of the Life of Christ (Grand Rapids: Zondervan Pub. House, 1981).

of his servants owed him ten thousand talents, an equivalent of millions of dollars in our modern day. Unable to pay and threatened with imprisonment for both he and his family he threw himself on the mercy of his master who took pity, canceled the debt and set him free. Then, this servant who had been forgiven, went out and found a fellow servant who owed him a hundred denarii, or a few dollars by modern standards. Without mercy he demanded repayment. Unable to pay, his fellow servant begged for mercy. But he scorned those pleas and had him imprisoned. Other servants witnessed this act of wickedness and in great distress reported the incident to their master.[539] Then, the unforgettable admonition by the master who had forgiven his servant: "You wicked servant. I canceled all that debt of yours because you begged me to. Shouldn't you have had mercy on your fellow servant just as I had on you?"[540] Angry at his servant's lack of mercy, the master had him imprisoned and punished until he could pay back his debt. Then, Jesus exhorts his disciples, "This is how my heavenly Father will treat each of you unless you forgive your brother from your heart."[541] God

---

[539] Mt. 18:21-31. For a discussion see Arno Gaebelein, The Gospel of Matthew (Neptune, New Jersey: Loizeaux Brothers, reprint 1961), 390-392; John Walvoord, Matthew: Thy Kingdom Come (Chicago: Moody Press, 1974), 136-140.

[540] Mt. 18:32-33. For a discussion see Gaebelein, Matthew, 390-393; Walvoord, Matthew, 138-140.

[541] Mt. 18:35. For a discussion see Louis Barbieri, "Matthew," in The Bible Knowledge Commentary, ed. John Walvoord and Roy Zuck (Wheaton: Victor Books, 1983), 62-63.

through Christ has forgiven us of our sin and fully accepted us.[542]
But, some Christians have a difficult time fully accepting others
who are different racially or ethnically. These Christians need to
acknowledge that the differences that non-Christians have with
the living and holy God are far greater than one race has with a
different race. God forgave the greater, therefore, the
beneficiaries of that grace should forgive the lessor.[543]

Forgiveness is a key element in one's anthropology. For it
is the theological connection with Christology on a practical basis.
Thus, for an accurate anthropology to be formulated there is a
need for a rethinking of the relationship between repentance and
forgiveness. According to Calvin, forgiveness is logically prior to
repentance. And both faith and repentance are our response to
grace not conditions for it. Repentance itself literally means to
have a change of heart and mind. Some object to this exclusion
of any conditional idea pointing to John's epistle, "If we confess
our sins, he is faithful and just and will forgive us our sins and

---

[542] Barbieri notes the significance of this lesson: "The Lord was teaching that forgiveness ought to be in direct proportion to the amount forgiven." (Barbieri, "Matthew," 62-63.) That is, when a Christian, who enjoys complete forgiveness of personal sin by God, ought to in turn forgive a fellow Christian who sins against him no matter how many times that sin is committed or repeated.

[543] Hoehner notes that this principle is made clear in Ephesians 4:32. There he explains that all Christians are to manifest three important qualities: kindness, compassion and forgiveness. The basis for this manifestation is that God has already been kind, compassionate, and forgiving to every Christian. (Hoehner, "Ephesians," 637.

purify us from all unrighteousness."[544]  And Paul's epistle to the Romans: "That if you confess with your mouth, `Jesus is Lord,' and believe in your heart that God raised him from the dead, you will be saved."[545]  However, the reformers disclaimed that these were conditions for salvation.  Instead, they acknowledged that in any relationships with humans that there was always some structure involved.  The "if" in these cases then was explained as descriptive not prescriptive.  That is, these passages describe the consequences of grace, namely, faith, repentance and confession.  To claim that these conditions are prescriptive, that is, prior to conversion, then, Rome was right and the Trinitarian reformers were wrong.[546]

This leads to the question of what then, from a proper Trinitarian view, is involved in the conversion of people?  Certainly, the answer to this begins with a clear distinction, namely, that the law never converts but the word of grace does.  Just as God has so freely and unconditionally loved us and

---

[544]  1 Jn. 1:9.  For a discussion see Zane Hodges, "1 John," in The Bible Knowledge Commentary, New Testament edition, ed. by John Walvoord and Roy Zuck (Wheaton: Victor Books, 1981), 885-886.

[545]  Rom. 10:9.  For a discussion see John Witmer, "Romans," in The Bible Knowledge Commentary, New Testament edition, ed. John Walvoord and Roy Zuck (Wheaton: Victor Books, 1981), 481.

[546]  For a further discussion see Torrance, "Campbell."  Torrance describes Campbell's perspective: " . . . faith and repentance and prayer are not conditions of grace, but the gift of the Spirit of sonship who so unites us with Christ in his communion with the Father that we might have grounds for rejoicing in God." (Ibid., 310.)

forgiven us so we are freely and unconditionally called to forgive one another in the same manner as we have been forgiven. A number of New Testament texts illustrate this perspective: "Accept one another, then, just as Christ accepted you"[547] Notice that the indicatives of grace are prior to the imperatives. Also, Paul exhorted, "Husbands, love your wives, just as Christ loved the church and gave himself up for her . . . "[548] Then again: "Forgive as the Lord forgave you."[549] Also, John instructs: "This is love: not that we loved God, but that he loved us and sent his Son as an atoning sacrifice for our sins. Dear friends, since God so loved us, we also ought to love one another."[550] And finally, Paul clearly indicates that it is "by grace"[551] that man has been saved. As a result of this factual indicative as well as the dividing wall of hostility between all men being broken down, then, Christians are to live in harmony and peace with one another. For Christ's explicit purpose in His grace was " . . . to create in

---

[547] Rom. 15:7. For a discussion see Hodge, Romans, 434-435; Murray, Romans, 203-204; Witmer, "Romans," 495.

[548] Eph. 5:25. For a discussion see Bruce, Ephesians, 115; Hoehner, "Ephesians," 641.

[549] Col. 3:13. For a discussion see Geisler, "Colossians," 682.

[550] 1 Jn. 4:7-11. For a discussion see Robert Candlish, First Epistle of John (Grand Rapids: Kregel Pub., 1979), 377-402; Hodges, "1 John," 898-899.

[551] Eph. 2:8-10. For a discussion see Bruce, Ephesians, 51-52; Hoehner, "Ephesians," 624-625.

himself one new man out of the two, thus making peace, and in this one body to reconcile both of them to God through the cross by which he put to death their hostility."[552]  On this basis then, to know who Christ is, the one who broke down the barrier between Jew and Gentile, is to be summoned unconditionally to accept one another and forgive.[553]

What God has already accomplished precedes the habits of all Christians who follow after God in faith.  So, as God has loved us so we should love one another. As God has forgiven us, so we ought to forgive one another.[554]  For four hundred years the Protestant tradition has emphasized the vertical plane of sola gratia.  God accepts us by grace and we receive salvation by grace.  This great heritage needs to have the balance of human response to one another within the church as part of the grace dynamic.[555]

---

[552]  Eph. 2:15b-16. For a discussion see Hoehner, "Ephesians," 626; Moule, Ephesians, 80-81.

[553]  I am grateful to Professor Torrance for this concept of applying a theology with Christology at its center to the problem of racial tension in the church.

[554]  During a personal interview Professor Torrance applied his view of Trinitarian theology.  He suggested that the Christian Church is meant to proclaim the Gospel of grace not only by word of mouth but also to proclaim it by the way we live by being a loving, believing, and accepting community of the world.  I am indebted to him for this thought.

[555]  I am grateful to Professor Torrance for his ideas on applying a Christological theology to the racial tensions in the church.  He suggested that since God has broken down the barriers that divide all men from God and that He has broken down the barriers that divide Jew and Gentile and just as clearly made black and white into one body in Christ, therefore, it is one of the unconditional imperatives to make that

## Anthropology Based upon Christ's Headship

God does not abandon a filial relationship with man due to the Fall but fulfills it all in His Son. And yet it would be an error to conclude that the son is merely the redeemer, a second part of a tragedy that needed a happy ending. No, this Son is both the incarnated One and redeemer.[556] He is the beginning and the end not only of all existence but also the alpha and omega of mankind. The reason God made man like His Son is so that man could mature into the likeness of Him. It is in Jesus Christ at His Resurrection that all men regained their true humanity.

Two doctrines are essential to this concept of headship. First, all parts of our salvation are complete in Christ. Sonship is realized in all Christians through Christ. Second, participation in Christ is gained by a Christian's response through the Spirit; that is, the two matters of participation and headship are inseparable. Jesus Christ made us what we are to make us into what He is. Hence, the incarnation of Jesus Christ was done to bring man to glory. He took what was man's and gave him what was His.[557] As creator, Jesus formed man out of the dust of the ground and gave him the breath of life. As redeemer, all races can look at the

---

visible in our church life and in our structures. Deliberate racial segregation in the church is a vast of denial of this theological indicative.

[556] Torrance, "Incarnation," 86.

[557] I am grateful to Professor Torrance for this idea.

one man, Jesus, and find in Him forgiveness and rediscover their human dignity in Him.[558]

For those who maintain that race or ethnicity is a reason for separation, the theological notion that grace presupposes or perfects nature is frequently present. According to this perspective anthropology is based on natural law, observed facts and limits. Making a critique of this perspective can take at least two possible courses. First, it is possible to criticize the natural law interpretation which is reflected in the American Constitution. Individual rights, one can argue, are all equal. However, this particular tact is weak since it operates on an anthropological basis and results in merely a difference of opinion. The early Dutch Reformed Church just did not believe that God made all men equal but instead made some white and some black and some masters and some slaves. And the Calvinists in America fought the Civil War over their disagreement of natural law as it surfaced in the slavery issue.[559] This view has its merits but also its limitations.

---

[558] This perspective of Christ as both creator and redeemer is described by Torrance, "He is the One by whom and for whom all things were created who fulfills in the New Covenant his purposes in creating man." (Torrance, "Incarnation," 92.)

[559] Torrance expands the implications of this distinction made between nature and grace in the historical setting of America: " . . . the separation of nature and grace, lies behind the American radical separation of church and state, and has been the ground of certain doctrines of `the spirituality of the church' where the church is concerned with `spiritual' matters like the preaching of the gospel, but civil matters like civil rights and race relations should be left to the state . . . " (Torrance, "Incarnation," 89.)

A second view offers a more effective critique. Simply put, this view argues that if a Christian knows who Jesus Christ is, then, he must ask what God's purpose for all humans is. Why did God create man? If in Christ there is no difference between black or white, Asian or Caucasian, then God created all mankind to have unity in their diversity. This demonstration of unity in diversity is to be seen in church for sure but also in creation as well. Jesus Christ is the key. He has broken down the wall to make all men one so that all who respond to His work of grace can have equal access to the Father. No justification for racially separating Christians from one another can be made if Christ is viewed this way.

## Separation and Hostility

Theology must always pass the test of the practical if it is true to its nature as a study of God. That is, when theory is applied to the church the consequential effect on the Christians involved and the effect on the surrounding community the true Gospel of Christ is clearly proclaimed. Human history has revealed that man's preferences and biases have been shaped by a faithful theology. But, this same theology seems to be susceptible to shifts and bends according to new issues or political crises. People find it practical to adapt their convictions.

Whatever the causes for the dynamics of developing a

theology, one principle must remain true; namely, the final product must be faithful to the beginning. That is, God in His love and grace should also be manifested in the theology that results from man's study of the Almighty. In this regard there is a certainty that any theology that concludes with the use of force, violence, hostility or injustice has gone awry somewhere in the dynamic process of developing. Significantly, Christians throughout the generations have asked if violence is an option against religious injustice. Can those who are oppressed take up the sword in the name of their faith and be blessed by God for their deed?

The answer to this inquiry is intricately intertwined with the meaning of the doctrine of the incarnation. Here the focus is that the Son of God became the brother of all Christians. This new union was formed in order that we, men and women, might receive the Spirit of adoption, sharing and participating in that relationship. Jesus comes to draw all men and women, rich and poor, black and white, in order that all might participate in His knowledge of the Father, in His love of the Father, in His communion with the Father.[560]     At the heart of the relationship between the Father and the Son in which all Christians share is the concept of "covenant." J. B. Torrance defines this vital theological term: "Theologically speaking a covenant is a promise binding two people or two parties to love

---

[560] I am grateful to Professor Torrance for these ideas. For a further discussion see Torrance, "Covenant or Contract?"

one another *unconditionally*."[561]  This description is portrayed in the marriage relationship.  A man and woman make a covenant together to love each other unconditionally; that is, "for better or for worse."  "Indeed the marriage service enshrines the fact that all true love and all true forgiveness are in fact unconditional, and there is no such thing as conditional love or conditional forgiveness."[562]

And it was in the context of Federal Theology that the debate over the permissible use of violence in a religious issue was allowable.  In France there were the Huguenots.  In England there were the Puritans.   And in Scotland there were the Covenanters.  All were prepared to take up the sword in defense of religious liberty.  But they knew that they must do so lawfully.  And so they appealed to the notion of covenant.  They reasoned that when a King and the people enter a covenant it is under law.  Both are obligated to fulfill the contracts of that covenant.  That is what the law requires.  If either breaks the covenant, that was tantamount to acting as if they were above the law.  And that would be condemnable behavior and violence could be justified in such an instance.  Thus, covenant was based upon law.  And nobody is above the law.[563]

---

[561]  Torrance, "Covenant or Contract?" 54.

[562]  Ibid.

[563]  I am grateful to Professor Torrance for this insightful interpretation of church history, Christology, and human justification for rebellion based upon theology.

And it was from this twin notion of law and covenant that spawned two great insights. First, it was the consensus that for all human society the choice was "right not might." Justice was supreme. And second, human society must be based upon human consent not force.[564] Tyranny should be resisted. When a government uses might to impose without consent what it feels is right upon the people, then it was an injustice that could legitimately be fought.[565]

Whenever separation is based upon a racial distinction, hostilities accompany it. Whether it is the majority that forces the oppression as it is in the Southern United States or the minority as it is in Pretoria, the result is the same. A group is set apart as different and inevitably inferior. This group suffers injustices and a degrading of their human dignity. And even in the Christian context of the church this separation is perpetuated by the forces of social pressure or even assumed theology. But, the reality is that every human being has been created in the image of God and the certainty of the inconsistency is bound to generate friction. Jesus Christ has in fact broken down the barrier, the dividing wall. Therefore, as the oppressed walk in the Spirit and

---

[564] I am indebted to Professor Torrance for this perspective.

[565] That is why those who stand in a reformed tradition find it deeply disturbing that the policy of Apartheid is supported by the Dutch Reformed Church. According to the tradition of the Puritans and Covenanters, South Africa is oppressed by a tyrannical government. A minority controls the government and uses force to impose its will on the majority. I am grateful to Andrew Konig for this idea.

sense this error of separation based on human limitations the objections will naturally be raised. Hostilities will come as surely as the social order of man seeking his individual freedom and expression has demonstrated them throughout history.

## Evangelism Should Reflect a Christological Focus

The mission of the church is clear in the minds of most theological thinkers and church leaders as well as in the minds of the average church member. Jesus Christ gave the church an evangelistic mandate. "Therefore go and make disciples of all nations . . . ."[566] "Go into all the world and preach the good news to all creation."[567] "You are witnesses of these things."[568] "As the Father has sent me, I am sending you."[569] There is no doubt that the mission for the church is made clear by these words of our Lord. However, the debate ensues when any plan is presented

---

[566] Mt. 28:19a  For a discussion see Barbieri, "Matthew," 93-94; Gaebelein, Matthew, 621-624.

[567] Mk. 16:15  For a discussion see John Grassmick, "Mark," in The Bible Knowledge Commentary, ed. John Walvoord and Roy Zuck (Wheaton: Victor Books, 1983), 195; W. Graham Scroggie, The Gospel of Mark (Grand Rapids: Zondervan Pub. House, 1976), 282-283.

[568] Lk. 24:48  For a discussion see John Martin, "Luke," in The Bible Knowledge Commentary, ed. John Walvoord and Roy Zuck (Wheaton: Victor Books, 1983), 264 and Plummer, Luke, 563.

[569] Jn. 20:21b  For a discussion see Blum, "John," 343.

for the church to carry out its mission. For some the enormity of the task calls for immediate and intense action. Their interests is in results, namely, numbers that rival the astounding figure of 3 billion non-Christians in the world. According to their feelings, if the churches are declining or are stagnant, then the masses will not be converted to Christ. In this desperate situation the Church Growth philosophy is to find where the Gospel is openly received and to concentrate efforts there for immediate results. Results is first on their priority: "Today's supreme task is effective multiplication of churches in the receptive societies of earth."[570] Unfortunately, this emphasis forces the church to operate from a "means and ends" philosophy. And this perspective misrepresents the meaning of grace, the center of the Gospel message.

From an interpretive stand point, the Church Growth Movement builds its case on a use of *ethne* that is highly suspect. They follow a rigidly literal derivation of the term without due regard for its contextual use. McGavran elaborates in his explanation of Romans 16:25,26. Note his understanding of the term: "For exact rendering of the Greek words panta ta ethne, `all nations' should read `all peoples.' The apostle did not have in mind modern nation-states such as India or America. He had in mind families of mankind - tongues, tribes, castes, and lineages of

---

[570] McGavran, Church Growth, revised, 41.

men.  That is exactly what ta ethne means both here and in Matthew 28:19."[571]  When Christ gave the "Great Commission" to His disciples, He was using the term that meant for these followers of His, all Jews, to take the Good News to the Gentiles. Once thought of as unclean and nothing better than dogs, Jews who were followers of Christ, now had a commission to tell the whole world that Jesus Christ had broken down the dividing wall between Jew and Gentile (ethne). And that eternal peace and human dignity, as those created in the image of God, was for all mankind.  And Paul, the Jew of Jews, was called by Jesus to be the apostle to the ethne.  If there were ever a living illustration of the broken wall then it was Paul's apostleship to the Gentiles. This is the kind of evangelism that the New Testament advocates. Evangelism should be lives building relationships with others, sharing the love of Christ in visible form, across man-made barriers of race, class, and status.  It is supported by the church where these kinds of Christians gather for mutual encouragement and edification of their faith.

Too often the issue of culture is injected in the discussion of evangelism as a point of confusion.  Some argue that the practical problems of culture demand that the principles of evangelism be altered.  Others stick rigidly to their formulas and ignore the practical matters.  This kind of tug-o'-war again breeds

---

[571]  Ibid., 56.

a dualism that is not found in the New Testament. Instead, it should be acknowledged that God did indeed give culture but its dynamics in no way justify any theological or political justification for separation. It is also unnecessary to debate an issue of "evangelism and social justice" as if the two were mutually exclusive from one another. They are not. Christians are called upon to hold out Christ to the world and let the people of the world see their humanity.[572]

How, then, is the church to demonstrate this kind of Gospel to the world? It is done by example in conjunction with proclamation. The church must reflect who Christ is. There must, as is made clear in Romans 6, be a mortification of sin, a turning away from it. And this includes everything that segregates; anything that prevents Christ from achieving reconciliation must be removed by true repentance as well.[573] Coming to Christ must, therefore, also mean dying to racism. It means dying to all that prevents Christ's reconciling ministry.[574] This understanding, then, calls for an evangelism effort that is theologically

---

[572] I am grateful to Professor Torrance for this idea which he elaborated on during a personal interview on 22 February 1989.

[573] There is a direct link between repentance and sanctification in a similar way that faith is linked to justification. Repentance calls for a Christian to turn away from sin; it is a conscious act. This attitude and subsequent act always exists in conjunction with true faith. Berkhof notes: "The two are but different aspects of the same turning, - a turning away from sin in the direction of God." (Louis Berkhof, Systematic Theology [Grand Rapids: Wm. B. Eerdmans Pub. Co., 1939.], 486-487.)

[574] I am grateful to Professor Torrance for this valuable insight.

responsible. That is, when the Gospel is being heralded to the world and people are turning to Christ, the church must not separate the matters of evangelism and reconciliation. They belong together. It is incorrect to attempt Christian evangelism and hope at some later date to see reconciliation take place. Therefore, to be theologically correct, a new convert to Christianity must also confront any racist attitude and turn from it as a part of his conversion. Salvation and good works are inseparably linked.[575] A Christian goes on to do good works but not as a moral obligation. Rather, good works are done as part of one's new character in Christ. In other words, the response of the Christian to ward off racism is a reflection of the Christological mandate not an ethical one.[576]

When the two issues of culture and theology are brought up in discussion their end ought to be the same. However, too frequently, the final product is segregation. Essentially, the

---

[575] James 1:22-25. For a discussion see James Ropes, A Critical and Exegetical Commentary on the Epistle of St. James, The International Critical Commentary, ed. Alfred Plummer and Francis Brown (Edinburgh: T & T Clark, 1916.), 174-180 and Robertson, James, 67-71 and Mayor, James, 69-75.

[576] This crucial difference may at first appear to be a subtle distinction, but, it has ramifications that are far reaching. It is a difference whose effect is rooted in the federal scheme of theology. Here with a radical dichotomy made between nature and grace there is natural separation between natural law and the Gospel. Consequently, the relationship between the Church and the world is no longer understood Christologically but in terms of Gospel and natural law. Torrance notes: "This separation between nature and grace amounts to a reversion to the pre-Reformation medieval view that grace presupposes nature - grace perfects nature - a departure from the great emphasis of the Reformation that nothing is prior to grace." (Torrance, "Campbell," 300-301.)

church must face culture and adapt with it. But, this flexibility that is built into the church of the New Testament must be done so that both thinking and behavior are controlled by Christ.

## *Conclusion of Chapter III, Part 2*

To construct a theologically accurate alternative for the church regarding the issue of race it is helpful to stand back and look at the total picture of the church through history. This perspective helps to identify two important features. One is that the problems of racial unrest are not new but even older than the church. Also, there is a confusion that exists among church leaders regarding what God really intended when He created a variety of ethnic groups around the world. For deep within the church's theological tradition is a system of thinking that is linked with the confusion that allows for racial unrest. These roots must be addressed and a theological response that is true to the Gospel must be refashioned and allowed to direct the church's mission to herald that Gospel. The following directions in this theological formulation on a practical level for actual church development and interpersonal relationships may prove helpful.

First, any church strategy for growth must adequately emphasize the truths of sanctification. This doctrine calls for an immediate change in light of a new relationship with Christ. The

234

ethical change in a new Christian convert is an appropriate response to a clear Christology. Now, "in Christ" a new Christian has the capacity to respond to his fellow man in love just as Christ has already graciously given unconditional love to him. Admittedly, learning in varying degrees will be required. But, the actual potential now exists where it did not before conversion. Without this transformation affecting daily life Christianity assumes a position of a purely historical or judicial doctrine.[577] Instead, each Christian, due to the love and grace of God, can grow in the Spirit. A Christian can confront each inconsistency between their sinful life and their new life in Christ as these matters are revealed and respond by conforming to Christ.[578] This process of maturation is ongoing for all Christians. When the doctrine of sanctification is related to the church and the problem of race, what is certain is that every new Christian has an immediate capacity to deal with the problem of hatred and bigotry.

The option available to them as a result of their conversion is completely different than their pre-conversion options. Namely, due to the pouring out of the Spirit and the ministry that the Spirit now has in each Christian, they can love as God has loved

---

[577] Harold Brown, "The Conservative Option," in Tensions in Contemporary Theology, ed. Stanley Gundry and Alan Johnson (Chicago: Moody Press, 1976), 356-357.

[578] Walvoord, "Augustinian-Dispensational," 215-220.

them.  The primary issue is " . . . whether they will submit completely to the will of God."[579]

Second, the church, which is in pursuit of sanctification, must be relieved of the influences of philosophical pragmatism. Where one begins the process of theological reasoning ultimately influences the final conclusions.  If the beginning point of theology is how to deal with a specific problem, then the end result will place man at the center of theology.  This leads to the search for the most efficient solutions for ecclesiastical problems, even at the expense of Biblical principles.  Man asks questions like, "What is the most efficient way to resolve the decline in church membership?"  In the hunt for an answer the hope is to produce a means to gain a working product:  "What works best?"   Too often the question evolves into "What works the fastest?"  Thus, when two different kinds of people are at odds with each other, then the quickest solution, under the guise of a temporary situation, is to separate these two.  People generally are biased according to their own ethnicity  to the point of disliking others who are different.   Thus, the easiest and quickest way to resolve this problem is to separate them from each other.   This kind of reasoning is very attractive to the minister who is scratching out a means of existence in a dying church and who is unduly pressured with the misguided idea that vast numbers are

---

[579] Ibid., 217.

equivalent to success. But, no matter how appealing these kinds of questions are, they are misleading.

Correct theology begins with the question of who Christ is. Once this is established, then man can determine that he will treat his fellow Christian and non-Christian as Christ has treated him, without favoritism. True love is impartial. The solution to man's biased treatment of his fellow man once entering into the kingdom of God is not to resort to pragmatic options which avoid problems but to deal with them Christologically. As Christ has accepted all unconditionally and as all who belong to Him are one with Him without differences, then racism from a Christological perspective is not allowable. Rather, a union of all regardless of race is by far the better picture over segregated or separated church congregations. For Christians not only have the capacity to accept others as realized through the process of sanctification, they also have the motivation knowing that they are one with each other in Christ.

Third, the church must avoid the dangerous tensions raised in the issues of ethnicity caused by the tension of civil religion. Unfortunately, the combination of religion and politics, together with that human quality of romanticism, leads to grave error. Romanticism is a quest for the ideal. It is so passionate for that ideal that the concept of sacrifices is utilized as the excuse for violence and the loss of life or liberty. When romantic ideas are wedded to religion, these ideas are given justification and divine

237

approval.  The motivation runs high to achieve the lofty goals. Then, if this volatile partnership is joined with civil pride, a dangerous product emerges: civil religion.  Power is now added to the passion.  And a cause is moved forward with the notion that "might equals right".  This powerful movement can be countered by a theology that properly replaces grace into the premier place over law.  If grace is prior to law, then, Christ and who He is as Creator and Redeemer, become the basis for responding to our fellow man.  Thus, since all Christians are one in Christ, and since there is no difference among those in Christ, then there is no theological basis for separating Christians based on race.  This is sanctification in action.

Fourth, the doctrine of the image of God teaches that there must be equality among all who are a part of the church. God values all men equally regardless of their ethnic background. And consequently, all men must love each other with equality as well.  This sense of unanimity must be the visible demonstration of the church to the world.  Certainly, this is the kind of light that the church is to shine out to the world.  Any arguments that suggest that God was ethnically biased toward Israel are in error. In fact God's use of Israel was not to the detriment of the Gentile world but to its benefit.  The exclusiveness of one human group over another is in error.  Human dignity is a part of the redemption blessing.  Christian must give that to each other.  Sanctification calls for this progressive acceptance of others who are equally identified by the image of God.

And fifth, it would be appropriate for the problem of race to be addressed by a theological clarification. In the opinion of this author the theological scheme of the church must refine its thinking. There must be a return back to a focus on the person of Christ as the center of theology. This Christological focus must be the hub from which all theology both philosophically and practically revolve. Separation of people in churches based upon their ethnicity is not a reflection of the one Christ who is the Savior to the world. But, a unity of spirit is.

All people who come to Christ must accept that what they now share in common with other Christians is far greater than their differences. Their new identity as citizens of heaven is far more powerful than their earthly heritage. Theologically, then, any alternative for the church's growth strategy must begin with Christology at its center to produce a church in the world that has credibility with the true Gospel message. It must not encourage the separation of human groups for the sake of human distinction alone for that is contrary to an accurate Christology. It must not foster a misleading sense of acceptability based upon a pragmatism that is not consistent with the Gospel of Good News. Instead, just as each individual regardless of race or class or language was accepted by the unconditional love of God, so the church must be as universal in accepting others into Christian fellowship.

Sanctification emphasizes a new capacity to love, Christology points to the reality of belonging to Christ, and Grace highlights the reality of unity among Christians, the absence of differences in light of what is shared in common. When this theological analysis is combined with the Biblical mandate of unity resulting from the broken wall, it gives the church a clear direction for its growth strategy. The very Gospel which it aims to herald to the world, that same Gospel that initiated their own conversion to Christ, must reach out to give man what Christ meant to give through His unconditional love. It is an eternal redemption through His grace that carries with it the renewal of the dignity of being in the image of God without any of the limitations that man has bludgeoned on his fellow man. The church must reflect the reality of this grace and Christology, the same grace that they each received. Each congregation of professing confessing Christians should reflect in visible form an attitude of mutual acceptance for all who come to the grace that Christ offers to all in the world regardless of race, class or language. The multi-racial, multi-class church becomes a testimony to the world what the grace of God can do.

## An Explanation of Mutual Acceptance

Mutual Acceptance is based upon the preceding biblical theological foundation. It constructs a philosophy from New Testament principles and theological considerations and then assesses the needs of people in light of those formulations. Upon an analysis of human needs in that perspective procedures or strategies are then developed for use in the church for its growth and functioning as well as in the mission field. At the heart of Mutual Acceptance is the sense of Christian community. Every assembly and all of its individuals together comprise a Christian community.

". . . people who are radically different take pleasure in and accept each other. Christian (and this means liberating) community then, no longer means only to sit next to those with whom I agree but also to sit next to those with whom I do not agree. Functioning with this meaning of community, we would no longer come together in order to confirm for each other the eternally same stories, jokes, and opinions, but would rather create an open and hospitable community which would bring friendliness into the unfriendly corners of this society."[580]  I am not suggesting that Christians pretend that differences do not exist nor that opinions cannot differ. Nor am I suggesting that contemporary animosity and enmity among professing Christians is not real. I am

---

[580]   Jurgen Moltmann, The Open Church: Invitation to a Messianic Lifestyle (London: SCM, 1978), 33.

241

emphasizing that what Christians do have in common in Christ is much more important than all of the issues over which they disagree. And this commonness enables them to meet on an equal level for genuine loving interaction. Christians are always growing. But, they first begin with always accepting.

It is not acceptable to Mutual Acceptance that Christian interaction be relegated to representatives on a denominational basis or deferred to an annual event of interchurch mass celebrations. Rather, the intensely personal level of New Testament *koinonia* is to be entered by all Christians with all other Christians. Basic to *koinonia* is the mutualness of the relationship. It requires that all Christians recognize that every Christian has a place in the church and that all Christians share something eternal in common. "The koinonia which is the church's proper life is two-way traffic, taking as well as giving, and it requires us both to share what resources of Christian insight we have and to take gratefully any further insights that others offer us."[581]

A glaring error in the church is that most Christians are very loving to themselves but not generous to others. But, the Christian faith advocates that this attitude should be just the opposite.[582] In a gathering or community of Christians all should

---

[581] Packer, "The Gospel," 103.

[582] I am grateful to Professor Roland Walls for this idea.

be fully accepted. There should be a marked difference between the world with its racism and an assembly of Christians with its *koinonia*. Everyone is welcomed to the church on an equal basis. This is what *koinonia* is. "In this fallen world where men and women are alienated through sin from both God and each other, God has acted to create for himself a new people who should live with him and with each other in a fellowship of covenant love and loyalty."[583] Impersonal organizational ties among Christians are not the emphasis. Convenience and similarity of doctrine are not the bonds linking Christians. Rather each Christian is ". . . united to every other Christian everywhere, by the closest of spiritual ties, communion in the one Spirit."[584]

A practical issue for the church with this regard is the care that must be taken to insure that as the church grows, its fellowship (Christian to Christian) is not selective. It must be accepting of any and all. "Only this attitude can give us a new orientation and break through our limitations so that we can spring over our narrow shadows. It opens us up for others as they really are so that we gain a longing for and an interest in them. As a result of this we become able actually to forget ourselves and to focus on the way Christ has accepted us."[585] Unity is a necessary

---

[583] Packer, "The Gospel," 105.

[584] Roland Allen, <u>Missionary Methods: St. Paul's or Ours?</u> (Grand Rapids: Wm. B. Eerdmans Pub. Co., 1962), 126.

[585] Moltmann, <u>Open Church</u>, 30-31.

Christian expression within the church as a demonstration of the single Savior and Spirit. As Christian relates to Christian in the church there must acceptance not selectivity. Even today, as it was in the days of the Apostle Paul, "[the] separation of Christians meant the dividing of Christ."[586]  Or to state this positively, " . . . the unseen God who revealed Himself in His Son now reveals Himself in His people, in their love for one another which is nothing but the love of God."[587]

---

[586] Allen, Missionary Methods, 128.

[587] Stott, Guilty Silence, 76.

CHAPTER IV

## THE APPLICATION OF MUTUAL ACCEPTANCE TO THE CHURCH AND ITS MISSION

### *Introduction*

It is generally agreed that the mission of the church is to win individuals from every corner of the world to Christ. And once that kind of conversion is realized, nurturing, which is also a part of the mission, is to follow with equal vigor and effort.[588] Furthermore, it is also agreed that the planting of churches must be a part of the nurturing process.[589] What remains unclear is the kind of church that should be planted. This issue is particularly relevant due to the racial tension that is present in the world. If

---

[588] For a discussion of the difficulty of defining "mission" see Sunday Aigbe, "Cultural Mandate," in Missiology: An International Review 19, no. 1 (January 1991): 32-33. Aigbe discusses many of the variables in determining an adequate definition. He then concludes with a general description of the mission of the church from the standpoint of "dynamic causality factor" and "common cause factor." The former refers to the impact made on an individual and the latter points to the change in a person's destiny.

[589] Peters identifies the proclamation of the Gospel and the subsequent planting of churches as basic features of the church's mission. (Peters, Missions, 249.)

racial tensions exist in a community should separate churches be established or encouraged? If they are, will the church be accused of masking racist policies? Or possibly, would such a distinction encourage Christians to deliberately avoid their racial biases. And is the church obligated to celebrate culture in a multi-cultural society by exclusive ethnic churches or is there a greater New Testament principle of multi-ethnic unity that should be pursued?

In chapter 3 an analysis of Ephesians 2:11-22 demonstrated that the spiritual heritage of every Christian is directly linked to his current union with other Christians regardless of race, language or class. Also, the peace that each individual Christian has with God is to be expressed in his relationships with other Christians. And, lastly, the union between Jew and Gentile by the Christ directly affects mutual relationships among Christians. Sociological preferences of culture or race are affected by conversion. It has been established that these are the changes that determine Christian association in the church not culture.

It is the position of mutual acceptance that while cultural factors are crucial in effective evangelism[590] those same elements do not necessarily maintain the same position of priority in the organization of a church[591]. In part 2 of chapter 3 the issue of

---

[590] My focus here is the relation of Christian to non-Christian.

[591] My focus here is the relationship between Christian and Christian.

sanctification was discussed. From that discussion it can be concluded that the church cannot accept total relativism about culture.[592] The Gospel ". . . endorses an immensely wide diversity among human cultures . . ."[593] and as such allows for cultural expression in churches and Christian groups. But, this allowance cannot be made into an absolute. Conversion causes sanctification. Sanctification causes cultural changes. This dynamic should not be minimized.[594] The church must be flexible in allowances for cultural expression with a balance between conversion absolutes and cultural expression.

It is helpful to note that the new community of believers by New Testament standards is simultaneously both culturally diverse and spiritually united.[595] But, how does this pattern fit in today's churches? From a Practical Theology perspective how does this balance of diversity and unity reveal itself in church life? When

---

[592] Leslie Newbigin, The Gospel in a Pluralist Society (Grand Rapids: Wm. B. Eerdmans Pub. Co., 1989), 186.

[593] Ibid., 197.

[594] Ibid., 184.

[595] Stott describes with precision the need to clarify church development in light of legitimate and effective evangelistic efforts. Acceptable mission strategies cannot be allowed to confuse Biblical ecclesiastical priorities. The line of conversion is a vital landmark to observe. This thesis and this application section focus primarily on the post-conversion activity of church life. In it no pre-conversion strategy for mission may be permitted to infiltrate the church with a perspective that tolerates or erects barriers in the Christian community that Jesus Christ has definitively abolished. (Stott, "Unreached People," 2.)

there are racial and ethnic tensions, how should the leadership, its individual members and the church at large address the sense of community with its varied demands?

The application of mutual acceptance will address these matters in two broad realms. First, it will be applied to the field of Missions. The mission of the church is to evangelize the world by making converts and planting churches. Mutual acceptance will be integrated into a missionary philosophy. Second, it will be applied to the existing church which has a varied history of racial and cultural tensions. Beyond the planting of new churches, how are today's churches to deal responsibly with matters of racial, cultural, and ethnic tensions? Mutual acceptance presents guidelines for the ethnic church, the multi-racial church, and the majority population church.

## *Part 1*

### *Applying Mutual Acceptance to Missions*
### *A Convergence of Culture and Theology*

The issue of culture is a significant factor in any church strategy for missions. On the one hand, past failure to address this matter has led to a damaging criticism of the church's missionary effort. On the other hand, efforts to rectify these problems have in some cases precipitated an extreme reaction resulting in even further problems.[596]   A balanced and flexible position is needed.  Missions must proclaim the Gospel to cultures and permit the new converts to experience the Good News with as little cultural threat as possible.  A way to achieve this must be accomplished without diminishing the good work that missions is currently doing.        At the outset, it is prudent to acknowledge the innate difficulty of evaluating culture.  Two factors are involved here.  First, total objectivity by an observer to culture is extremely difficult since any person is first and foremost culturally influenced himself.  Second, the New Testament does not directly address the subject of culture.[597]   While these two areas of difficulty are

---

[596] Fundamental to McGavran's thinking is the struggle to make room for the cultural influences that appear to stifle church growth.  From his personal experience as a missionary to India, he drew from the Indian tendency to move toward Christ according to their caste.  He then began to utilize this pattern for his missionary enterprise.

He asked questions regarding a society's observance of endogamy, where marriage was limited to a particular social unit.  How did conversion to Christianity occur under such boundaries?  He also asked how evangelism could enter such a tightly knit society without inferring or demanding that disloyalty to one's caste was a prerequisite.  Also, that joining the church was not tantamount to entering a new cast.

"His concern, among others, was to alert the Christian community to the slowing-down effect that one-on-one traditional method, associated with the mission-station approach of the past, had on the rapidity with which such groups could be harvested for the gospel.  He saw past approaches as leaving converts with the feeling that they had betrayed their people." (Harvie M. Conn, "Looking for a Method: Backgrounds and Suggestions," in Exploring Church Growth, ed. Wilbert R. Shenk [Grand Rapids: Wm. B. Eerdmans Pub. Co., 1983], 79.)

[597] Marshall notes the difficulty of evaluating culture while being "a prisoner of his own culture."  And he also notes that in addressing an area like culture that is not specifically detailed in the New Testament is similar to the problem when a Christian searches for a Biblical response to abortion.  Since the subject was never a part of the consciousness of the New Testament writers. (Howard Marshall, "Culture and the New Testament," in Down to Earth: Studies in Christianity and Culture, ed. Robert Coote and John Stott [Grand Rapids: Wm. B. Eerdmans Pub. Co., 1980], 18)

admitted, the effort to discuss the topic is not necessarily futile. Cultural changes and influences are a part of man's history. For example in advance of the New Testament times, Alexander the Great through his conquests, was forcing the Greek culture on the known world. These cultural changes are a part of the New Testament scene.[598]

The two matters of cultural influence and Biblical perception are not always easily discernable. The more complicated a culture is the more difficult it is to evaluate the distinction. A society that is immersed in a complex cultural milieu may not only defy definition but also seriously tax any reasonable Western cultural application. And just as certain, the more conflicting a host culture is to the culture of a missionary, the more difficult it is to ascertain accurate guidelines for cultural respect. Newbigin reflects on his own experience as a missionary to India: "As a young missionary, I was confident that the critical evaluations I made about Hindu beliefs and practices were securely founded on God's revelation in Christ. As I grew older, I

---

[598] Marshall observed that " . . . while the Greek element was always obvious, the local manifestations could vary considerably." (Marshall, "Culture," 18.) But, it is also clear that this cultural flux was not necessarily bad nor a part of the church's responsibility preserve it. "We can hardly fathom the riches of the Gospel they proclaimed without appreciating something of the cultural mix which characterized their time and place." (Ibid., 17-18.) For a further discussion on the Greek and Roman influence on that day see Robert H. Gundry, A Survey of the New Testament, revised edition (Grand Rapids: Zondervan Pub. House, 1981). In particular note chapter 2, "The Secular Setting of the New Testament," 21-32 and chapter 3, "The Religious Setting of the New Testament," 33-53.

learned to see that they were shaped more than I had realized by my own culture."[599]  Such an acknowledgement is not a verdict against the church carrying out its mission cross-culturally but a caution against cultural assumptions when the Gospel is spread to the whole world.

## Scope of Culture

Culture has been the historical subject of much attention in the realm of missiology.  It first rose to the attention of theologians and church leaders because of the negative effect that some missionary efforts were having around the world.  Along with bringing the Gospel of peace to people around the world, missions also experienced a clash of cultures, namely Western versus third (or two-thirds) world.  The Gospel was often swallowed up in the confusion.  The missionary message became known not as the "Good News of Christ" but as the "white man's religion."[600]  Hence, Christian leaders eventually began to rethink and restrategize their

---

[599]  Lesslie Newbigin, Foolishness to the Greeks: The Gospel and Western Culture (London: SPCK, 1986), 21.

[600]  Western missions was locked into its own culture.  Kraft reflects:  "As missionaries we have steadfastly maintained that God is more than simply `the White Man's God'.  Yet, because our understanding of him and of Christian theology is so culture-bound, we often find ourselves unable to give any other impression to members of other cultures."  (Charles H. Kraft, Christianity in Culture: A Study in Dynamic Biblical Theologizing in Cross-Cultural Perspective [New York: Orbis Books, 1979], 21.)

response to the Great Commission in order to continue the fulfillment of Christ's last command to His disciples.

The subject of culture and Christianity is far beyond the scope of this volume. And even the topic of culture and the mission of the church is extraneous to the goal of this chapter.[601] What is within the scope of this paper, however, is to isolate the conclusions from a cultural study that defines a perspective of cultural respect, which allows for missionary enthusiasm to continue to flourish while minimizing the distracting clashes of contrasting cultures. The hybrid concept of contextualization[602] is a helpful term in this regard and will be an important part of this discussion.

## Western Culture and the Church Mission

Another issue that will be a part of this discussion is the dominance of Western culture in defining the church's mission. The material for missiology has almost exclusively dealt with the movement of Western Christianity into the Third World. The concern has been for Western missionaries to responsibly respect the cultures into which they are entering. Also, when large groups

---

[601] Remarkable works like Christ and Culture by Richard Niebuhr (London: Faber & Faber Ltd., 1952) or the earlier volume of Modern Missions and Culture: Their Mutual Relations by Gustav Warnack (noted earlier in chapter 2, note 129) or the more recent writing of Christianity in Culture by Charles Kraft (see previous note) represent the intensity of the culture issue throughout the history of missiology.

[602] Refer to chapter 1, "Liberation Theology," for an earlier discussion of the definition of "contextualization."

of non-Western people immigrate for example to North America, language is often a need that encourages the establishment of ethnic churches. These churches set the tone for what is acceptable. For what is common becomes what is acceptable. Furthermore, often immigrating people find that a church organization helps to preserve their ethnic identity. They have ethnic leadership, convenience of language, and comfortable social contact. But, if these issues contradict the New Testament principles of the church, then they must be challenged.

Rather unique in the plethora of writings on this matter has been Lesslie Newbigin's Foolishness to the Greeks. While the church of the West is busily pouring its energy, resources and effort into missions away from itself, Newbigin simply asks whether the Gospel, which churches are carefully analyzing and grooming and exporting, has any bearing on its own society.[603] Certainly the decline in Christianity in the West compared to the spectacular growth in certain parts of the Third World warrants such an assessment. Adding to Newbigin's significant insight is yet another issue to be seriously contemplated, namely: What Biblical Theological guidelines are there for the non-Western immigrants who settle in the Western

---

[603] Newbigin argues through his thesis in six points. He examines the issues raised by cross-cultural communication of the Gospel, looks at the essentials of Western culture, faces the reality of Biblical authority in Western culture, asks how the Gospel affects a scientific Western culture, discusses the Gospel's affect on a politically-minded West, and inquires how the church of the West must embark upon the challenge of its own need to be confronted by the Gospel. (Newbigin, Foolishness, 4.)

culture?   If the principles of contextualization direct Western missionaries to adapt the Gospel to the culture in which they enter should the same apply in the reverse?   Is the factor of immigrant compared to missionary an exclusion from these guidelines or an even greater requisite?   Much writing has concentrated on sending the Western message and messenger of Christianity to the Third World.   Newbigin has broached the subject by reversing the direction of the message, bringing it back to the West.   This subject can be examined further by looking at the messenger, Christians from the third world who enter the West to live.

This section will apply mutual acceptance to missions theory.   It will interact with the concept of contextualization, examine the place for ethnic churches,   and acknowledge the changes that conversion brings to culture.

## Contextualization is a Helpful Concept in Directing Church Missions

The historical development of the missionary philosophy of the Christian church is a global reaction against the ill-effects of a culturally dressed Gospel.   In an effort to curb the future repetition of culturally flavored missionary enterprises the perspective of contextualization has emerged.

Contextualization addresses the importance of allowing a receiving culture the dignity of hearing the Gospel in its own cultural context. While contextualization is not easily defined with conciseness, it is consistently described. It is a shifting of cultural interpretations to better understand the immutable value of the Gospel. From each culture's variant perspective of the same "Good News" individuals hear in the context of their own culture and receive the truth in that same context. Every culture " . . . transforms elements of [its] cultural milieu, bringing these under the lordship of Christ."[604] Newbigin says that it is " . . . the placing of the gospel in the total context of a culture at a particular moment."[605] Two elements are a part of contextualization. One is the truth of the Gospel, accurately stated, faithful to God's revelation. Second is an effort to insure that it is

" . . . meaningful to respondents in their respective cultural existential contexts."[606] From the hard lessons of mission field failure, contextualization attempts to balance culture with the Gospel proclamation.

---

[604] Dean Gilliland, "Contextualized Theology as Incarnational Mission," in The Word Among Us: Contextualizing Theology for Mission Today, ed. Dean Gilliland [Dallas: Word, 1989], 12-13.

[605] Newbigin, Foolishness, 2.

[606] David Hesselgrave and Edward Rommen, Contextualization (Grand Rapids: Baker Book House, 1989), 200.

## Historical Struggle of Missions: Indigenize or Contextualize?

The early missions' watchword in dealing with culture was "indigenize". But, that watchword fell on hard times. Even though the term contributed significantly to the missionary enterprise, it had application problems. Also, indigenization tended to relate the Gospel to "traditional cultural forms"[607] to the neglect of modern influences and changes.

## Problems with Indigenization

In the early 19th century missionary churches modeled their organization and worship on the churches in the sending country. Churches on the mission field became mere replicas of the churches "back home".[608] It was in this context that Henry Vern, Rufus Anderson, and Roland Allen argued in favor of "indigenous" churches. Their argument followed a three-self guideline: self-governing, self-supporting, and self-propagating.

---

[607] Newbigin, Foolishness, 2.

[608] The pattern for church life was exported and willingly followed by new converts who wanted to be Western. Padilla observes that "Western missionaries have often assumed that their task is simply to extract the message directly from the biblical text and to transmit it to hearers in the `mission field' with no consideration of the role of culture in the whole interpretive process." (C. Rene Padilla, "Hermeneutics and Culture: A Theological Perspective," in Down to Earth: Studies in Christianity and Culture, ed. Robert Coote and John R. W. Stott [Grand Rapids: Wm. B. Eerdmans Pub. Co., 1980], 77.) As a consequence, Christianity is perceived in many parts of the world as an ethnic religion - "the white man's religion." (Ibid.)

They illustrated from Paul's own missionary example pointing out that the apostle planted churches, he did not found mission stations. While indigeneity became a watchword for missions, it proved to have practical limitations.[609] It eroded when local leaders were trained in western ways of thought and procedure.[610] The desire of the indigenization concept was on target with regard for foreign missions but no one could foresee the logistics problem that culture would place upon its efforts.[611] William Smalley correctly points out that indigeneity is the proper direction for missions to take but it needs careful definition. As he critiques the three selves of indigenization, he notes that the meaning of them "

---

[609] Kraft notes that when indigenization was attempted the end result was training indigenous personnel to think like a Westerner. The concept was superficial and theoretical but failed in actuality. For a further discussion see Charles Kraft, "The Church in Culture: A Dynamic Equivalence Model," in <u>Down to Earth: Studies in Christianity and Culture</u>, ed. Robert Coote and John R. W. Stott (Grand Rapids: Wm. B. Eerdmans Pub. Co., 1980), 213.

[610] <u>The Willowbank Report</u>, 1978 Lausanne Committee for World Evangelization, in <u>Down to Earth: Studies in Christianity and Culture</u>, ed. Robert Coote and John R. W. Stott (Grand Rapids: Wm. B. Eerdmans Pub. Co., 1980), 329.
   This examination maintains a favorable acceptance of the views expressed in <u>The Willowbank Report</u>. For a response to the report please see Peter D. Latuihamallow, "Response to the Willowbank Report on Gospel and Culture," in <u>Southeast Asia Journal of Theology</u>, 19, no. 2 (50-62), 1978. Latuihamallow valued the document as a whole. He desires more of an explanation of the person of the Holy Spirit in relation to culture. Also, he questions why more theological development was not offered in light of the bounty of anthropology.

[611] Kraft identifies a biased cultural view that was common in traditional missionary strategy. It was monocultural and ethnocentric. It was also paternalistic. For a further discussion see Kraft, "Church in Culture," 212.

. . . strongly points to the need for a deeply <u>functional</u> kind of indigeneity in contrast to a merely surface-level approach."[612]

## Provincialism and Syncretism

While the church should be encouraged to grow around the world according to the indigenous concept, there is also a danger of celebrating the gospel in each culture according to mediums followed in that culture.[613]   Culture certainly has to be respected but it must not be allowed to overshadow the theological priorities that delineate the nature of the church.  The church must guard against an over emphasis on culture that allows itself to slip into provincialism.  Several points can be raised in explanation of this position.

First, the point must be emphasized that a call for a multi-racial or non-racial church is not an unreachable ideal but a realistic possibility.  The community sense of the church around the world clearly testifies to an assembly of Christians that is thoroughly multi-ethnic.[614]  If the church at large is clearly universal

---

[612]  Kraft, "Church in Culture," 213.

[613]  Culture can assume several postures that are not acceptable.  In extreme cases it can become chauvinistic, that is, boastful of itself or assertive over others.  Also, it can absolutize itself and thus become idolatrous.  What is more common, however, is the problem of provincialism, " . . . that is, such a retreat into their own culture as cuts them adrift from the rest of the church and from the wider world." (Willowbank, 333.)

[614]  I argued in part one of chapter three that every church is a component of the universal church.  By God's grace the church is a community that is international, inter-

in its inclusion, then it seems appropriate to speculate that the local church in a given geographical area is also capable of the same kind of universal inclusion by way of mutual acceptance. Perhaps more if not most churches, ministers, and denominational leaders should be looking and planning to express this mutual acceptance in their churches through visible activities on an on-going basis. Pulpit-sharing, choir-sharing, joint educational events, joint youth celebrations are some ways that this could be done.

Second, God is culturally diverse. That is, He can be worshipped by any person in any country in any language and in any culture. There is an equality that all Christians share in their relationship with the living God. Certainly, if this is the case, then all Christians must be able to value each other in spite of their cultural differences.[615] This point is vital. It is not just the leaders or the official statements of a church body that are under scrutiny here. Rather every individual Christian, even more importantly, each individual Christian's attitude is being challenged. Christians should pursue a bi-cultural even a multi-cultural existence as an

---

racial, multi-ethnic, and multi-cultural. Barriers to a new humanity were abolished by Christ. Racism has no part in the Christian society. This is the basis of the message found in Ephesians 2.

[615] Newbigin explains that no individual is in isolation. Every person is linked in his being to his community, language, and culture. This identity is part of God's order of creation and must be mutually respected. For a further discussion see Lesslie Newbigin, The Open Secret: Sketches for a Missionary Theology (London: SPCK, 1978), 157-160.

enrichment of the very humanity that God has injected with His own image.

Third, an attitude of openness must be developed by every church and by every Christian. Whether some, many, or even most churches are homogenous is not the crucial issue. Whether the reality of homogeneous churches is a fact due to a dominant culture or close-knit ethnic group is not the crucial issue. What is germane to all churches is each church's responsibility to be open to all Christians. Barna notes that a person's attitude toward others may be the most important indicator of a person's character. And essential for the church and Christians is to love others before self. In contrast to a society where racism exists and will persist Christians must show in their churches a caring and serving priority for others different from themselves.[616]

Another danger that church leaders must guard against in the balancing of the Gospel and culture is syncretism.[617] Culture has to be respected. Each new culture must be allowed to celebrate the Gospel in its own way.[618] But, just as importantly,

---

[616] Barna, Frog, 166-167.

[617] Hesselgrave makes the following definition: "When respondents choose parts of the Christian message which appeal to them and, rejecting other parts of the message, incorporate the accepted elements into non-Christian religious systems to make a new whole, the result is syncretism." (David J. Hesselgrave, Communicating Christ Cross-Culturally [Grand Rapids: Zondervan Pub. House, 1978], 112-113.)

[618] This is the emphasis of "contextualization". Thus, a person with an Argentinean ethnic heritage should be able to celebrate the Gospel in his Argentinean-ness. And a person with a Korean ethnic heritage should be able to celebrate the Gospel in his

the Gospel cannot be celebrated with means that are in conflict with its fundamental nature.[619]  It is here that the concept of contextualization is very helpful.  For the transmission of the Gospel must be achieved within a set of parameters[620] defined by God's revelation.  This insight expands an understanding of contextualization to two conflicting elements.  From a positive perspective contextualization seeks to place the Gospel into any culture in an understandable and acceptable form.  And also, from a precautionary perspective contextualization deliberately avoids syncretism.[621]

## Thinking About New Terms

In light of this discussion another point must be raised. And that is to commend the flexibility of the church to adjust its dialogue when a problem arises.  After missionary thinkers realized that the application of indigenization merely circumvented

---

Korean-ness.  Or a person with a Nigerian ethnic heritage should be able to celebrate the Gospel in his Nigerian-ness.

Some perceive this perspective as too ideal or even culturally naive.  For a discussion of this alternate view see Kraft, "Church in Culture," 211-212.

[619]  The Willowbank Report attempts to balance the complexities of this issue by making a distinction between intrinsic evil and association with evil.  The former is syncretism and cannot be permitted.  The latter is not, however, and can be assimilated into the church.  For a further discussion see Willowbank, 334.

[620]  Hesselgrave and Rommen, Contextualization, 203.

[621]  John Connor, "When Culture Leaves Contextualized Christianity Behind," in Missiology: An International Review 19, no.1 (January 1991), 22.

the emphasis on Western culture by the training of native leadership with Western thinking, the response was to discontinue ineffective terms and to develop a more accurate expression. The term "indigenous" did not functionally convey the desired missions concept.[622] To describe a church as indigenous limited the kind of change in a community desired by the Gospel. Making the church identical to a non-converted community is not the intent.[623] Realizing fundamental changes in individual Christians who are being sanctified yet still within the community is the desire.[624]

Practically, it is the concept of mission and the implementation of that concept that is important, not a loyalty to a particular term. However, allowing for the fact that "indigenization" has been tainted with Western cultural chauvinism and dubbed with the notorious reputation of being archaic and entrenched in the past, it has limited benefit.[625] Currently, the popular term is

---

[622] Kraft explains what authentic indigeneity is: "Authentic indigeneity lies in the manner in which such selfhood is expressed." (Kraft, "Church in Culture," 213.)

[623] Smalley does not believe that it is possible for a church in any culture to be absolutely indigenous. The fact that the church is "inevitably intrusive" in any culture is his basis for this conclusion. For a further discussion see William A. Smalley, "What Are Indigenous Churches Like?" Practical Anthropology 6 [1959]:137, quoted in "The Church in Culture: A Dynamic Equivalence Model," in Down to Earth: Studies in Christianity and Culture, ed. Robert Coote and John R. W. Stott (Grand Rapids: Wm. B. Eerdmans Pub. Co., 1980), 214.

[624] The participants of the Willowbank Report agree with this assessment. They conclude, " . . . a more radical concept of indigenous church life needs to be developed, by which each church may discover and express its selfhood as the body of Christ within its own culture." (Willowbank, 329.)

[625] Hesselgrave notes that the Gospel is " . . . not native to any culture . . . " and

262

"contextualize". But regardless of which term is utilized the goal is the same: "The supracultural truth of Christ becomes meaningful within any cultural system as it takes on the various forms of that system: linguistics, personal, social, and ecclesiastical."[626] And in this goal the lordship of Christ must remain over culture. Properly understood, contextualization follows all of these guidelines. When properly applied it will make the Gospel " . . . message meaningful, relevant, persuasive, and effective within the respondent culture."[627] The term "contextualization" speaks more precisely to the goal of missions than does "indigenization." It is the accurate transfer of the Gospel to a culture, as it is in a point of time. Also, it avoids damage to the Gospel due to syncretism[628]. But, how is this delicate balance accomplished?

---

hence the term "indigenize" may communicate more than what the church is attempting in its mission. For a further discussion see Hesselgrave, Communicating Christ, 83.

[626] Hesselgrave, Communicating Christ, 84.

[627] Ibid., 86.

[628] Barna defines syncretism from a historical perspective. It is a religion which ". . . takes the best facets of each religion they encountered and formed a new, blended faith." (Barna, Frog, 121.) He also observes that when such a phenomena occurs among Christians, that those who practice syncretism believe that they have improved Christianity.

## *Challenge of Cultural Inclusion*

Ignoring culture while attempting to fulfill the mission of the church leads to tremendous problems. But, to give culture a controlling place in the theology of the church leads to confusing compromise. Somewhere there is a proper balance that theologians can enthusiastically endorse and missionaries can eagerly apply.

## Definition of Culture

The point has been made that culture must be a factor that is given serious consideration in the church's strategy for development. It would be appropriate at this point that a definition of culture is attempted. Marshall notes six features that are included in understanding culture:

1. Man's life as it expresses itself in controlling his environment for his own use
2. Man's appreciation and effort in the realm of aesthetic appreciation which exists beyond the basics of mere survival
3. Man's development of values
4. Man's phenomenal social interaction
5. Man's process and patterns of thought

> 6. Man's ability to combine or separate various features of his life[629]

To this helpful description of culture a seventh may be added:

> 7. Culture is capable of being transmitted from one generation to the next. If this feature is absent, then that culture is dying.[630]

The details of what makes up a culture are fundamental to defining it and effectively introducing the Gospel to it contextually. Linking these details together is possible by isolating the essentials of a culture. Weaving the various details of the complexity of culture into a manageable definition is extremely difficult. However, when it is attempted it must blend both the objective observable facets of a people along with the unseen spiritual values. Padilla's suggestion is helpful when he writes that an understanding of culture ought " . . . to include, not only technical skills, life-style, attitudes, and values of a people, but also their thought patterns, cognitive processes, and ways of learning, all of which ultimately express a religious commitment."[631] Those present for the composition of the <u>Willowbank Report</u> have

---

[629] Marshall, "Culture and the New Testament," 18,19.

[630] Newbigin, <u>Foolishness</u>, 3.

[631] Padilla, "Hermeneutics," 63.

constructed a thorough definition of culture: "Culture is an integrated system of beliefs (about God or reality or ultimate meaning), of values (about what is true, good, beautiful and normative), of customs (how to behave, relate to others, talk, pray, dress, work, play, trade, farm, eat, etc.) and of institutions which express these beliefs, values and customs (government, law courts, temples or churches, family, schools, hospitals, factories, shops, unions, clubs, etc.), which binds a society together and gives it a sense of identity, dignity, security, and continuity."[632] Newbigin offers a more concise and manageable definition of culture: " . . . the sum total of ways of living developed by a group of human beings and handed on from generation to generation."[633] He also notes that the " . . . most fundamental element in culture is language."[634]

## Theological View of Culture

Culture is not exclusively a sociological topic. It is also a theological matter as well. From the Genesis account man's interaction with other men has been directly related to God's

---

[632] Several additional factors are involved in the Willowbank Report perception of culture. It is received from the past, "learned afresh" by each succeeding generation. The home is the primary location for the subconscious absorption of these factors. (Willowbank, 312-313.)

[633] Newbigin, Open Secret, 159.

[634] Newbigin, Pluralistic Society, 185.

commands and guidelines. And the complications due to man's perversions are inherently interwoven in the sovereign plan of God to bring about man's salvation.[635] Thus, culture must be viewed from its dual origin. It has both the stamp of divine approval but also the flaw of human sin.[636] Both features must be acknowledged and blended into a balanced theological perspective. As well, the humanity of man calls for a sensitivity to the need for man to act as a social creature. That too is a divine quality built into the spectrum of human existence. Theology recognizes man's essential psychological needs.

### Incarnational Model

One of the most helpful models of how culture and the Gospel can be blended together by the messenger is Christ's own incarnation. Jesus Christ set aside all of His glory to be born as a man. This is contextualization of the message and the messenger for the benefit of the receptor society at its highest degree. Tabor notes that a contextualization based upon the incarnation will

---

[635] I am referring here to man as a fallen creature. His self-centeredness and thus his culture as well cannot be brought under the Lordship of Christ without drastic changes. For a further discussion see Willowbank, 311-312.

[636] This dual perspective emphasizes the need for cultural change and cultural respect which was the conclusion of chapter 3. For a further discussion of this see James I. Packer, "The Gospel: Its Content and Communication: A Theological Perspective," in Down to Earth: Studies in Christianity and Culture, ed. Robert Coote and John R. W. Stott (Grand Rapids: Wm. B. Eerdmans Pub. Co., 1980), 103.

produce a ". . . profound implications for missionary methodology."[637]

## Strategy and Attitude

One of the key features of this mission's perspective is that the strategy itself is reflected through the life of the messenger. How the messenger approaches people to deliver the Gospel is more important than any theory outlined on paper. The collection of missions leaders at Willowbank believe that the key ingredient to the Gospel's effectiveness is ". . . to be found in the communicators themselves and what kind of people they are."[638] Acting with the humility of Christ is the key.[639] This attitude not only accomplishes the desired goal but it also acknowledges the actual limitations. Pride of one's own culture is almost a part of every culture. To set this attitude aside by taking the deliberate steps to learn another person's culture is an act of humility. And to accept people as they are, realizing that their current cultural state

---

[637] Charles R. Tabor, "Contextualization," in Exploring Church Growth, ed. Wilbert R. Shenk (Grand Rapids: Wm. B. Eerdmans Pub. Co., 1983) 117.

[638] Willowbank, 321, 322.

[639] Paul, as a missionary, modelled this principle in his exhortation in 2 Corinthians 10:1. He urged the Corinthians to action "by the meekness and gentleness of Christ." Hodges explains the text to mean that these two qualities "belonged to Christ." (Hodges, 2 Corinthians, 327) Meekness is viewed by Hodges as a person's "inward virtue" while gentleness is seen as one's "outward expression." (Ibid.)

is as good as one's own and perhaps in some ways even better is a massive step in lowliness.[640]

## Key Features of the Incarnational Model

When the intricate blend[641] of the Gospel and culture is attempted, the incarnational model is very helpful. When it is defined properly, there are four particular emphases that rise to the surface. These four elements of the incarnational model are humility, a new mind, a renunciation, and a new identification. First and foremost of these incarnational elements is Christ's own example of willingly being sent[642]. Second, the model of Christ's life displays a new way of thinking. Jesus was not self-absorbed. He did not worry about losing His own status but instead was overcome with an unending interest in His assigned mission, bringing the Gospel to mankind. It was far more than a mere

---

[640] Willowbank, 322-323.

[641] This term "blend" is used with some reservation. It is not intended to indicate that the Gospel and culture are equal. Nor is it intended to indicate that mutual compromise is required by either element. Rather, just as Christ was incarnated, He neither became identical with humans nor did He compromise any part of His character. Rather, as an act of humility, He identified with humans out of love for them without any selfish or egotistical expressions.

[642] This example of Jesus' own humility expressed in His incarnation as a model of contextualization is described in His own words to His disciples: "As the Father has sent men, even so I send you." (John 20:21) There is a humility inherent in being sent. It assumes submission to a higher authority. And it often speaks about a lower of oneself in order to carry out the mission that has been assigned. Godet describes the impact of this text: "There is properly only one mission from heaven to earth: it is that of Jesus. He is the apostle." (Godet, John, 421.)

thinking of others as equals, it was elevating them to a higher consideration than Himself.[643] This is Christ demonstrating a sanctified life, a life that is a model for all Christians to reproduce. And at the center of this sanctified life is a Christian's thinking. For the mind of Christ is to be the mind of all Christians as well. Tenney notes that there is a close connection between a Christian's sanctification and his commission.[644] As Christ was sent into the world, He was now commissioning His followers to a mission as well. Sanctified thinking calls for humble attitudes. No culture is superior to another's. Being sent to another people does not assume that those who are the beneficiaries of the Good News are lesser people.

Third, a renunciation has to be made. Christ came to earth as a Galilean Jew but He first "emptied himself". There was a definite sacrifice made in incarnating Himself as a man. Jesus renounced his status, his independence, and his immunity. Voluntarily Jesus Christ set aside His rightful status. He has no room for any status symbols. And Jesus Christ also willingly gave up a favorite Western commodity that is cherished almost as much as status, namely, independence. He lived on the money of

---

[643] This demonstration of practical humility is not unlike Paul's exhortation for Christians to prefer one another in honor (Romans 12:10). This is an admonition " . . . directed against the conceit by which we assert ourselves above others." (Murray, Romans, 130) It is a practical demonstration of Christian love directed toward others.

[644] Tenney, John, 248.

others. He was completely dependent on the finances of others to sustain His physical well-being. Jesus lived in their homes, used their boats and ate their food because He had none of His own.[645] This feature of the incarnational model is closely linked with the original concept of humility. Pride, the evil selfish kind, is at the root of much racist activity and feeling. There is an unseen presence of pride in the attitude of "I'll do it my way" or "I'll do it myself." Jesus willingly subjected Himself to being vulnerable. He gave up His divine immunity and willingly accepted the difficulties that plague the human being.[646]

A fourth and last feature of the incarnational model is identification. That is, Jesus had a real solidarity with man by becoming a true human being, ". . . a genuine partaker of flesh and blood."[647] And He did so "in like manner" with them. Man in his life experienced both life and death, so Jesus also experienced life and death.[648] But it was not just what Jesus did that leaves all

---

[645] The vast experience of the Willowbank authors can be seen in their comments on this matter. They strongly advise all first year missionaries to take deliberate steps in learning how to depend on others. The incarnational model calls for a toning down of an independent spirit and a quiet expression of true humility in service achieved through dependence on others. (Willowbank, 324.)

[646] The missionary is to follow the pattern of Christ. He willing exposes Himself to hardship and trouble for the sake of communicating the Gospel. (Willowbank, 324).

[647] Bruce, Hebrews, 48.

[648] Bruce describes this act of humble identification: "He became man, then, in order to help men. When the Son of God, the Creator and Lord of angels, humbled Himself, He passed by the angelic estate and stooped lower still, becoming man for men's salvation." (Bruce, Hebrews, 51.)

Christians an amazing example to follow; rather, it was the extent to which He did what He did. And every church leader has His example to follow. Jesus became one with those to whom He served. By His example Christians, who act as a herald of the Gospel to a particular people, should immerse themselves into the host culture, learning how to think and feel as those people think and feel.[649]

The incarnational model is a splendid pattern for all church leaders, church planters, and Christians to follow. Christ who is the head of the church is also the example to follow in propagating the church. Some may hesitate and argue that self-identity is lost in such a scheme; but that is far from true. Even though Jesus went to great measures to identify with mankind, it is presumptuous and erroneous to extrapolate that He lost His individual identity. Christ assumed true humanity but He never lost any of His deity.[650] No compromise ever affected Jesus' person in

---

[649] This does not mean that all Christian missionaries should "go native" for such an effort may be perceived as not authentic but as play-acting. At the same time conspicuous disparity between the life style of the missionary and those being sought is also an extreme to be avoided. "In between these extremes, we see the possibility of developing a standard of living which expresses the kind of love which cares and shares, and which finds it natural to exchange hospitality with others on a basis of reciprocity, without embarrassment. A searching test of identification is how far we feel that we belong to the people, and - still more - how far they feel that we belong to them." (Willowbank, 324.)

[650] Padilla makes a helpful explanation on this point: "It is only as the Word of God becomes `flesh' in the people of God that the Gospel takes shape within culture. According to God's purpose, the Gospel is never to be merely a message in words but a message incarnate in his church and, through it, in culture." (Padilla, "Hermeneutics and Culture," 78.)

His incarnation. While He talked, felt, and thought like those to whom He brought the Gospel, He never succumbed to their evils like favoritism, racism, oppression or pride.

Initiating people contacts across racially bitter barriers, Jesus shared the Good News of the Kingdom to women in public, Samaritans, Gentiles, Roman soldiers, and the unclean of society. He respected the culture that was His in the incarnation but He demonstrated that the message was the master not the culture. "Insofar as we can exercise control, we should not be offensive as to dress, speech, or culture, but the moment we announce the Gospel we take on the offense of the Cross (Gal. 5:11). The message is a stumbling block; the messenger should not be."[651]

## Adaptability by the Messenger

A balanced perspective regarding culture and how it is effectively interwoven into an evangelistic strategy will aid every missionary, church planter or church leader. As a priority, the Gospel must be at the center of any evangelistic message and methodology. This central position will allow the Gospel to speak to each different culture in a way that culturally bound missionaries cannot decipher.[652] When this kind of evaluation is applied, the

---

[651] Ryrie, Basic Theology, 336.

[652] The nature and content of the Gospel indicate that it has some contribution to the

Gospel will be a message of expectation as well as good news. The Gospel expects that the response of faith will be accompanied with a radical change.[653]  Both reconciliation and identification are at the forefront.  Christ identifies Himself with those who put their faith in Him and each convert is reconciled with God and with every other Christian.   There is no allowance for divisive differences or people preferences.  Entrance into the Good News of the Kingdom is an entrance into a reconciled body of people from all nations, languages, and ethnic groups.[654]

## The Cross-Cultural Challenge

At the same time the skill in communicating the Gospel necessitates a grasp of the culture that is to receive the message.[655]  This is the cross-cultural challenge.  The Gospel message must be faithfully expressed into a culture by some

---

means of its communication in any culture.  For a further discussion see Robert L. Ramseyer, "Christian Mission and Cultural Anthropology," in Exploring Church Growth, ed. Wilbert R. Shenk (Grand Rapids: Wm. B. Eerdmans Pub. Co., 1983), 108.

[653] Ramseyer emphasizes the two features of "reconciliation" and "identification" as essential to the communication of the Gospel.  See Ramseyer, "Cultural Anthropology," 108-109.

[654] As was demonstrated in part 1 of chapter 3 ,the Gospel can only be communicated in a way that breaks down barriers not one that builds them up or tolerates ones that already exist.  See further Ramseyer, "Cultural Anthropology," 109.

[655] It is granted that separation between the "pure" Gospel and the communicating culture or the receiving culture is an ideal.  Whatever balance can be struck is difficult to achieve. (Marshall, "Culture," 24.)

means that will insure that the message is accurately received. Two major problems face missionaries in such a situation. First, the Gospel may not be received well in the beginning due to a common cultural phenomenon: fear and conflict. The genuineness of the "Good News" may not be the issue but its threat to a peoples' familiar and secure way of life may be.[656] Second, missionaries, steeped in their own culture and at times naive about other cultures may unwittingly communicate by culturally alien forms. Instead of attracting new converts their presentations may in fact stimulate just the opposite response.[657]

## The Vital Blend

The two issues are plain. The Gospel must be faithfully represented when it is proclaimed. However, it will not be successfully delivered if its messengers ignore the culture into which it is being introduced. Blending the two is vital. Blending them correctly is the challenge. Some may suggest that the study

---

[656] Fear is a real response by lesser cultures to dominant ones. If it is the dominant culture that is the sending culture regarding the Gospel, then contextualization places a high priority on missionaries " . . . to take the concrete human context in all its dimensions with utmost seriousness. The particularity of each milieu becomes the starting point . . . " for concern for evangelistic respect for another culture. (Taber, "Contextualization", 119.) Marshall also notes that Christianity brings with it ethical and moral standards which will challenge many culturally-ingrained customs, some which are part of the essence of a culture's solidarity. Conflict between the Gospel and culture in this sense is inevitable. (Marshall, "Culture," 29.)

[657] Tabor, "Contextualization," 120.

of techniques used by the modern communication industry may help.[658]   But before the blend is made between the Gospel and culture this caution should be well respected.   Essentially, communication techniques attempt to exploit people's lives with commercial advertising.  A target group of a selected population is identified according to buying tendencies that already exist.  This is followed by specialized advertising and other marketing techniques to boost sales in a particular product. They desire a kind of change and utilize their communication techniques to achieve it;  but, the change is based on already present tendencies.  The presentation of the Gospel is very different from this.  When a person is confronted with the Gospel it is a matter of facing the reality of judgment.  An old way of life is not merely altered, adjusted, or influenced.  Instead, a radical change occurs and this same change becomes the basis for a calling to righteous living.[659]

Perhaps the greatest challenge of culture and the Gospel is the language factor.  At the heart of human identification is the ability to converse.  This mode of interaction is the most basic to all

---

[658]   However, there is a caution to be observed here for its methods " . . . tend to proceed as though any technique can be made suitable for a given communication task, irrespective of the message to be conveyed.  But   . . . a technique may bring formal clarity at the surface at the cost of indepth understanding."  (Packer, "The Gospel", 98.)

[659]   The Gospel must be seen as an evaluation of one's life.  It must result in a "radical and far-reaching" commitment for every person who follows Christ.  For a discussion see Packer, "The Gospel," 98.

people groups. And it is the means by which the Gospel must be communicated. Apart from all of the trappings of cultural colors, heirlooms, and history there lies the need for verbal interchange. If the Gospel is to affect any culture it must be adaptable to this fact. And if church leaders would acknowledge it, the Gospel also is essentially verbal.[660]


## Spiritual Conversion Will Require Cultural Changes

As the church continues on its mission to bring the Gospel to new cultures, it must face the reality that conversion always brings "change". What changes are demanded by a relationship with Christ? What aspects of culture are by necessity altered as a result of conversion? And it is in fact this latter topic, namely, conversion, that is at the heart of the "change" issue. The term conversion literally means "to turn around"[661]. Closely connected with "conversion" is the term "repentance" which literally means to "change your mind"[662]. Each concept indicates a radical alteration

---

[660]   Packer identifies any number of varied means in order to make the Gospel understood in some audible form for the benefit of the listener. See further Packer, "The Gospel," 98.

[661]   William Arndt and Wilbur Gingrich, A Greek-English Lexicon of the New Testament and Other Early Christian Literature (Chicago: University of Chicago Press, 1952), 778-779. Also see W. E. Vine, An Expository Dictionary of New Testament Words (Old Tappan, New Jersey: Fleming Revell Co., 1966), 238-239.

[662]   For a discussion see Arndt and Gingrich, Lexicon, 513-514 and Vine, Dictionary,

of a life. It is not a change that is an addition to a past life but it is a completely new life that has been begun.[663] This realization and sensitivity is mutual acceptance in operation with missions.

## *Culture's Effect on the Gospel and Visa Versa*

Missionaries must cognizant of two important questions that govern the logic of this section. First, what effect does conversion have on the culture of its converts? And the corollary, what effect does our culture have on our understanding of conversion? In the traditional evangelical view of conversion, culture has been more influential than commonly admitted. It is important that conversion be given a biblical understanding. When culture has wrongly intruded, then it is important to challenge it.[664]

The conversion experience is biblically explained as a radical change. There can be many gradual steps leading up to it and the time factor for its actual consummation may follow many moments of development. However, the actual moment of conversion is instantaneous and requires a radical alteration. The radical nature of this change must not be overlooked as a trivial matter. Rather it is to be ". . . the outward expression of a

---

279-281.

[663] 2 Cor. 5:17. For a discussion see Hodges, 2 Corinthians, 280-281.

[664] Conversion must be seen as a process as well as a crisis. And as such, it has "consequent public and social responsibilities." (Willowbank Report, 325.)

regeneration or new birth by God's Spirit, a recreation, and resurrection from spiritual death."[665]

## The Resurrection and Conversion

While, as it has been acknowledged, that there are different patterns leading up to conversion there is a measurable landmark for all persons coming to Christ, namely, the Resurrection.[666]  The difference between Christianity and any culture can be most clearly seen when the Resurrection of Jesus is considered.  This confrontation of history and man provides a way of giving meaning to the life of the individual and the life he now shares with others in the Christian community.[667]  As a result of this event in a person's life, there is a major change that occurs: conversion.[668]  Every missionary encounter of the gospel calls for a conversion of the individual.  It is a radical change that is required.[669]  Jesus Himself warned that those who would follow

---

[665] Willowbank, 325.

[666] Willowbank, 325.

[667] The resurrection serves as a basis for assurance for all believers.  It verifies their place in history and with "the sovereign Lord of history". (Newbigin, Foolishness, 63.)

[668] Conversion results in separation with one's past.  It is a complete separation that is described as death. (Newbigin, Foolishness, 63.)

[669] It is valid to describe conversion as a radical change since it affects every part of a person: the mind, the volition and the emotions. (Newbigin, Foolishness, 64.)

Him would run the risk of losing family and possessions.[670] And in the culture into which Jesus entered as a man, every Jew found identity in his family[671] and in his family inheritance or land possessions.

## Lordship and Change

This expectation of a radical change comes under the theological heading of "lordship"[672]. Conversion is related to

---

[670] Lk. 14:25ff. Plummer refers to this section of verses 25-35 as "The Conditions of Discipleship." It is a warning against being half-hearted in following Christ. For a further discussion see Plummer, Luke, 363-367.

[671] The matter of family and how this relates to an individual's conversion in a potential sense raises the topic of "people movements." The most casual studies of culture and conversion must acknowledge that the Biblical evidence should place this phenomenon high on the expectation list in evangelistic efforts. "It is evident that people receive the gospel most readily when it is presented to them in a manner which is appropriate - and not alien - to their culture, and when they can respond to it with and among their own people." (Willowbank, 326-327.) There is no theological compromise in adapting methods or strategies to cultural features that are amoral. In fact there is wisdom and Biblical consistency to present the Gospel as a welcomed friend that demonstrates its universal application to the world. Thus, in cultures where strong family, tribal, or community ties exist, then "people movements" are not to be discounted. Instead, it is completely acceptable to acknowledge that " . . . the covenant theme of the Old Testament and the household baptisms of the New should lead us to desire, work for, and expect both family and group conversions." (Willowbank, 326-327.)

Each time the issue of conversion is evaluated it must undergo the scrutiny of comparison. That is, it must match well with the essence of what conversion is, namely, " . . . that personal commitment to Jesus Christ is foundational. In him alone we find salvation, new life, and personal identity. Conversion must also result in new attitudes and relationships, and lead to a responsible involvement in our church, our culture, and our world." (Willowbank, 326-327.)

[672] A practical problem facing the church today is the presence of Christian profession without an accompanying commitment demonstrated through personal values and morals. The discussion that attempts to align these two matters is the topic

280

making a commitment to Jesus Christ as lord of one's life in a number of ways. Initially, it acknowledges His deity.[673] And it also includes a "subjective lordship"[674] or dedication[675] that may either occur simultaneously or subsequent to one's initial conversion.[676] Thus, making Jesus Christ Lord of one's life will also require one's past culture to be progressively scrutinized and with very few exceptions, to have parts of that culture abandoned as no longer

---

of "lordship." On the one hand, there is a realization that a newness must be reflected in the life of a believer. On the other hand, salvation by grace cannot be compromised. For a discussion of the former see John MacArthur, Jr., The Gospel According to Jesus (Grand Rapids: Zondervan Pub. House, 1988). For the latter see Zane Hodges, Absolutely Free! (Grand Rapids: Zondervan Pub. House, 1989).

[673] Westcott provides the following helpful explanation of what it means "to confess Jesus" or to confess "Jesus as Lord" which can only mean to acknowledge the union of both divinity and humanity in the one Person, Jesus Christ. (B. F. Westcott, The Epistles of St. John (Cambridge: Macmillan, 1892.), 142.

[674] Ryrie distinguishes between an objective lordship and a subjective lordship. The former is the acknowledgement of who Christ is, in His Person and position. The latter describes the master relationship that Christ has with His believers. Christ, from the objective lordship perspective is who He is regardless of any human acknowledgement. However, the subjective lordship is possible only when a Christian acknowledges Christ as master of his or her life. For a further discussion see Charles C. Ryrie, So Great Salvation (Wheaton: Victor Books, 1989.), chapter 7, "Of Course He is Lord," 67-77 and in particular 71-72.

[675] For a discussion of "dedication" see Charles C. Ryrie, Balancing the Christian Life (Chicago: Moody Press, 1969.), chapter 7, 75-83. Also, for a discussion of a presentation that reflects a constant commitment see Murray, Romans, 109-116.

[676] Ryrie makes a helpful explanation of Peter's predicament in Acts 10:14. Peter illustrates one who's life acknowledged the lordship of Christ for his life in general but there were some specific areas that still needed to be included. For a further discussion see Ryrie, Salvation, 73.

morally acceptable. Great care is required for this submission to lordship to be properly accomplished.[677]

There is an inevitable clash when a person's allegiance it cast toward Christ. The culture of that person's past is immediately challenged.[678] Basic beliefs and morals and values have been shaped by one's culture from birth. These matters now are challenged by a new system of beliefs and morals and values. Lordship is an exclusive position. It cannot be shared by Christ and a past form of life once the inconsistency has been revealed.[679]

When Jesus Christ is Lord of one's life there is an observable change of behavior.[680] Moral standards and whole

---

[677] Extremes in lordship cannot be allowed. But, efforts to avoid excesses should not erode into "soft-pedalling" necessary choices against cultural carry-overs that oppose the person of Christ. (Tabor, "Contextualization," 127.)

[678] Repentance is a part of the Christian experience. While there is a variation the specifics of each Christian's ethical and moral life that is challenged by repentance, there is the universal that " . . . there can be no repentance without ethical content . . . " (Pasadena Consultation, 6.)

[679] A converted Christian becomes morally obligated to live according to God's standards. It is not a legalistic issue but an ethical one. And it becomes natural and desirable. This is the Christian call to repentance, a " . . . call to enter into harmonious relations with God." (Hodges, Free, 145.)

[680] To follow Christ as one of His disciples can only be done at great cost. It is not easy to do so. Ryrie describes the nature of true discipleship: "It cost (1) supreme loyalty to Him even above family, (20 willingness to die for Him, and (3) literally forsaking everything (not just being willing to do so) to be able to accompany Jesus from place to place." (Ryrie, Salvation, 75-76.)

ethical lifestyles become the product of a repented life.[681] Perhaps most evident in the changed life of a repented soul is a new capacity to love.[682] From a practical standpoint this calls for a submission to Christ as Lord over our interpersonal relationships.[683] A massive change is not out of the question when spiritual conversion is seen for what it is: a total alteration of a person's life.[684]

## Dynamic Equivalence Model

The writers of the Willowbank Report present a hopeful solution to the search for a pattern that the church may follow in the quest for a balance between conversion and culture. They refer to it as the "dynamic equivalent model." According to these

---

[681] Mt. 3:8. For a further discussion see Pentecost, Words and Works, 87-90 and Alfred Edersheim, Life and Times of Jesus the Messiah (MacDonald Pub., Co.), 119-128.

[682] Conversion in the New Testament liberates a person to love. (Willowbank, 326.)

[683] Acts 2:40-47 points to "the new believing community" of which Christians were now a part. Their relationship together was founded upon their common faith in Christ as their Lord. For a further discussion see Bruce, Acts, 78-81.

[684] At the same time, while recognizing the need for a radical change when conversion takes place, there is a limit when cultural changes are expected. On the one hand, all aspects of one's culture must come under the Lord's scrutiny. Yet, on the other hand true conversion does not "de-culturize a convert." Conflicts and misunderstandings are unavoidable. The judgments by Christ of one's culture may be interpreted as treachery by non-converted cultural fellows. It is a tragic clash. When such does happen, the convert must do whatever is possible to continue to identify with his culture in the ways that are acceptable to Christ. (Willowbank, 326-327.)

individuals, " . . . a `dynamic equivalence' translation . . . seeks to convey to contemporary readers meanings equivalent to those conveyed to the original readers, by using appropriate cultural forms, [also it seeks] to express these in forms equivalent to the originals but appropriate to the local culture." Furthermore, this perspective identifies what is foreign or false and dismisses those items. Principles from the New Testament dominate as patterns for procedure over tradition or culture. And the local church is the preferred place for these applications.[685]

## *Growth in the Church: Balance Between Reality and Theology*

A true balance is possible between accurate theology and its application to the church as it attempts to fulfill its mission by evangelizing the people of the earth. To promote a methodology that "succeeds" at numerical growth but "fails" to validate itself theologically is irresponsible. But, to theologize about truth without significant application to life is to verge on being disobedient. Both of these extremes must be avoided by those who follow Christ as Lord. Nor are the options limited to these two. The very essence of the term "theology" necessitates it is truth and therefore applicable to the lives of people who belong to God. Those who

---

[685] Willowbank, 331.

are made in God's image can find out how to fulfill their destiny by beginning with the truth given by their creator.

## Sense of Community

To begin with there is an unavoidable and ever present sense of community for all people. Humankind finds its definition in community. Several key concepts are noted by Conn. First, evangelism must demonstrate itself in a visible form of unity among those who follow after Christ. A resulting "new humanity" which includes all kinds of people functioning and living together must be seen by the world. This product of the Gospel is a "demonstration-sign" of that good news. Second, a realistic perspective of the Christian community must be kept in focus. Due to man's fallen condition evil will be present even in the Christian community.[686] Third, care must observed in addressing the matters of Jesus as Savior and Jesus as Lord[687]. Any distinction between them must not put them at odds with each other. Fourth, a position which places community as a high priority, is not also advocating ethnocide or cultural imperialism.

---

[686] A church can also be excessive. On the one hand, it may demand a loyalty that exceeds New Testament standards, making the idolatrous. On the other hand, it may "freeze out" outsiders and thus become self-oriented. Examples of "demonic homogeneity" are "racism, tribalism, and oppressive wealth." (Conn, "Method," 86.)

[687] As discussed earlier, "lordship" calls for submission to the values and disciplines modeled by Christ and described in the New Testament. A new lifestyle must emerge and a new community must be entered. (Conn, "Method," 86).

Reconciliation among all people with Christ and with each other is the goal. But a "commitment to the liberating justice of Christ"[688] is a prerequisite to this kind of Christian community.

## Growth, Life, Faith, and Change

Once these matters are understood, then there is a need to determine what kind of growth in a church should be pursued. For growth always produces change; but, change is not always accepted. Any additions or deletions in form, content, tradition, even language are a part of any culture changes.[689] Besides the clear connection between growth and change there is also another feature that accompanies growth. That feature is the process of life. Whatever is alive will develop, grow, and change.[690] This analogy between church growth and physical growth can be taken even further. For just as in the realm of nature not all growth is desirable so too the organism of the church does not always benefit by certain kinds of growth.[691]

---

[688] Conn, "Method," 86.

[689] For a further discussion of the inter-relationship between "growth" and "change" see Orlando E. Costas, "A Wholistic Concept of Church Growth," in Exploring Church Growth, ed. Wilbert R. Shenk (Grand Rapids: Wm. B. Eerdmans Pub. Co., 1983), 96.

[690] For a further discussion of the relationship between "life" and "growth" see Costas, "Wholistic," 97.

[691] Rarely can an illustration be pushed to illogical extremes. So it is in the area of growth. For some, growth is unacceptable, even dangerous to the point of self-destruction. For a further discussion see Costas, "Wholistic," 98.

The reality of this danger strongly suggests that theologians formulate an accurate criterion for evaluating church growth. Growth is desired but it must be the right kind of growth that aligns itself with the truth of accurate theology. It is this kind of growth, characterized by beneficial change that must be the aim of the church. The proper beginning for a search to properly understand growth is in the origin of the church.[692] This supernatural origin of the church clearly calls for a corresponding response by people. Essentially, the church's growth calls for a distinct commitment on the part of all who desire it to grow.[693]

## Features of Theological Church Development

When growth is properly identified and labored toward by a group of Christians in a church, a number of features will be very distinctive. All are theologically identifiable and are consistent with an accurate development of theology. They are spirituality, incarnation, and faithfulness. First, consider spirituality. And, as the term indicates, this feature concentrates on the presence of the Holy Spirit in the life of the church.[694] As proper church growth

---

[692] Costas, "Wholistic," 100.

[693] The emphasis here is as discussed in chapter 3, that is, growth is first emphasized in spiritual changes. Thus, it is a personal and individual growth that is the church's priority.

[694] Growth in the church must be related to the operations of the Holy Spirit. (Costas, "Wholistic," 101.)

is linked with change and life, the ongoing source of these dynamics are maintained by the abiding presence of the Holy Spirit.[695] Second, the person of Christ is necessarily a part of church growth. He must be seen in all that occurs in His body. This visual presence is in the character of the individual Christians who make up the church. ". . . [We] must ask to what extent the church is experiencing a growth that bears a concrete (incarnate) witness to the commitment and comprehensive presence of Christ among the harassed and helpless multitudes of the world."[696] Third, a primary feature that displays itself in proper church growth is consistency with what God has done for the church in previous generations. God is certainly not fickle. Hence, when His church grows in each generation there will be standards that are kept all of the time and across different cultures. This is the kind of faithfulness that is to indicative of the church.

## Measures of Church Growth

Besides these three qualities that typify proper theological growth in the church there are also several ways in which the church should grow. Costas lists four ways: "in the reproduction of its members, the development of its organic life, the deepening of

---

[695] Gal. 5:22. For a discussion see Lightfoot, Galatians, 213.

[696] Costas, "Wholistic," 101.

its understanding of the faith, and the efficacy of its service in the world."[697]

The most common of the four dimensions that nearly all Christians would list is numerical growth. It is the most obvious.[698] The clear concern here is the addition of new people into the church via the process of conversion. Second on this list of church growth dimensions is organic change. Unfortunately, there is a polarization between advocates for numerical growth and organic growth, when in fact these are not issues in opposition to each other but in tandem with each other.[699] Third, growth within a church calls for a deepening of knowledge. After all, loving God is the purpose of Christian living and to know God is to love God. Maturity is growth in the assimilation of knowledge into a believer's life. Costas calls this "conceptual growth".[700] Last, growth requires a development in conscience. In sharp contrast to the

---

[697] Costas refers to these four dimensions as "numerical, organic, conceptual, and diaconal." (Costas, "Wholistic," 102.)

[698] Numerical growth refers to "membership reproduction" through evangelistic responses. (Costas, "Wholistic," 102.)

[699] Organic growth refers to the "internal development" of a local church. This includes form of government, financial practices, leadership patterns, style of worship, et cetera. (Costas, "Wholistic," 102.)

[700] Conceptual growth identifies the area of spiritual depth. It refers to matters such as Scriptural understanding, doctrinal awareness, and environment sensitivity. (Costas, "Wholistic," 102.)

world's proneness to self-indulgence, the church adopts the loving concern of the Christ who is her head.[701]

## *Part 2*

## *Application of Mutual Acceptance to Existing Churches*

The principles of equal acceptance have particular application as an aid for churches that are already in existence. They have been derived from a Scriptural foundation in order to guide the organization of Christians around accurate principles that lead to obedient activity. Too frequently a compromise of principles in the beginning stages of a church can result in strong resistance to change when accurate ideas are eventually discovered or even taught. The "we've-always-done-it-this-way" syndrome can scuttle renovation efforts. Or a church may be reluctant to change from past patterns, reasoning that such a shift would be tantamount to an admission of years of acting in error. More than theorizing on ideas and confusing the church in operation, practical theology acts to give firm and clear guidance for church leaders. Thus, it is clear that as accurate a foundation as possible for Christian living must be a part of a church's

---

[701] Diaconal growth measures the effect that the church is having on its surrounding community. This dimension builds the church's "authenticity and credibility" which gives the Gospel a hearing in the community. (Costas, "Wholistic," 102-103.)

philosophy and instrumental in evaluating how a church is progressing in its development.


### *Are Ethnic Churches Biblically Justifiable?*

The formulation of a church strategy for development, as it relates to the matter of race, cannot avoid addressing the issue of existing ethnic churches. If the essential message of the Gospel calls for a unity among all Christians, then the ethnic churches that are operating in a culture that is different from them are in a predicament. For example, in the North American western culture, do Christians with an ethnic Chinese heritage have a Biblical basis for operating a culturally oriented church? There is the obvious reason of language that legitimizes the existence of some ethnic churches. And it is understandable if Christians in the dominant society "freezes out" a racially distinct group of people, then those disenfranchised believers organize their own churches. But, where racial tension is less than flagrant bigotry and where language is not a limiting factor, should a multi-racial priority not only be the strategy but should it not be one of the church's testimony priorities to its particular community?[702] This question

---

[702] Yamamori finds biblical, historical and strategic support in including both evangelism and social action in the ministry of the church. While they are "separate in function", they are also "inseparable in relations" and "essential to the total ministry of the Church." For a further discussion see Tetsunao Yamamori, "Toward the Symbiotic Ministry: God's Mandate for the Church Today," in <u>Missiology: An International Review</u> 5 (July 1977): 265-274.

must be answered according to the findings of the New
Testament.

## The Effect of the Gospel on Culture

The New Testament acknowledges from background
studies that the Jewish culture from which the Gospel grew was
influenced by the Hellenism of the first century.[703] Bearing this in
mind, then it has to be accepted that when the Gospel came into
being it was culturally influenced. Because, as was noted earlier,
that the Gospel is verbal and that culture is language, then culture
does significantly have an effect on the Gospel's communication in
language and thought-forms.[704]

In the effort to sort out the blend of the Gospel and culture
it is important to give recognition to the essence of the Gospel's
divine origin. That is, there are certainly features about the Gospel
that are universal to all of mankind and therefore will fit in every

---

[703] Marshall explains: " . . . [It] is important to bear in mind that the cultural
relationships of Christianity were part of a broader process of cultural assimilation in
Palestine which was still going on in the first century, and which also provides a
background against which we can assess the nature of what was going on in the early
church." (Marshall, "Culture," 21.)

[704] Unger traces the dissemination of Hellenistic culture due to Alexander's
conquests. Greek language, philosophy, art and literature affected the entire known
world, even influencing the Jews of the Diaspora. For this cultural influence was
instrumental in the translation of the Old Testament into the common Greek of the day.
And that work " . . . became an important factor in the formation of the New Testament
. . . " (Merrill F. Unger, Archaeology and the New Testament [Grand Rapids:
Zondervan Pub. House, 1962], 35.)

culture.[705] It is also worth keeping in mind, as well, that the Gospel never ignored nor deliberately damaged a culture. In fact both Jesus and His Twelve are examples of how adaptable the Gospel is in a culture while still maintaining its effectiveness to change individual lives for eternity.[706]

Adaptability, however, should not be confused with compromise. Nor should it be expected that the Gospel should never be offensive. The radical change demanded by the Gospel is adaptable to every culture but it can also be offensive. Jesus Himself stood against the culture in which He was incarnated. Regarding the Sabbath violations and rules of cleanliness Jesus was criticized for causing offense.[707] And, of course, Jesus offended the culture into which He was born by His acceptance of the Gentile. Racial prejudice was ingrained in the Jewish culture but that was an evil that Jesus stood unreservedly against.[708]

---

[705] Ethnicity and culture are not antithetical to holy living. In fact, they are part of the celebration of God's beauty in creating all of mankind. "Each church, if it is to be truly indigenous, should be rooted in the soil of its local culture." (Pasadena Consultation, 3.)

[706] Marshall notes that the disciples of Jesus followed a lifestyle typical of Palestinian Jews. It included a strict observance to the Jewish law which governed every aspect of Jewish social and religious life. These followers of Jesus lived according to the law. (Marshall, "Culture," 27.)

[707] Marshall, "Culture," 27.

[708] As an example of this, Jesus openly received the centurion in Matthew 8:10ff helping to prepare the way for Gentile inclusion into the church. See further Marshall, "Culture," 27.

When the church's effect on the first century is evaluated it is clear that the Church left a massive impact on the culture from which it emerged. This point is illustrated by noting that two of the most culturally oriented features are related to the race debate. "(1) Gentiles did not need to be circumcised or keep the law of Moses but only to believe in Christ (with all that that involved) in order to be saved; and (2) Jew and Gentile stood on an equal footing, so that Gentiles no longer ranked as `unclean' in relation to Jews."[709] Jesus Himself impacted culture to such an extent that it was forever changed; yet, those changes cannot be considered evil. The New Testament does not condemn culture nor does it commend it. It does at certain points, however, come into conflict with it. "We do not forget the Scripture which declares that `the whole world is in the power of the evil one' (1 John 5:19)."[710] Culture is mentioned in a parallel sense when the term "world" is used.[711] The term "world" as it is used in 1 John 2:15 refers to a sinful human society. No Christian behavior is acceptable when it participates in this system.

The New Testament must be consulted on this matter of culture and the Gospel, for how the first church was impacted in its

---

[709] Marshall, "Culture," 27.

[710] "Pasadena Consultation," 5.

[711] The term "world" (*kosmos*) identifies the life that man has organized for himself. It is the nearest New Testament word for culture. Furthermore, it represents man's society as it stands against God. See further Marshall, "Culture," 28.

culture is the same manner in which modern cultures should seek to interact with the Gospel. The challenge of hermeneutics is to transpose the message from its original historical context into the context of present day readers so as to produce the same kind of impact on their lives as it did on the original hearers or readers.[712] This historical factor is indispensable. For an accurate application of the New Testament leads Christians to a point of pleasing the living God. Padilla observes, "Without a sufficient awareness of the historical factors, the faith of the hearers of the Gospel will tend to degenerate into a `culture-Christianity' which serves unredeemed cultural forces rather than the living God."[713] In a world of conflict and in a church with a history of racial failure, the task is a massive one, yet, it still must be the aim. The ultimate goal of Christianity, in spite of the church's poor track record, must be to please God by doing what is right.[714]

## The New Testament Definition of a Local Church

One of the most important themes in the New Testament is the topic of the church. Christ built the church, He sacrificed His life for it, He sent the Spirit to indwell it, He promises to take it as

---

[712] Padilla, "Hermeneutics and Culture," 65.

[713] Padilla, "Hermeneutics and Culture," 65.

[714] Marshall, "Culture," 30.

His bride, God the Spirit gave gifted men to establish it and guide it and He equipped every Christian with gifts to insure the church's smooth operation. How the church is defined in the New Testament is immensely helpful in the issue of culture and in the formulation of a church strategy for growth. For the very meaning of "church" in the New Testament defies any inclusion of racial or ethnic separation in its usage. If the definition of a church demands unity among its members on the basis of race or ethnicity, then any strategy that attempts to separate church members on the basis of race or ethnicity is false and artificial.

**The Term "Church"**

The term "church" is derived from the Greek term *ekklesia*.[715] And there are three levels to the development of this term: heathen, Jewish, and finally Christian. The basic sense of the term or the heathen use of *ekklesia* is descriptive of the etymology of the term. Literally meaning "called out ones" the sense of the term has two parts. First, they were summoned, thus, "called". But, they were also, called "out". That is, they were summoned "out of the whole population".[716]

---

[715] There are terms which existed before the church that were adopted by it for use. They were in a sense consecrated. The term Church is one of those ennobled terms. See further Richard C. Trench, Synonyms of the New Testament (Grand Rapids: Associated Publishes and Authors, Inc.), 1.

[716] For a further discussion see Trench, Synonyms, 2.

The Jewish use of *ekklesia* was mixed with the later Christian use. For the term synagogue, the center of Jewish gatherings, was slowly phased out and replaced by *ekklesia*. While the church had its beginnings among Jews, it was increasing its presence among the Gentile nations. It was natural to allow the shift of terms to adapt to this development as well. The term synagogue, definitely expressing Jewish identity, was steadily replaced by the term church.[717]


**A Mixed But Equal Gathering**

From this overview of the etymology of the term "church" the single clear understanding is that it has to do with an assembled group. Now, an observation of the uses in the New Testament will reveal two important aspects of the term; namely, a description of those who assemble and an explanation of the focus or reason for the gathering.[718] Some New Testament uses do not refer to Christians at all.[719] Others speak of a gathering of people all of whom are converted. In some cases this gathering is

---

[717] The replacement of the term "synagogue" by the term "church" was made palatable by the familiarity of the latter term to "Greek ears." (Trench, Synonyms, 5.)

[718] Ryrie, Basic Theology, 394.

[719] Acts 7:38. For a discussion of ekklesia in this context see Bruce, Acts, 152 and corresponding footnote 53, and Stott, Acts, 137. Also, Acts 19:39,41 illustrates the broad use of this term. For a discussion of the secular use of ekklesia in this context see Bruce, Acts, 401-402.

inclusive of all Christians on earth and in heaven.[720]    The passages that are of particular interest to this study are those that give a definite sense of a localized group of people who profess a faith in Christianity, or "local churches".  An examination of these texts reveal a pattern that describes what the foci of churches should be: "One was geographical.  Another was that profession of faith in Christ.  Another was the observance of baptism and the Lord's Supper. Another was the exercise of group responsibilities, like teaching."[721]    There is no evidence in the study of a New Testament local church that would allow for a church to adopt the characteristics based upon pre-conversion sociological comfort.  In fact, this study demonstrates that the church should display a universal inclusion of any people within a geographical area who profess faith in Christ and desire to observe the ordinances.[722]

---

[720]  Eph. 1:22-23.  For a further discussion see Moule, Ephesians, 63-64 and Abbott, Ephesians, 34-38.

[721]  Ryrie, Theology, 394.

[722]  Perhaps the Catholic Church may have a better understanding of this truth than does the Protestant Church.  I am grateful Professor Roland Allan for this insight.

    Pallen notes: " . . . [The Church] is a divinely constituted society consisting of members from every race and nation, all holding one faith . . . " C. B. Pallen, "Catholic Church," The New Catholic Dictionary (N.Y.: The Universal Knowledge Foundation, 1929), 180-181; quoted in Charles C. Ryrie, Basic Theology (Wheaton: Victor Books, 1981), 394.

## Challenging Ethnic Ecclesiastical Separation with a New Testament Understanding of Culture

Proponents of separate ethnic churches place a great emphasis on the importance of culture as a determining factor in strategizing for church growth. However, it has been demonstrated in this study that culture is an important factor in fulfilling the mission of the church but not a sovereign one. Culture must be seen in its proper theological perspective. It should not define the application of theology but visa versa. Theology must define the limits of culture and its influence on the application of ecclesiology.

## Blending New Testament Principles and the Dynamics of Culture

As a beginning point in the blending of culture and New Testament principles Conn makes the following observation: "All people want to affirm and reject God-given authentic community without losing social and ethnic identity."[723] This helpful suggestion points to the tension that exists in this issue. It addresses both the flaws in elevating culture above New Testament principles as well as affirms the divine source of the essence of human culture. Conn correctly points out that to regard

---

[723] Conn, "Method," 86.

culture as morally benign is a mistake.[724]  It too has been affected and is misused by evil.  At the same time it would be an error to assume that there is a complete separation between culture and religion.[725]  Culture is a product of man's living on this earth.  And man, created in the image of God, has produced his culture.  Man is definitely on a quest.[726]  Theologians and church leaders must guide mankind in that search.  However, the object of our search is supernatural not natural.[727]  These same differences are the ones that are cited as a reason for separating different kinds of people in different local churches; yet, they should be seen instead, as a theological imprint that is a result of man's fallenness. Nevertheless, these items serve as a protection from man perverting his humanity beyond a certain point.

## Common Headship

Clearly, then, man has a commonness with his fellow man. But, where is the root of that commonness?  "They are not simply

---

[724]  Ibid.

[725]  Matters of location, ethnic identity, language and social behavior are all expressions of man who is in the image of God.  And hence, all are in some way religious.  For a further discussion see Conn, "Method," 86.

[726]  Conn, "Method," 86.

[727]  For a discussion of the Babel text in Genesis 11 see Allan Ross, "Genesis," in The Bible Knowledge Commentary, Old Testament Edition, ed. John Walvoord and Roy Zuck (Wheaton: Victor Books, 1983.), 44-45.

in any sociological connection abstracted from its more basic covenant character. Rather, the heart of homogeneity is solidarity in religion as covenant."[728]   Theology makes it clear that all of mankind shares together in an origin that makes their relationship with each other stronger than their shared culture, as strong as tradition and cultural links are.[729]   This theme is also consistent with the New Testament.   Paul develops the theme of the universal kinship of all mankind in his sermon at the Areopagus. The apostle proclaimed that all of mankind came from the one man, Adam.

At this point it must be acknowledged that a separation between culture and theology is more imaginary than factual. Man's social environment is not separate from theology.   The demonic side of the issue of culture must be addressed.   There is an ongoing struggle with the powers described by Paul in Ephesians 6.  No unit in any culture is free from being tainted by sin.[730]   Every "nation" indicates that culture is subservient to something greater that all humans share in common; namely, an original head of the human race.[731]

---

[728]   Conn, "Method," 87.

[729]   Ibid.

[730]   To speak about barriers to conversion solely from a social perspective then, is theological imprecise.  See further Conn, "Method," 88.

[731]   Acts 17:26-27.  For a discussion of this text see Bruce, Acts, 357- 359 and Stott, Acts, 286.  Along this same theme Conn observes: " `God has made of one man

## Ethnicity and Unity

One of the difficulties that the subject of culture and theology presents is determining the balance between acknowledging the differences in ethnicity[732] and the necessity of unity in the body of Christ.[733] In his struggle to balance diversity

---

every race of men to live on all the face of the earth. . . . ' From covenant headship flows covenant kinship or solidarity." (Conn, "Method," 87.)

[732] Regarding the matter of ethnicity and the events at Babel, it is erroneous to assume that social pluralism was God's creational intent and that there is no other divine intention for God's created people. (see Wagner, Our Kind, 112.) For instance, it is unlikely that all cultural diversity can be attributed to the events of this account. For a further discussion see Conn, "Method," 90.

Furthermore, in viewing the Babel account it is inaccurate to demand that the text either be taken positively or negatively. Rather " . . . this dispersion movement of Genesis 10 appears as a curse, a centrifugal force separating people and retarding the subjugation of the earth (11:6b). Yet in sin's context this curse proved a blessing. God's intervention had an ultimately saving purpose for the nations." (Conn, "Method," 90.) The divine plan was for man to spread throughout the earth with the maintenance of their inward unity. But, sin had broken that relationship already and could not be reversed by man's outward efforts. (C. F. Keil and F. Delitzsch, Commentary on the Old Testament, vol. 1, transl. by James Martin [Grand Rapids: Wm. B. Eerdmans Pub. Co.], 173.) For a further discussion see Nahum M. Sarna, Understanding Genesis: The Heritage of Biblical Israel, (New York: Schocken Books, 1966), chapter 3, 63-90, with special note of 67-68.

As well, it is a false assumption to then take a view from Genesis 10 and apply it to the New Testament term ethne. With regard to the concept of "people" it is certain that " . . . the major emphasis of the New Testament, in connection with peoplehood, is generally of a judgmental sort." (Conn, "Method," 90.) Jesus came and redirected the thinking of all those who followed Him. Instead of catering to the ethnicity of Israel, which would have been a logical avenue if the HUP theory were true, He instead diverts the reasoning of His disciples in the opposite way. To love one's neighbor is not a command that can be restricted ethnically (Lk. 10:36-37). Perhaps the balance is kept in perspective by this statement by Conn: "The church plants churches in the homogeneous units of Jerusalem, but the church cannot forget that its final ethnic attachments are with the New Jerusalem. That understanding . . . controls the mission method." (Conn, "Method," 91.)

[733] Conn notes the application of this discussion in light of church strategy for growth and the tenets of the HUP theory: "McGavran's HUP makes the concept of human diversity the keystone of God's strategy for the nations. From that keystone pivot he

302

with unity, McGavran begins by asking the wrong question. Hence, the HUP theory reveals an inadequacy. "The ultimate orientation of any HUP must not be structured around the ethnic or sociological unit but around the catholicity and unity of the church as essential attribute. Thus, the crucial issue is not so much, `How much diversity can the church allow while remaining the church?' but rather, `How shall the church fully express its nature as one and catholic and do justice to those God-given, but sin-warped, dimensions of covenant solidarity still displayed in the peoples of the world'."[734] Essentially, then, it is the unity of the church that must remain central in any strategy for the church and her mission around the world not the diversity of man's ethnicity.

Regardless of the value placed on peoplehood, it cannot replace the importance of theological priorities for the church. The topic is important but if the focus of discussion and strategy development is shifted to peoplehood a problem arises; namely, has the recognition of peoplehood been so exalted by the methodology that it has become ultimately and solely a beneficial principle? Even a matter as vital as ethnicity can be improperly elevated to a point of distraction.[735]

---

struggles with its compatibility with the unity of the body, flowing out of its catholicity." (Conn, "Method," 87.)

[734] Conn, "Method," 89.

[735] Conn, "Method," 89.

## Possible Models of Mutual Acceptance in the Church

Mutual Acceptance is built upon the philosophy that the New Testament clearly calls for unity and koinonia in the Christian-to-Christian relationship. This relationship is to highlight mutual acceptance just as each was totally and fully accepted by Christ. Yet, this philosophy also recognizes that human needs vary greatly due to pre-Christian cultural and environmental influences. Some of these influences are legitimate others are inherently evil and have no part in the Christian community. Mutual Acceptance calls for wise discernment of these distinctions. As such, it urges that efforts to bring Christians together for worship and fellowship be creative and sensitive to peoples needs. But, the precepts of New Testament oneness must be allowed to guide the process.

### Existing Ethnic Churches

The application of mutual acceptance to ethnic ministries is precluded by a number of already established principles. First, it has been firmly acknowledged that ethnic churches are in fact real churches. There is no need to debate their genuine character. Also, they contribute an immense amount of life into the church at large and in their community. And their theological right to exist is not open to discussion and there is unquestionable sympathetic understanding for their existence as well. However, it has also been noted that ethnic churches are temporary. The need that

304

they serve dissipates for each passing generation. At the same time it is clear that their need ebbs and flows with the immigration quotient of any particular geographical vicinity. As long as immigration exists so will ethnic churches. The pertinent question is what should the church do to address the vast population of assimilated and acculturated believers.

A look at the historical formation of the New World highlights the role of immigration patterns on developing religion. As ethnic traditions were introduced, so religious trends began.[736] In this sense the social form of religion and ethnic churches are closely connected.[737] Two perspectives dominate the attempt to correlate ethnicity and religion, as described by Mullins.

First, there is the functionalist theory of religion.[738] According to this view religious forms such as beliefs and ritual have two affects. They provide a bonding among people and they also provide a social context in which these same traditions and values can be transferred to others.[739] It is observed by this

---

[736] For a discussion on this observation see Will Herberg, Protestant, Catholic, Jew (Garden City, New York: Anchor Books, 1960).

[737] Mullins observes that the study of ethnic churches has been largely ignored by sociologists in recent decades. He supposes that a "preoccupation with the nature of Protestant sectarianism, new religious movements, and secularization has probably led to this neglect of an area equally important in the sociology of religion." (Mullins, "Ethnic Churches," 321.)

[738] For a more detailed study of this perspective see Emile Durkheim, The Elementary Forms of the Religious Life (New York: The Free Press Edition, 1965).

[739] Mullins refers to this as "the traditional functions and integrative consequences of

perspective that while there are many institutions that contribute to the preservation of a particular ethnic group, the ethnic church is usually at the forefront.[740] Such a phenomenon is expected for there are many functions of religion that lend themselves to ethnic preservation. Anderson and Frideres list several of these religious features: religion plays a major part in establishing personal identity, it can easily assume the role as the protector of ethnic identity, it is recognized as a promoter of social integration, it serves as a validation for ethnic values and customs, it gives ethnic members a place to have their individual dignity affirmed when they may be considered as lower in status by non-members, it promotes a conservatism that is conducive for ethnic preservation, and it condones deliberate social exclusiveness from outsiders.[741] Second, ethnic churches are perceived as adapting organizations rather than cultural preservers. This viewpoint

---

religion for ethnic groups in modern pluralistic societies." (Mullins, "Ethnic Churches," 322.)

[740] From the context of multi-ethnic Canada Millett states, " . . . of all the institutions supporting the survival of distinctive cultures, the church is usually the strongest and the most active." (David Millett, "Religion as a Source of Perpetuation of Ethnic Identity." In Sounds Canadian: Languages and Cultures in Multi-Ethnic Society, ed. Paul M. Migus [Toronto: Peter Martin], 105.) Others have the same sense of the situation. Mol describes the effect of immigration with certainty: " . . . migrant churches have always been the most effective bastions of ethnic preservation." (Han Mol, Identity and the Sacred [New York: The Free Press, 1976],174.) The church in South Africa is also an example of the church acting as the protector of ethnic identity. For a further discussion see Moodie, Afrikanerdom.)

[741] Alan Anderson and James Frideres, Ethnicity in Canada: Theoretical Perspectives (Toronto: Butterworths, 1981), quoted in Mullins, "Ethnic Churches," 322.

306

assumes that the natural process of assimilation transforms an ethnic group over a period of time. The generational landmarks are especially noteworthy in these changes. Initially, every ethnic group resists change and attempts to preserve the "old way" of life.[742] However, the final result is described by Mullins: " . . . the history of immigrant churches reveals that the tendency toward conformity is ultimately the dominant force shaping their character. The process of assimilation forces the churches to choose between accommodation and extinction."[743]

Of these two perspectives, Mullins finds greater validity in the second. He bases his selection upon the viewpoint of contemporary sociologists who have observed the pattern that ethnic churches make significant organizational adaptions in order to survive. In particular, ethnic churches have organizationally accommodated its latter generations, which are progressively lost to the natural process of cultural assimilation. The culture of the majority will produce an inevitable influence on the offspring of immigrants through education, economics, recreation and religion.[744]

---

[742] At the outset, ethnic groups have an aim to maintain their distinctions from other groups. However, group survival will cause traditions to bend and adapt to the acculturated generations. For a further discussion on this see Niebuhr, Social Sources.

[743] Mullins, "Ethnic Churches," 323.

[744] Mullins cites three studies that point to the influence of the assimilation process. (Mullins, "Ethnic Churches," 322-323.) First, he cites the ethnic study of Howard Palmer done in Alberta, Canada. A pattern among ethnic churches was clearly observed. Organizational adaptions were made with the specific aim "to stem the

Based upon these observations Mullins constructs an ideal-typical model of ethnic church development. He describes three different stages as an ethnic church experiences the assimilation process. In stage one, ethnic churches focus attention on meeting the needs of the immigrant generation.[745] Language is a major feature in this stage. When the new country of the majority culture do not offer services in the mother tongue of an immigrant group, the natural reaction is to initiate churches with

---

defection of the second and third generations." (Howard Palmer, Land of the Second Chance: A History of Ethnic Groups in Southern Alberta [Alberta: The Lethbridge Herald, 1972], 239-242.) The "old way" was assumed in the formation of churches by immigrants. But, the normal pressures of educating children (second generation in the land or first generation born in the new land), socializing children in extra-curricular activities, immersing into the economics of a new land with co-workers and business associates, learning to communicate in a new language, deciphering cultural innuendoes, and enjoying a new culture's recreation and entertainment mean a lessening of the "old way" and an adapting to the new.

Second, Mullins cites a work reflecting a similar observation on American soil by Stephen Steinberg. Steinberg alludes to the inevitable loss of the "old way" and points to the adapting efforts of ethnic churches as a curtailment of losing successive generations but not as a sure means of stopping it. Steinberg notes that " . . . ethnic subsocieties must adapt to the prevailing culture to curtail the loss of more assimilated members." (Stephen Steinberg, The Ethnic Myth: Race, Ethnicity and Class in America [New York: Atheneum, 1981], 67-68.)

Third, Joshua Fishman observes that developing religion in an ethnic setting will be a part of the assimilation process. The measure of religious success is directly proportional to lessening of ethnicity in the church. Fishman states, " . . . the more `successful' religion becomes, the more de-ethnicized it becomes." (Joshua Fishman, Language in Sociocultural Change [Stanford: Stanford University Press, 1972.], 621.)

[745] The immigrant generation gravitate to services where their own first language is utilized and where the church leadership have their origin in the old country. Mullins notes, "The strong leadership of the first generation with their cultural and language differences provides the motivation and resources necessary for ethnic churches to be established." (Mullins, "Ethnic Churches," 323.)

this ethnic emphasis.[746]   Yet, two powerful elements force a tension on ethnic churches during this stage. One is the reality of religious organizations being very slow to change. They are poor at adapting to the pace of their surrounding environment.[747]   The second is the generational problem. Each new generation that is born from that ethnic group is assimilated into the host society. They are reared with a bilingual base and live the majority of their lives in a culture that is identified more and more with the new society and foreign to their ethnic roots.   These observations identify the ethnic church as an organization that has a temporary purpose.   Its constituency is unique and subject to inevitable change with each generation born into the host society.   Mullins accurately states, "Generational change is at the root of all the organizational problems which confront ethnic churches."[748]

Two features increase their influence on the first stage ethnic church. They are the processes of cultural assimilation and the natural change in language emphasis, away from the mother-

---

[746]   There are negative reasons that facilitate the development of ethnic churches as well.   Racial tensions are regularly fed by prejudice and exclusion even in church settings. When these attitudes are expressed by the churches of the host society, then ethnic churches are bound to be established.   Such ethnic churches, Mullins notes, are "the only realistic alternative." (Mullins, "Ethnic Churches," 323.)

[747]   Mullins, "Ethnic Churches," 325.

[748]   Mullins, "Ethnic Churches," 325. For a further discussion see M. J. Yinger, The Scientific Study of Religion (Toronto: Collier-Macmillan, 1970.) and Milton Gordon, Assimilation in American Life: The Role of Race, Religion, and National Origin (New York: Oxford University Press, 1964.).

tongue and toward the language of the host society. As a result, a second stage for the ethnic church emerges. Dominant in this stage is the effort to provide a bi-lingual ministry. Leadership, services and materials assume a multi-language dimension. But, this emphasis is not smooth. Rigidity against change as opposed to flexibility to new ideas is usually the attitude in most ethnic churches.[749] Even when the painful decision to adapt is made, practical matters such as available leadership or resources may not be readily available. And economic demands for such a shift may not be within the church's reach. But, it is a certainty that when a church has reached this level of struggle but fails to adapt to the language and cultural assimilation shift, it will face a gradual decline in its membership. For an ethnic church to survive, then, it must be able to adapt to the changing needs of its members and the target group with which it is identified.[750]

The third stage of ethnic church development is characterized by the influences of structural assimilation[751]. This stage can be identified by the movement of its constituency into

---

[749] For a further discussion see William Starbuck, "Organizational growth and development," in Handbook of Organizations, ed. by James March (Chicago: Rand McNally and Co., 1965.) and J. E. Eldridge and A. D. Crombie, A Sociology of Organizations (London: George All and Unwin, 1974).

[750] For a further discussion and an illustration of this type of organizational adaption see Mayer Zald and Patricia Denton, "From Evangelism to General Service: The Transformation of the YMCA," in Administrative Science Quarterly 8, no.2 (1963): 214-234.

[751] Gordon, Assimilation, 70.

the host society as fully accepted members. Barriers to clubs, neighborhoods, schools, et cetera have been reduced. And the processes of acculturation have had time to change the values and reorient the perspectives of the ethnic population. Ethnic churches again feel the loss of its members during this stage. Its purpose of fulfilling social and ethnic identification can now be equally met by organizations of the host society. Along with education and social adaption comes social mobility. And social mobility is accompanied by necessity, geographical mobility. This shift breaks up the ethnic community.[752] Furthermore, this third stage of the ethnic church also faces the increase of intermarriage among its later generations. Both of these trends lead to an increase in the de-ethnicization of these churches.[753] And in contrast to the first stage ethnic church the absence of the immigrant generation also means the absence of the mother-tongue as the primary means of communication. The church is monolingual but with the language of the host society.

---

[752] For a further discussion see Darrel Montero, "The Japanese Americans: Changing patterns of Assimilation Over Three Generations," in American Sociological Review 46, no. 6: 829-839.

[753] Mullins notes that if a large number of exogamous marriages are included into the ethnic church, then the ethnic flavor of the church will diminish by the introduction of more and more who do not share in that ethnic heritage. However, it is also observed that exogamous marriages do not tend to gravitate toward ethnic churches, but in fact seem to discourage active participation in them. Exogamous marriages move away from the ethnic community. (Mullins, "Ethnic Churches," 326.) For a further discussion see Darrel Montero, Japanese Americans: Changing Patterns of Ethnic Affiliation Over Three Generations (Boulder, Colorado: Westview Press, 1980).

The process of change for ethnic churches is in large part sociologically inevitable. Internal matters of language and culture bring these kinds of churches into existence but when they cease to be needs, then, the reason for the churches to exist disappears as well. And when the negative use of discrimination and racism are diminished, the external pressure for ethnic churches to exist also disappear.[754]

**Planning More Ethnic Churches**

The preceding argument shows the sociological forces at play in the ethnic church. It serves to emphasize the temporary nature of the ethnic church. Yet, it must be carefully restated that the temporary nature does not mean that the ethnic church is in any way inferior or less than a real church. In particular, when the external forces of the host society subject a particular group to racism or discrimination, the initiation of their own culturally oriented church is understandable. Or, when the internal forces of ethnic identity are of an immigrant nature, it is understandable that there will be ethnic churches. However, from an organizational and a sociological perspective, ethnic churches lose their reason for existence when their original goal of serving the needs of the

---

[754] Mullins, "Ethnic Churches," 326.

312

immigrant generation no longer exists. Churches in this situation face three possible alternatives.

First, a fresh wave of immigrants can enter the country or a renewed expression of discrimination can erupt. Either of these would stimulate the sagging clientele and membership of an ethnic church. Or second, the church could insist upon maintaining its ethnic emphasis in spite of its diminishing need. Should it choose this avenue, it will most likely disappear.[755] A third alternative is for the ethnic church to reformulate its goals. With its original purpose for existence no longer relevant any desire to survive must be based on a new constitution of goals.[756] Less and less emphasis must be placed upon the church's ethnicity and tradition. In their place broader goals which include the needs of its acculturated constituency and non-ethnics must be established. Creating more churches of any kind is not the solution to reaching the un-churched. Rather, it is making the church a source of quality and

---

[755] Mullins quotes Kayal in describing an ethnic church's insistence on maintaining its "ethnic enclosure and support" as an element that will lead to a church's eventual demise. (Philip Kayal, "Religion and Assimilation: Catholic `Syrians' in America," in International Migration Review 7, no.4: 424, quoted in Mullins, "Ethnic Churches," 327.)

[756] For a further discussion on organization survivability see David Sills, The Volunteers: Means and Ends in a National Organization (Glencoe, Illinois: The Free Press, 1957) and Richard Hall, Organizations: Structure and Process (Englewood Cliffs, New Jersey: Prentice Hall, 1972).

relevance in life.[757]  It is possible that the likely scenario for this gradual transition is conversion into a multi-ethnic church.[758]

## Multi-Ethnic Church

A helpful example of how one church addresses the subject of a multi-racial or multi-cultural ecclesiastical effort is The Rock of Our Salvation Evangelical Free Church in Austin on the West Side of Chicago. Demographically, this area of the city is 95% black; but, the church is comprised of a white and black mix - approximately 30% of the membership of this new congregation is white.[759]  It is an unusual combination of both white and black members from the inner-city and commuters[760] drawn to its commitment to a wholistic emphasis. That is, the church takes the

---

[757] Barna, Frog, 140.

[758] Mullins illustrates the phenomenon of ethnic church dissolution or multi-ethnic adaption from two ethnic groups: the Japanese Conference of the United Church of Canada and the Buddhist Churches of Canada.  He notes that without any new immigrant wave or new discrimination uprising the only two options for their future is dissolution or multi-ethnicity. (Mullins, "Ethnic Churches," 329.)

[759] The Rock of Our Salvation Evangelical Free Church was established in October of 1983.  (Robert Kachur, "Fudge Ripple at the Rock," in Christianity Today [March 4, 1988], 22-23.) Its pastor admits that it is a black church both in focus and outreach but then quickly points out that a substantial percentage of its members are white. " . . . we're not exactly a traditional black or a traditional white church. We're a hybrid." (Ibid., 21.)

[760] In this regard, the Rock of Our Salvation Evangelical Free Church is an illustration of more than a racial mix, it is also an example of a class mix. Yet, the point could be made that it is virtually impossible to completely separate the two issues.

314

initiative to provide the neighborhood " . . . with everything from emergency housing to family counseling."[761]  Once they are involved, white members find an additional attraction, namely, a new spiritual dimension that before was lacking in their personal spiritual walk.[762] Commonly this added dimension is described as a faith that goes beyond talk and enters into the realm of personal experience.[763]

What began this unique ministry was a friendship between Raleigh Washington, a black pastor, and Glen Kehrein, a white executive, director of Circle Urban Ministries.  Their companionship seemingly has a great influence on this multi-ethnic ministry.  What they are themselves committed to individually and corporately, is what they bring into the church. Kehrein recalls, "All my adult life I had been searching for a black pastor who was committed to holistic ministry and who wasn't threatened by associating with a white brother."[764]  This attitude is duplicated in Kehrein's life as well.  Neither friend is threatened by a racial or ethnic association.  In fact, they deliberately reach out to embrace others of another ethnic background.  They sense a

---

[761] Kachur, "Fudge Ripple," 22.

[762] Ibid.

[763] It is common to hear a white member of the Rock describe how satisfying it is to see so many people helped in so many different ways through the activities of different kinds of Christians joining together to help them.

[764] Kachur, "Fudge Ripple," 21.

personal calling to be bridge builders in this realm of racial segregation in the church.[765] This common calling for both men is firmly implanted with past experiences of racial pain.[766] Washington relates to his enduring of a "racially motivated attack"[767] of his military career as a lieutenant colonel in the U.S. Army. Kehrein grew up in Wisconsin and never saw a black person until he moved to Chicago at 18. There he involved himself in Circle Church. At the time it was an interracial church. But, the church split in 1976 due to racial issues. Kehrein suffered through that painful division. Together, these two men found a common cause and vision together. Their individual dreams of seeing a multi-racial church ignited into a single quest when they met each other. They model their mutual acceptance in their personal relationship.[768] This example is an indication of one necessary ingredient in a multi-cultural church. A successful effort

---

[765] Kachur, "Fudge Ripple," 21.

[766] Kehrein reflects over the value of these painful experiences as a basis for their current commitment: "The Lord had to put Pastor (Washington) and me through certain experiences to understand the commitment it takes to be partners in cross-cultural ministry." (Kachur, "Fudge Ripple," 21.)

[767] Other white officers blocked Washington's rise in rank, hoping to prevent him from becoming the first black General in the Adjutants General Corps. Subsequently, Washington was accused of wrongdoing. White investigators, who shared these racist fears, then contributed to Washington's unjust departure from the military. (Kachur, "Fudge Ripple," 21.)

[768] Kehrein notes that he and his pastor placed special effort in their relationship for the church to emulate. They desired to demonstrate that "blacks and whites can serve God together." Their relationship was one of deep personal commitment. (Kachur, "Fudge Ripple," 23.)

by the church which will stand against history, tradition, and man's bent toward the sin of racism begins with the church's leadership. "Leadership will be a key component if the church is going to progress."[769] Personal relationships by leaders that reflect the importance of multi-cultural relationships are part of the development of a multi-cultural church.

Besides a leadership commitment on a personal level, a ministry philosophy that recognizes mutual acceptance is vital to any effort that challenges the racial tension among Christians and churches. It must be addressed directly as an ongoing effort by the church. Not all are so sure of this effort. Carl Ellis, black pastor of the Presbyterian Church of America, believes that humans are naturally sinful. And, if the problem of race were eliminated some other expression of that sinfulness would take its place. His reticence here is further fueled by a suspicion that his black culture would be discarded some where along the way.[770] Yet, a church, an assembly of converted Christians, must operate according to God's intent for the church. And, it is clear that God did not intend for Christians to gather according to their pre-converted preferences but according to a new community of

---

[769] Barna, Frog, 148.

[770] Frame, "Race," 16. Frame suggests that such feelings illustrate the complexity in resolving the problems of race in the church. He suggests that there are no "simple answers." And, he furthermore points to this complexity as a major culprit in the continuing problem of racial unrest in the church.

people that He has chosen among the peoples of the earth. The church must be a visible demonstration of the power of reconciliation not only of the individual to God but also of each Christian with his fellow Christian.[771] Washington elaborates, "I disagree with some of the writers who are saying that the homogeneous church is the way to go. Homogeneous churches may be easier, but I don't think they're God's intent."[772] Every Christian church and assembly should actively address the matter of mutual acceptance as part of its agenda for ministry.

One course of action for a church in this situation would be to be involved in extensive evangelism to a particular ethnic group that is different from itself. It would not have to be an exclusive effort but an emphasis nevertheless. The target group would be one whose needs are not currently being met by any other church agency. Such a target group would also be one with which the church could more easily identify than another. Either the church at large or a group within the church could take responsibility for such an ongoing effort.[773]

---

[771] While this perspective is not new, Kehrein notes that Christians do not have a vehicle to act on that reconciliation. Furthermore, he observes that church-growth models stress homogeneity as the best means to achieve church growth. So we have Bible-believing evangelicals who at their core are very racist, yet they experience very little contradiction with that because they're never challenged." (Kachur, "Fudge Ripple," 23.)

[772] Kachur, "Fudge Ripple," 23.

[773] For a further discussion of target group evangelism within a church philosophy of ministry see Frank Tillapaugh, Unleashing the Church (Old Tappan, New Jersey:

318

But, more than just a ministry philosophy there must be an emphasis on reconciliation between individuals. This feature of a ministry that is based upon mutual acceptance is apparent from Kehrein's analysis of the problems leading up to Circle Church's racial split. That experience emphasized to him that philosophy was a good beginning but insufficient by itself. Individuals have to work out their reconciliation with each other one on one.[774] Acknowledging this need consequently formulates a realistic perspective regarding racial tension. Programs, meetings, and ideals meet a prime ingredient for their eventual success or failure when the individual is the focus. At the rock, there is a realization that in a multiracial setting "the potential for conflict and misunderstanding is high."[775] Individuals must make the difference. No church can depend upon a generally accepted idea and make a multi-ethnic church advance beyond the normal distractions of racial tension. The philosophy is needed but individuals and the relationships that they share with others needs to actualize that philosophy. Mutual acceptance operates as a

---

Fleming H. Revell Co., 1979).

[774] Kehrein makes the helpful comment: "If your commitment is to a philosophy, an idea, or a dream rather than a person, you won't make it through the difficult times." (Kachur, "Fudge Ripple," 23.)

[775] Washington observes from his own experience, "Any time there is a difference between a black and a white, no matter what that difference is, no matter what caused it, it ends up being a racial conflict." (Kachur, "Fudge Ripple," 23.)

perspective; but, it must operate in relationships between and among people who are reconciled to each other.

Once the leadership of the church model their conviction regarding mutual acceptance and the church actively addresses the matter in its regular philosophy of ministry and the membership participates in the reality of reconciliation with one another measures to manage the stresses in a racially sensitive society must be observes. Managing mutual acceptance in the church calls for a realistic expectation of problems which are race-related. Real conflicts call for deliberate action in the church program. Such action must be adjusted by the church leadership to fit in with the church's structure. But, essentially members must be allowed to communicate in an edifying forum what their struggles are with the church's racial dynamics.[776] The aim of such encounters must be understanding not demand-meeting or bias-compromising. Each session has the preemptive hope of drawing people closer together and tearing more barriers down.[777]

---

[776] The Rock's solution is to organize church calendar events that provide its members with the opportunity to express their feelings about racial circumstances in the church. They are called "chocolate" and "vanilla" meetings. Both blacks and whites are invited to discuss what bothers them about the church's racial dynamics over a bowl of fudge ripple ice cream. (Kachur, "Fudge Ripple," 23.)

[777] The Rock intends such sessions to be preventative rather than prescriptive. Both church leaders are also ready to deal individually with those who do not feel comfortable in a racially mixed situation to express their feelings. Again both men are committed to dealing with the problems of racial anxiety with a loving and bold approach. Their goal is to prevent anything that can be racially divisive. Washington reflects, "We've often marveled at how God has used one of us to resolve potentially divisive issues." (Kachur, "Fudge Ripple," 23.) For a further discussion of specific

320

## Churches of the Majority

When the church faces the problem of racism, the solution is too frequently left to the ethnic churches or to the occasional multi-racial church. Functionally, the majority church avoids the issue. Admittedly, the problem of racism has its origin in the community. However, when the church assumes the same posture as the community regarding this "open sore"[778] then, it also becomes a problem in the church. The church is to be distinct from the world not an image of it. Members individually and corporately are responsible to make their uniqueness visible to the world. This uniqueness possessed by Christians is a kind of unity that is essential to its being a light for Christ.[779]

A practical outworking of the church's essential theology is the divine design for the church. That is, the church perceives humanity as a single race originating from Adam as the progenitor. All members of the single human race are so related. In the same vein, the church recognizes that all Christians are related to each other through Christ, who is the progenitor of a " . . . new race whose members are in Him, sharing in His salvation act and being

---

examples of racist feelings being replaced with mutual acceptance see Kachur, "Fudge Ripple," 23, in particular the final column entitled, "Is heaven homogeneous?".

[778] United Methodist News Service, "Racism," 42-43.

[779] Light is more than a reference to displaying something. Rather, it is also a reference to essence of being. All Christians are not only in the light, but also "penetrated by it, so that they themselves became `the light of the world,' Matt. v.14." (Abbott, Ephesians, 152.)

dominated by His personality."[780]  Those in Christ are part of a flock with Him as the shepherd.  And this flock is composed of sheep from every ethnic background and culture.  "The sheep of the New Testament church from every nation are one flock because of common relationship to the one Shepherd."[781]  A reciprocal result is a part of this common relationship.  For all Christians not only share a reciprocal love with God but also with each other; that is, they are brothers together in the same single family.  Implied in this brotherly relationship is a "personal equality before the Lord."[782]  This togetherness of equality is unique to the church in comparison to the world.  It is fundamental to the church's identity.  Therefore, it is a part of what the church must be striving to display to the world.  This task is for all of the church. Each local congregation of Christians is obligated to pursue this task.  It is inadequate to assume that another congregation's effort to display Christian unity among its members of differing ethnic backgrounds is a credit to any other congregation.  For any church in a multi-cultural situation to be a true local church, it ". . . must be manifestly functioning as a sign and foretaste and instrument of

---

[780]  Robert Saucy, The Church in God's Program (Chicago: Moody Press, 1972), 21.

[781]  Saucy, Church, 50.

[782]  Saucy illustrates this equality and unity from Matthew 23:8.  Matters of seeking titles or positions placing oneself over others was not to be sought.  Rather, a brotherly or equal relationship is to be pursued.  For a further discussion see Saucy, Church, 23-24 and Barbieri, "Matthew," 73-74.  Also, see Robertson, Epistles of Paul, 591.

God's purpose to draw those of different cultures into his one family."[783]

Also, unity among church members must be developed as well as maintained. It must be made visible while it is energetically nurtured " . . . to grow up into the fullness of unity in Christ."[784] No church can remain in isolation from the race problem in the community and be complete in itself. Any church regardless of size or homogeneous make-up can with the application of mutual acceptance " . . . reflect the universality and diversity of the Body of Christ."[785] But, where does the church begin? How does the majority church enter into the world of contrasting cultures of its community and make its impact on the world as the light of Christ?

A simple beginning is to bring a church into a close working relationship with an existing ethnic or multi-ethnic church. Together there can be plans for shared celebrations of their common faith. Such relationships must be allowed to be creative with the aim at the demonstration of " . . . Christian love,

---

[783] Newbigin notes that a claim by a church which argues that its members have unity in themselves but does not relate to its multi-ethnic community is a false claim of church unity. True local church unity requires "movement" in the direction of unity. (Lesslie Newbigin, "What is `A Local Church Truly United?'," in Ecumenical Review, 29 [April 1977], 125.)

[784] "Pasadena Consultation," 4. For a further discussion of this idea as it relates to Ephesians 4:13-16 see Salmond, "Ephesians," 332-338.

[785] "Pasadena Consultation," 4.

brotherhood, and interdependence."[786] Cultures vary in degrees due to generational factors as well as population demographics. Hence, flexibility is necessary within the application of mutual acceptance. What remains a constant, however, is the priority for the church to identify with its community by reaching out into it with an attitude of equality and brotherhood. Any paternalistic disposition patronizes the mutual acceptance principle and compromises the theological basis for unity.[787]

Two other suggestions which require a greater degree of involvement are for a local church to establish culturally distinct fellowship groups among its own members or to embark upon a totally integrated church. These distinct groups would be free to develop their own identity and utilize ways of creative worship and outreach to those who identify with their cultural ways. This program can occur on a midweek schedule. Then, on every Lord's Day all of the church's members can meet and celebrate together.[788] Meeting jointly in conjunction to separate fellowships is a task that must face certain obstacles as well. For the flavor of the worship, the symbols for celebration, the style of music, the

---

[786] "Pasadena Consultation," 5.

[787] I am indebted to Patrick Sookhdeo for the thoughts in this discussion which arose during a personal interview (London, 1989) on the matter of the church's responsibility toward issues of racial tension.

[788] "Pasadena Consultation," 5. This is the second of three suggested models.

manner of the preaching, <u>et cetera</u> must be edifying to all who worship together. But, what principles guide this kind of situation?

## Leadership is a Key

"Giftedness" in leadership and specialized service take priority over culture. Just as theology supersedes ethnicity, so the functioning and operation of the church must be based upon Biblical priorities. The two matters, however, of ethnicity and giftedness may overlap. For example, in the area of music, it is right for the musically gifted[789] to be the directors of that aspect of a church's worship regardless of their ethnic background. Also, regarding leadership the principles of elder qualifications in the New Testament ought to guide the acknowledgment of who the church leaders are.

At the same time sensitivity ought to be exercised as well. It is difficult for ethnics to believe that a church is eager to display the reconciliation of Christ in a multi-cultural community when all of the church leadership are of the majority or controlling culture. Transition time for maturing of leaders is one matter, but, it cannot be a permanent excuse. Racial minorities are too familiar with such excuses. Circle Church in Chicago serves as an example. Its effort toward a multi-racial church was commendable and

---

[789] It is a given that church leaders and specialized servers are Christians who are spiritually committed as well as particularly gifted.

courageous but was noticeably lacking in multi-racial leadership. There was a multi-racial pastoral staff but the understanding of equality was different.[790] On the board, which made the church's major decisions, there were no Blacks. Ortiz identifies both of these leadership tensions as contributors to the eventual demise of Circle Church.[791] The issue of "power" is a primary blockade to true racial reconciliation in the church. White evangelicals are generally unwilling to give up their control to ethnic minorities. Hence, little movement toward this Gospel essential of unity in the body of Christ will actually be realized.[792] Thompson suggests two helpful ideas related to this problem. One is to turn from the "secular point of view" regarding power. The Christian perspective is one where power has changed lives, made individuals into new people.[793] The second is to obey God's command of reconciliation. This kind of obedience calls for deliberate and daily

---

[790] The "team concept" among its pastors of different ethnic backgrounds was not understood in the same way. Hillard, the black pastor, understood "team concept" to mean that all the pastors were equal. Mains, the white pastor, understood "team concept" to mean he was the senior pastor with whom the other ministers worked. (Manuel Ortiz, "Circle Church: A Case Study in Contextualization," in Urban Mission [January 1991], 12-14.)

[791] Ortiz, "Circle Church," 14.

[792] Barbara Thompson, "The Gospel in Black & White," in Christianity Today (March 4, 1988), 19. Parker notes that while some whites participate in doing good things to help other ethnic groups, those same individuals " . . . might be uncomfortable submitting to black leadership or taking orders from someone at work who is not white." (Frame, "Race," 17.)

[793] Thompson, "Gospel," 19.

action in building relationships. In Johnson's estimation it is not possible to claim to be God's people and " . . . reject another part of the body of Christ."[794] At "the Rock" Washington and Kehrein believe that racial reconciliation is built on individuals being reconciled with one another. Therefore, as leaders in their church their personal commitment to each other is a "model" and it is "bedrock" in their ministry commitment.[795]

## *Conclusion of Chapter IV*

Mutual Acceptance philosophically and practically applies to missions in several ways. First, it acknowledges the need to be flexible in the use of methodological terms. Indigenization was helpful in pointing to the importance of missionary intent but limiting in its ability to emphasize communication of the Gospel with enough regard for the receiving culture. It is important for a church to develop its own character within its cultural climate but, when pushed to extremes indigenization can cut off Christian interaction with fellow Christians of a different culture. Webster notes, " . . . some leaders, both missionary and national, have made the mistake of looking upon the establishment of indigenous churches as the end and goal of missions and the final answer to

---

[794] Ibid.

[795] Kachur, "Fudge Ripple," 23.

327

nationalistic pressures. The fallacy of this, however, became apparent when some churches became so indigenous, so nationalistic, that they no longer had room for anything foreign, including missionaries and Christians of different racial and national origins."[796]

Second, the term contextualization is very useful in that it balances the importance of accurate Gospel presentation. That is, the sending culture is careful to present the revelation of God as clearly as possible, as free from cultural interpretation as possible. The receiving culture can accept the Gospel in their own context. And just as important, contextualization argues for an awareness of the syncretism. Nothing in a receiving culture that is contradictory to the revelation of God can be condoned nor tolerated. Truth cannot be compromised or it is no longer truth. Thus, if a receiving culture incorporates matters of racial, ethnic or class prejudice, then the Gospel and Christianity cannot accept such behavior or attitudes. Any such adaption of compromise would be in conflict with the essence of the Gospel. Third, lordship is a part of the conversion result. Missionaries must act upon this result. It is not their place to condone or qualify customs that must be brought under the rule of submission for the new life of a converted Christian. In particular, matters of racial acceptance are a part of the Gospel of reconciliation. Cultural

---

[796] Warren Webster, "Mission in Time and Space," in Church/Mission Tensions Today, ed. C. Peter Wagner, 93-110 (Chicago: Moody Press, 1972), 98.

features that identify with selective or prejudiced association must be confronted once individuals are a part of the Christian community. This is not tantamount to ethnocide. Culture can be and must be celebrated in its beauty by Christians; but, the fallen nature of man and that influence on culture must be rejected.[797]

Fourth, the application of mutual acceptance for the existing church is also a part of practical theology. How the church operates in the lives of people is the ultimate benefit of theologizing. Three areas of application are treated here. First, mutual acceptance applies to the ethnic church. Predominant here is the generation problem. The need for ethnic churches in a multi-ethnic community is temporary. Language needs is a major element here. But, when the normal processes of assimilation transpire, the need for ethnic churches passes. Without a new influx of immigrants or a resurgence of racial oppression, the temporary nature of ethnic churches must be accepted.

Also, churches that are deliberately multi-racial can apply mutual acceptance as well. A key ingredient here is the caution against a "melting-pot" mentality. Integration in the church does not mean that theology teaches that individual ethnicity is wrong. The two worlds of a multi-racial church and one's individual celebration of his or her ethnic identity can exist side-by-side. In fact, the individual nurturing of one's own ethnicity can prove to be

---

[797] For a further discussion of this balance of culture and Christianity see Newbigin, Pluralist Society. In particular note chapter 15 "The Gospel and Culture," 184-197.

an effective evangelistic tool. After successful evangelism results in a number of converts through ethnic identity in community centers, hobbies, sports events, et cetera, spiritual nurturing can include an introduction to a multi-racial church as part of the sanctification development.

Finally, the majority population churches must also apply mutual acceptance. A true local church must be reaching into its community, including its varied cultural backgrounds into its own body. It is essential that the Gospel of reconciliation be taught and modeled by the church leadership and taught to its individual members. Since the church universal is inclusive of all ethnic backgrounds, then this same universality must be accepted in every geographically defined local church.

## CONCLUSION

### *The Wall: Jesus destroyed the wall of hostility; His church must never rebuild it.*

This book has addressed a sensitive discussion in the church. Should the church continue to function with ethnic segregation? If there is clear Biblical instruction where oneness overrides separation, then should we make changes in our practice? What place do ethnic churches have in the plan of God? Are they different than churches that do not have an ethnic emphasis? Should the intent of evangelism be an adequate reason to target a special part of a community's population?

In order to explore these questions, a critique of the Homogeneous Unit Principle theory is presented as a starting point for a discussion. This evaluation serves as a beginning with the goal of discovering a strategy which the church can follow for its own development and fulfillment of its mission. Beyond theory, this discussion strives to find a practical plan which can be implemented. It is a plan that is Biblical, not with a cursory look at the Scriptures but with a rigorous theological understanding of what Christ accomplished at the cross.

Two matters are directly related to this study. The individual and his perception of his fellow man are pertinent regardless of that person's ethnic background. Also, existing ethnic churches,

331

their legitimate existence and future role is also germane to the conversation.

Several guidelines have served as important priorities in this analysis of how people perceive each other and how the ethnic church is to understand its place. First, any church development strategy must be consistent with basic New Testament principles. It is with certainty that an argument for the development on any local church must be grounded in the teachings of the Scripture. Jesus Christ is the head of the church and His redemptive work formed the basis for the church to exist. Second, an essential principle from the New Testament is that the church is to be salt and light to the world. That is, the church is to have moral impact on the world not by default but by initiative. This is not a new concept. For example, the church has played a major role in effectively addressing other moral issues as slavery an abortion.

Then, in order for the church to carry out this spiritual responsibility it must be aware of the existing moral turmoil. Such astuteness to the present issues will aid the church in choosing a strategy to continue its Biblical role as an institution that will make a moral impact and to avoid the implementation of ideas than can be too easily misapplied.

Fourth, the issue of racism and racial tension both inside and outside of the church is a moral issue that must be addressed. Christianity holds no common ground with form of bigotry.

Fifth, in order for the church to make an effective impact on this moral issue it must insure that its members acknowledge and implement the conversion in their life. For conversion demands that the initial feature of sanctification be manifested concurrently with an entrance into Christianity.

Sixth, while the topic of racism is too broad for a discussion of this nature, the matter of addressing racial tension in the church is not. Human relationship can be perceived in several ways. All people are categorized as either non-Christian or Christian. When non-Christians are guilty of racial discrimination toward non-Christians, the church finds it morally reprehensible. When a Christian is guilty of racial discrimination toward a non-Christian, then the church should find such attitudes and actions nothing short of dastardly. But, when a Christian is guilty of racial discrimination against his fellow Christian then this is the height of moral repulsion. If God's grace redeemed all people who by faith came to Christ, then each one of these should be as receptive to whoever has been rescued and redeemed as well. This is the focus of this book.

Seventh, the celebration of culture and ethnicity are acknowledged as a part of humanity given to each person by divine providence. The changes of sanctification do no obliterate such distinctions nor do they demand the adoption of a new culture. Sanctification has a focus on life-change. What is immoral must be jettisoned and there must be a submission to moral values.

Last, ethnic churches cannot be evaluated on a single level of either inclusion or exclusion. Their existence is legitimate as long as their essential purpose is founded on Scriptural principles. The greater issue is to acknowledge that the resent purpose and legitimacy may not necessarily argue for permanent status or unchanging status. On these matters, then, the HUP theory will be under critique.

Of particular concern to this author has been the interest shown by Asian churches in implementing the HUP theory as a rationale for perpetuating more ethnic churches and the preservation of their culture. The influx of Asian groups to the West in the last century (Chinese, Japanese, Korean, SE Asians, Filipino, etc.) has resulted in significant numerical church growth among these ethnic groups at varying times. But, are these examples a proof that the HUP theory is valid? Is there any Biblical Theological inadequacy inherent in the theory? Is the theory adequate in addressing the ecclesiastical essentials of the ethnic church?

It is in this light that the Biblical Theological critique of the UP theory is offered from a Practical Theology perspective. When a minister incorporated the HUP theory to a particular church situation, will visible results be gained at the expense of

334

New Testament principle and Theological priorities?  In an effort to find some measurable success does the implementation of the HUP theory in effect compromise other major moral issues fundamental to the purpose of the church?

## Chapter 1

An explanation of the "Homogeneous Unit Principle" is objectively presented in this initial chapter.  I wrote it thinking that those who espouse and embrace this view would agree that I had represented their position fairly.  My goal was to explain not only their conclusion but also how they reached their conclusion.

A passion for world evangelization is the driving force behind Church Growth efforts.  Proponents of Church Growth perceive that the opportunity is at hand for Christians to be a part of God's "final push in global evangelization."[798] Developing a strategy to take advantage of this opportunity is premier.

The Church Growth philosophy is built upon the concept of viewing the world as a large mosaic.  Each piece of the mosaic represents a different segment of society identified by language, economy, ethnic roots, cultural distinctive, etc.  While each piece is distinct, all of the pieces make up the large picture

---

[798] Ralph Winter, "Time is Running Out! Time to Get Tough with Terminology.  Time to Take Stock.  Business as Usual Won't Work!" editorial in <u>Missions Frontiers</u>,vol. 12, nox. 6-10 (June-October 1990), 1.

of the world. Into this picture Christ commissions all Christians to bring His Gospel.

The "Great Commission" of Matthew 28:18-19 is interpreted according to the illustration of the "vast mosaic." It is interpreted that the "all nations" (*ta ethne*) refers to each language, tribe and people group. Based upon this perspective, the strategy is designed to disturb these defined groups as little as possible, and to introduce the gospel to each in the context of their own peoplehood. The effort emphasizes the priority of protecting the elements necessary for conversion from the distractions of cultural offense. Instead, each of these mosaic segments will be Christianize in itself.

Attempts to communicate the Gospel that do not give attention to the features of any particular people group will result in evangelism failure. People will actually be driven away from the church outside of his own homogenous unit will not be successful since each congregation is culturally distinctive,. Those in the same mosaic parameters of an established church can comfortably hear and receive the Gospel without cultural offense. Hence, based upon these conclusions, churches within each piece of the mosaic must be established in order to attract others of that homogenous unit and thus fulfill the evangelistic mission of the church.

Concerns raised regarding the issue of church unity are answered on two levels. First, brotherhood is a part of every

336

church in every people group.  It is the goal of every Christian group in each mosaic piece.  Since it is a mutually share priority each group, it is part of the unifying link among all Christian groups regardless of homogeneous group distinctions.  Creative means for denominational representative and national meeting enhances this unifying feature of the church.  Second, the demonstration unity will take place in the future before the throne of the Lamb.  Members from each homogeneous unit will stand before Christ all distinguished Christians and all distinguished by their people group.

This perspective of viewing the world as a mosaic is essential to the Church Growth philosophy and foundational for the HUP theory.  People are naturally I distinct groups and these distinctions do not melt away nor should they be ignored in the evangelistic process.  Every person is a member of a group with distinctives. These distinctives have durable significance.[799] Subsequent to conversion the distinctions continue and are a good advantage in reaching yet others within the HU parameters of an established church.  This meeting of the Gospel with the "real world" is in view of the HUP theory supporters the kind of test that proves a valid theology.[800]

---

[799] Ralph Winter, "An Insider's View of McGavran," in Mission Frontiers, vol. 12, nos. 6-10 (June – October 1990), 6.

**Chapter 2**

The debate over ethnicity as a leading identity of a local church is not a new one. It has raged both in practice and dialogue for generations. Nor is the development of the HUP concept a recent phenomenon.

In this second chapter a review of the history that is pertinent to the HUP theory is traced. Key proponents in the debate were gathered together under the auspices of the Lausanne Theology and Education Group for a consultation on the topic of the HUP theory. Ideas were exchanged over five areas: methodology, anthropology, history, ethics and theology. It was clear that those who challenged the validity of the HUP theory had a great affinity to many of the intents of Church Growth. There was a substantial amount of common ground on the value placed on culture, evangelistic creativity and the urgency to fulfill the evangelistic task.

However, several areas of disagreement remain unsettled in the debate over the validity of the HUP theory. First, the observation that non-Christians prefer to come to Christ without crossing racial, linguistic or class barriers is not agreed to be pertinent to principles that direct the church. The observation is helpful as an evangelistic technique but not for ecclesiastical guidance. That is, as Christians introduce the Gospel to a non-Christian audience, this matter is applicable.

---

[800] Ibid., 7.

However, the dynamic of Christians interacting with Christians is not germane to the conversation. The literature suggests an apparent adjustment on the part of the HUP theory supporters on this point. Later publications indicate a great emphasis on using the HUP theory for evangelistic purposes. However, their attempts at implementing of their view are not clear. According to Church Growth supporters of the HUP theory, "evangelism" includes the establishing of new churches as well as the renovation of stagnant churches. If the local church does not primarily exist for the purpose of institutional evangelism, arranging itself for the ethnic or racial preferences of the non-Christian or making Christians feel comfortable with their previously unredeemed biases then organizing churches around ethnicity needs to be reconsidered.

Second, while culture is to be valued as a part of God's gift to humanity, it is not the church's responsibility to be the primary curator for culture. Details on this subject are addressed in chapter four with a discussion of the church's mission and contextualization.

Third, the practical difficulty of addressing the emotions and conflicts regarding interracial marriage is left unsettled. Matters dealing with anthropological and sociological mores are helpful. But, issues of marriage taboos cannot be made an absolute and then utilized in determining an ecclesiastical direction.

From the perspective of a Biblical Theological discussion there are several continuing issues for discussion as well. While the explanation of *ta ethne* as a reference to the pieces of the world's ethnic groups is a possibility from an etymological perspective, the context of the Matthew 28 is not as supportive to the HUP theory as suggested. Nor does the explanation of unity by the HUP theory satisfy the New Testament presentation of brotherhood that is to be experienced on earth by Christians in different languages, race and class distinctions. Neither representative fellowship nor future unity in heaven satisfies the New Testament revelations on *koinonia*.

Finally, while the world is still embroiled in racial tensions of various degrees and configurations, it is morally crucial for the church to address that matter when both victims and perpetrators of those tensions are converted and enter the church. Racial tensions in the community are too rampant and too much a part of lives, especially of ethnic minorities, for the church to ignore the issue or to construct a church growth philosophy that allows for this matter to be avoided or hidden.

On a daily basis Christians who are ethnic minorities experience bigotry and prejudice due to racist attitudes by those around them. They learn to survive and fend for themselves. Sometimes they resist, other times they retreat. The natural question in their minds is whether the church is any different. They believe that God is different but the church has the same

340

appearance as the world in which they live and separate from for protection against racist attitudes. While a measure of ethnic pride and cultural emphasis exists, there yet remains the safety in meeting with those of like ethnic heritage just to avoid additional pain. If the HUP theory contributes to the former, then there is merit. But the latter is too prevalent a problem to promote a concept that even remotely condones such an environment.

## Chapter 3

A two-part study comprised this chapter. In part 1 an exegetical study of Ephesians 2.11-22 revealed several New Testament priorities for the church's operational philosophy. Fellowship between ethnically distinct groups as the Jews and Gentile has been established as a real relationship. "There could be o such things as a Christian baptized into Christ Jesus not in communion with all the other membrs of the body of which Christ was the Head. If a member was united to the Head he was united to all the other members."[801] Then the unity established between all men in the church is to be a visible unity.

Basic to the mission of the church is the proclamation of the oneness that is accomplished by the Gospel. Peace

---

[801] Allen, Missionary Methods, 128.

between all men was achieved by the death of Christ and is to be part of the reality of the church in the world. Mutual acceptance does not argue that such cultural of ethnic distinctions are nullified. Rather, it calls for recognition that such differences are not the priority determination of fellowship between Christian. They exist, they may have been a significant part of a person's pre-Christian past. But, now Christians share more in common through Christ's love than the difference they used for the purpose of separation prior to conversion. It is this commonness of love that the church is to find as it center of fellowship. "God as love, however, can only be witnessed to and experienced in a congregation small enough for members to know each other and accept one another as they are accepted by Christ. The gospel of Christ crucified for us puts an end to religion as power and opens up the possibility of experiencing God in the context of genuine community as the God of love. Justification by faith puts an end to religious bondage and creates freedom in fellowship."[802]

Then in part 2 several features are presented that are non-optional in formulating a strategy for church development. One is that an adequate emphasis on sanctification must be present. A clear Christology calls for an ethical change upon

---

[802] Jurgen Motmann, "The Life Signs of the Spirit in the Fellowship Community of Christ," in Hope for the Church: Moltmann in Dialogue with Practical Theology, ed. Theodore Runyon, 37-56 (Nashville: Abingdon, 1979), 40.

342

conversion. Another is that the need to emphasize mutual acceptance by following the model of Christ Himself. All Christians are one together in Christ and their organization into the church should depict that essence. Also, any tendency to err on the matters related to civil religion must be checked. There is not theological basis for separating members of Christ's Church because of ethnicity or race. Mutual humanity as reflected the *imago dei* calls for mutual respect for each other's humanity with those ethnic features. Such differences call for acceptance not separation. Finally, a Christological center of theological commitment will aid in the demonstration of Christian unity.

This presentation establishes the priorities that are part of the alternative to the HUP theory. Each of these features is pertinent to the church minister. Furthermore, the discussion is set in the context of being acceptable to ministers of a minority church. I have referred to this approach as Mutual Acceptance. First, a strategy for church development must adequately address the elements of sanctification. Whether a person maintains a Reformed, Keswick, Pentecostal, Wesleyan or Augustinian-Dispensational view of sanctification there is general agreement of a past separation due to Christ's completed work. This past work enables a holy life to be pursued in the present and persevered in as a result of a future culmination. A present expression of God's love is a real

343

experience. Success in this process is assured through the promises of the Bible and the power of the Holy Spirit. Christians can love other kinds of Christians now because of sanctification.

Second, the theological center of a church ministry must be reevaluated. If the church's main effort is to deal with the problems of people, then it will have anthropology at its theological core instead of a Christological focus. Mutual Acceptance maintains that a theological philosophy must be established first according to principles found in the New Testament. Then, the needs of people are evaluated through that philosophy. Finally, subsequent programs are designed to resolve these problems consistently with a New Testament philosophy.

Third, a practical danger of justifying a separation of races in ecclesiastical or theological reasoning must be avoided. The historical dangers of civil religion have contributed to such efforts and the church must not adopt such thinking. Acknowledging the reality of the *imago dei* gives the potential of such theological practicality and realism in the church. With Christ breaking down the wall of racial prejudice all Christians can share a common fellowship with each other. When minority Christians are made to feel that they are excluded due to the ethnicity, then the Gospel message has been compromised. Dressing up separation among Christians in worship with the

344

description that such a choice enhances cultural celebration is too often made a pretense. It is far better for a church to add ethnic or cultural emphases while making sure that it welcomes all Christians to worship.


## Chapter 4

Mutual Acceptance is applied to two major areas of Christian concern: missions and church development. In the area of missions, Mutual Acceptance is in agreement with efforts to define and follow the concept of contextualization. That is, when the church sends the Gospel to another culture, it must make every effort to allow the receptors to receive the Gospel in their own way. This is a value or habit that is inherently evil they cannot be condoned or allowed to be incorporated in the new cultural church of the Christians that are organized in the new community.

The missionary must be careful not to allow his cultural ways to confuse the Gospel presentation. Humble adaption and service to the receiving people is of premier importance. Just as important is a Christian's attitude when immigrating to another country. Excessive demands to preserve one's own culture in one's Christianity when immigrating may be too great a cost to pay if the cause of the Gospel then brings offense. Perhaps Eric Liddell's admonition to the church on their matter would be the proper guide: "We are all missionaries . . . We carry our religion with us, or we allow our religion to carry us. Wherever we go, we either bring people nearer to Christ, or we repel them from Christ."[803]

Helpful in this transformation processes the matter of lordship. Acknowledging the lordship of Christ as a part or result of the conversation experience calls for radical changes in one's cultural past. For some cultures such changes will be minimal. On the other hand, some may find the demands drastic if not radical. The minister and church elders are they key persons to make this transformation possible. When they guide and shepherd the flock, helping converts to accept the unconditional love of God, then they can teach, counsel, admonish, and guide new Christians to reciprocate that same love-received to other Christians of a different ethnic group whom they once despised before their conversion.

Lastly, Mutual Acceptance is applied to three of the most common church situations: ethnic churches, multi-ethnic churches and churches representing the majority culture in a given geographical area. Regarding the ethnic church, Mutual Acceptance points out that there is a generational influence in such churches. Sociological studies demonstrate that such churches have been the result of a umber or combination of

---

[803] D.P. Thomson, Eric H. Liddell: Athlete and Missionary (Perth: The Research Unit, 1971), 114.

elements: a desire to preserve ethnic identity, religious expression in an oppressive society, and language limitations of family members not quickly assimilated into the new host culture. In the early stages of a recent immigration these features are understandable. But, Mutual Acceptance points out that these are temporary needs. These needs in light of Ephesians 2.11-22, suggest that subsequent generations of distinctively ethnic groups should be welcomed into churches of the host society. These culturally and linguistically distinct churches should be willing to either shift to the preferred New Testament model of a multi-ethnic church or cheerfully allow its subsequent generations to relocate into churches of the host society.

Churches that choose to be deliberately multi-ethnic face unique tensions. Mutual Acceptance views such deliberate attempts at church development as commendable because the problems of separation are often purposefully ignored. The church is to be a light in the world, showing what difference the love of Christ can make in the world. Yet, it is vital that such mixed efforts not falsely assume a "melting pot" disposition. Ethnicity is real and it is part of each person's humanity and is therefore a good thing. But, there are legitimate values or styles with each culture or sub-culture that will clash and call for wisdom in maintaining unity. Such difficulties are not; however, reason enough for separate Christian worship or fellowship. This again shows the priority that Mutual Acceptance places on establishing a philosophy of ministry based up New Testament principles first, then applying it to problems in a given situation.

The church that represents the majority population of any society has a unique challenge. Mutual Acceptance understands that the problem of racism in the world is acute. New converts that are minorities are from such an environment. Terror or past stress in such circumstances are common and do not disappear with conversion. There is an eventual openness that the same Christ who accepted them as individuals, even though they are a minority, will accept them into any of His churches. This hope must be nurtured. It is a common experience for a Christian who is also a minority to wonder why there cannot be more fellowship beyond ethnic limitations because of commonness in Christ. " . . . [A] truly Christian church is not one without a foreigner in it, but one in which a believer is treated like a brother; or more precisely one in which all believers – without distinction of nationality, race or cultural background – fellowship as members one with another in the household of God."[804]

Christians must be careful not to adopt the pragmatic philosophy where fellowship is based on the criteria of what seems comfortable. It is not always wrong to do so but it can easily compromise the essence of Christian love. Aristotle's ancient adage "Birds of a feather flock together" may reveal a

---

[804] Wester, "Mission in Time," 98,99.
348

sociability of human interaction but it is limiting and not reflective of New Testament Christianity. This idea results in racial segregation, religious separation, class isolationism and educational arrogance. If an individual can fit into one of these defined groups, then, such a pattern of behavior may seem natural and right. But, as Moltmann observes, ". . . those on the 'outside' feel excluded, degraded, and wounded. We get in a stew about showing special care for those people who are included in our own circle – and then "stew in our own juices'."[805] On bridging the gap with minorities, such churches should regularly participate in cross-cultural evangelism and seek to organize joint worship celebrations with ethnic churches. But, they should also realize that ethnicity in a church shifts with successive generations.

Visible differences do not always mean language or cultural variation. Mutual Acceptance encourages shared leadership with a visible difference. Pulpit sharing, leadership exchanges, ministry specialty cooperatives, and internal leadership development beyond a homogeneous line will encourage the congregation to follow suit. Leadership example is a key feature in Mutual Acceptance. One of the beginning places is the training level for church leadership. If the teaching staff of theological schools is the visible example for future church leaders to follow, then the more multi-ethnic (from a

---

[805] Motmann, Open Church, 30.

visible standpoint) the representation is and the more helpful the experience will be for ministers to model in the church.

Mutual Acceptance is based upon a mutual relationship among all Christians because a commonness in Christ. "He [Paul] taught his converts to recognize every baptized Christian as a brother. He taught them . . . the duty of mutual responsibility one for another."[806] Mutual Acceptance believes that this type of interactive *koinonia* can be applied in a local church that is comprised of a mixture of people from all different backgrounds. "[The] more mixed the congregation is, especially in 'class' and 'color', the greater its opportunity to demonstrate the power of Christ that is very different from the world around them. Truly inter-racial, inter-social Christian fellowships, whose members evidently cares for one another and bear one another's burdens, is in itself an eloquent witness to the reconciling power of Jesus Christ."[807]

Accepting one another is the badge of Christian love regardless of racial, linguistic, or class differences. Mutual Acceptance advocates that this is a present experience for Christians today. All Christians are beneficiaries of God's gracious acceptance regardless of race, language or class. Entrances into God's family as converted Christians, sanctified and unified, calls for all to accept each other as they themselves

---

[806] Allen, Missionary Methods, 134.
[807] Stott, Guilty Silence, 75.

have been accepted. Merciful love was received. Merciful love is all that is asked of each recipient to share. "In the depths of his suffering we perceive the greatness of his passion for us. We are disarmed whenever we recognize the suffering of God, which has borne and still bears his passion to us. [As a result, we] . . . can mutually accept each other because Christ has accepted us to the glory of God."[808]

---

[808] Moltmann, Open Church, 31.

24715277R00212

Made in the USA
Lexington, KY
29 July 2013